PENGUIN BUSINESS
SCALING MOUNT UPSC

Author and bureaucrat Sajjan Yadav is a 1995-batch Indian Administrative Service officer of the AGMUT (Arunachal Pradesh–Goa–Mizoram and Union Territory) cadre. His last book, titled *India's Vaccine Growth Story: From Cowpox to Vaccine Maitri*, is a national bestseller and has been translated into and published in Spanish as well as sixteen Indian languages. He has also extensively published in reputed international and national journals, magazines and newspapers.

Yadav earned his doctorate in public health from the prestigious London School of Hygiene and Tropical Medicine, a master's in public policy from the University of Minnesota, USA, and an MBA from the Faculty of Management Studies, Delhi University.

He is currently additional secretary in the Department of Expenditure, Ministry of Finance, Government of India. Yadav has a rich and diverse experience of thirty years in policy formulation and implementation, as well as in senior leadership positions in the Government of India and state governments.

In the Central government, besides the finance ministry, he has also worked in the ministries of health and family welfare, women and child development, heavy industry, and public enterprises and corporate affairs. Important assignments handled by Yadav in the past include tenures as mission director of the National Nutrition Mission (POSHAN Abhiyan), director of the National Rural Health Mission, commissioner of food and supplies in Delhi, CEO of the Delhi Jal Board, Value Added Tax (VAT) commissioner, commissioner of excise, entertainment and luxury tax, and commissioner of the East Delhi Municipal Corporation. He has worked in the states of Arunachal Pradesh, Mizoram and Rajasthan, and the Union Territories of National Capital Territory (NCT) of Delhi, Dadra and Nagar Haveli, and Daman and Diu. He has further served as district magistrate/deputy commissioner of East Kameng and Tawang districts of Arunachal Pradesh, and of the South Delhi district of NCT of Delhi.

Yadav has been conferred several awards for exceptional work in public service, including the National e-Governance Award for 2017–18 and the President of India's medal for outstanding work in census operations.

ADVANCE PRAISE FOR THE BOOK

'This book gives an unmatched portrayal of the struggle of the participants coming into civil services. The author of the book himself has been a strong traveller of this route, so he has given a clear voice to the fire required within to conquer this battle'—**Manoj Kumar Sharma, India Police Service, inspiration for the film** *12th Fail*

'This book vicariously takes the reader down the path of every aspirant who has struggled to scale "Mount UPSC"—from vulnerability and self-doubt to having the temerity to see light at the end of the tunnel. Stories of grit, tenacity, hard work, persistence and the indomitable human spirit inspire the reader to keep pushing the limits of what is possible and to go beyond. A must-read for anyone'—**Shivin Chaudhary, Indian Revenue Service**

'The narration of seven Union Public Service Commission (UPSC) heroes' sojourn is novel-like, and that makes this book a compelling read. In fact, in places, it offers such an immersive experience that a reader involuntarily starts imagining the characters and hearing their voices as well. The inspiration quotient of the book is not restricted to UPSC aspirants alone but has a universal appeal. In three words, this book is enlightening, energizing and entertaining'—**Balaji D.K., IAS officer and author**

'As someone who has recently cleared the UPSC exam, this book truly resonated with me on a personal level. The stories of these seven toppers brought back memories of my own struggles, doubts and triumphs during the preparation. The book brilliantly captures the emotional roller coaster this exam puts you through—the sleepless nights, the endless revisions and the constant pressure. What sets it apart is how it showcases the human side of this journey, making you realize that with perseverance and resilience you can overcome even the toughest odds. A deeply inspiring read for any aspirant aiming for this difficult path!'—**Aniruddh Yadav, IAS 2022**

'This book captures the varied and relatable journeys of IAS aspirants from Kashmir to Kerala who got it all right in the end by their sheer grit and determination. Tackling challenges ranging from family responsibilities and modest beginnings to physical impediments and career risks, each story comes alive with characters we know or situations we can relate to. Moreover, every story ends with practical advice and inspiration, and most importantly, it also explores the initial experiences with public service following the exam. In my opinion, this book must be read by anyone who aspires to be a civil servant and who wants to make significant contributions in their careers and beyond' —**Vikas Divyakirti, founder, Drishti IAS Coaching Institute**

'This book succeeds in giving a great overview of the exam and the struggles associated with it. By focussing on seven incredible stories, it rightly brings out the common factors of grit and perseverance playing the most imperative parts in the success of the candidates. I highly recommend the book to all the aspirants involved in the UPSC journey'— **Anudeep Durishetty, IAS officer and author**

'This book is going to inspire millions of youth from ordinary families who try every year to enter into the premier government service and it is a must-read for them'— **Shyamlal Yadav, senior associate editor,** *Indian Express*

SCALING MOUNT UPSC

INSPIRING STORIES OF YOUNG IAS OFFICERS

SAJJAN YADAV

PENGUIN
BUSINESS

An imprint of Penguin Random House

PENGUIN BUSINESS

Penguin Business is an imprint of the Penguin Random House group of companies
whose addresses can be found at global.penguinrandomhouse.com

Published by Penguin Random House India Pvt. Ltd
4th Floor, Capital Tower 1, MG Road,
Gurugram 122 002, Haryana, India

First published in Penguin Business by Penguin Random House India 2025

ISBN 9780143466116

Typeset in Adobe Caslon Pro by MAP Systems, Bengaluru, India
Printed at Thomson Press India Ltd, New Delhi

www.penguin.co.in

To
My lifeline, Sunita
My darling daughter, Siya
and
My loving son, Karan

In loving memory of my late parents,
Savitri Devi and Subedar Major Raghubir Singh (Retd),
whose values and wisdom continue to guide me every day

Contents

Foreword

India's youth possess boundless potential, a profound ambition to serve and the determination to rise above adversities. Nowhere is this more evident than in the aspirants for the Indian Administrative Service (IAS), who, year after year, display an unparalleled commitment to crack one of the most challenging exams in the world—the UPSC Civil Services Examination. This book, *Scaling Mount UPSC*, narrates the extraordinary journeys of seven young individuals who have conquered this monumental challenge.

The IAS is not merely a career; it is a call to nation-building, an opportunity to serve the people of this great country and drive transformative change. The aspirants who dare to take on the rigorous journey of the Civil Services Examination are bound by a shared dream—to contribute to India's development, to be an integral part of an ecosystem that shapes our nation's future. These seven stories reflect that very spirit of resilience, perseverance, and sacrifice.

Each story in this book is a testament to the strength of the human spirit. From overcoming economic hardships and social obstacles to sacrificing personal comforts and enduring failures, these young achievers show us that no dream is too big if pursued with passion and grit. They remind us that success is not just about securing a rank but about the journey, the lessons learned, and the courage it takes to rise after every fall.

India is on the cusp of becoming a global leader in the 21st century, and our civil servants are at the forefront of this transformation. The future of our nation rests in the hands of such determined individuals who are willing to dedicate their lives to the service of the people. Their ability to innovate, reform, and implement policies will define India's journey towards becoming a $30 trillion economy and a developed nation by 2047.

I hope this book serves as an inspiration to countless aspirants who dream of serving the nation. The stories of Minnu P.M., Satyam Gandhi, Bharat Singh, Lavish Ordia, Anjali Sharma, Waseem Ahmad Bhat and Shruti Sharma will resonate with every reader, encouraging them to strive for excellence in whatever path they choose.

To the future aspirants who pick up this book, remember that the road to success is often paved with challenges. But with unwavering determination, discipline and belief in oneself, even the tallest of mountains—like Mount UPSC—can be scaled.

22 October 2024

Amitabh Kant
IAS (Retd)
G-20 Sherpa and former CEO of
NITI Aayog
Government of India

List of Abbreviations

AIEEE	All India Engineering Entrance Exam
AIIMS	All India Institute of Medical Sciences
ATI	Administrative Training Institute
BDO	Block Development Officer
BDS	Bachelor of Dental Science
BIPARD	Bihar Institute of Public Administration & Rural Development
BPSC	Bihar Public Service Commission
CAD	Computer-Aided Design
CAPF	Central Armed Police Forces
CASRAE	Centre for Advanced Studies & Research in Automotive Engineering
CAT	Common Admission Test
CBSE	Central Board of Secondary Education
CGM	Chief General Manager
CPI	Cumulative Performance Index
CSAT	Civil Services Aptitude Test
CSE	Civil Services Examination

CV	Curriculum Vitae
DAF	Detailed Application Form
DG	Director General
DTC	Delhi Transport Corporation
DTU	Delhi Technological University
EWS	Economically Weaker Section
GS–I	General Studies–I
GS–II	General Studies–II
HSC	Hamdard Study Circle
IAS	Indian Administrative Service
IFS	Indian Forest Service
IGNOU	Indira Gandhi National Open University
IIM	Indian Institute of Management
IIT–JEE	Indian Institute of Technology–Joint Entrance Examination
IMechE	Institution of Mechanical Engineers
IPS	Indian Police Service
Interview	Personality Test
JNU	Jawaharlal Nehru University
LBSNAA	Lal Bahadur Shastri National Academy of Administration
MH	Modern History

MPPSC	Madhya Pradesh Provincial Civil Service
NAB	National Association for the Blind
NABARD	National Bank for Agriculture and Rural Development
NCERT	National Council of Educational Research & Training
NHAI	National Highways Authority of India
NIT	National Institute of Technology
ORN	Old Rajinder Nagar
PG	Paying Guest
PHQ	Police Headquarters
PIB	Press Information Bureau
PWD	Public Works Department
RBI	Reserve Bank of India
RCA	Residential Coaching Academy
RDO	Rural Development Officer
RML	Dr Ram Manohar Lohia
SDM	Sub-Divisional Magistrate
UGC	University Grants Commission
SSB	Services Selection Board
SDGs	Sustainable Development Goals
UIDAI	Unique Identification Authority of India
UPSC	Union Public Service Commission
VSSC	Vikram Sarabhai Space Centre
YASHADA	Yashwantrao Chavan Academy of Development Administration

Prologue

Heroes of the World's Toughest Exam

Maa, I Have Become a Collector

Every year, over a million Indian youth passionately pursue a shared dream: cracking the revered Civil Services Examination (CSE) to join the coveted Indian Administrative Service (IAS) and other premier civil services. Conducted by the Union Public Service Commission (UPSC), it's one of the world's most competitive, extensive and arduous exams.

Three decades ago, I was among those aspirants, deeply engrossed in the colossal preparations required to conquer this Mount Everest of exams. With my modest background set in Haryana, I had nurtured the dream of becoming an IAS officer since my school days. Winning a university gold medal in academics had further bolstered my confidence. Yet, tales of engineering prodigies from the Indian Institutes of Technology (IITs) achieving sky-high scores in the optional subjects left me uneasy.

My first tryst with UPSC was in 1993. The journey began with promise as I sailed through the first two phases, opening the doors to the majestic Dholpur House, the UPSC headquarters in New Delhi, for the crucial Personality Test. But, as life often reminds us, success is a rollercoaster. The initial euphoria was abruptly shattered when my name was conspicuously missing from the list of victors, sending shockwaves through my spirit.

This setback, however, did not crush my spirit; it became a powerful springboard for doubled determination. With unwavering resolve, I reevaluated my approach and immersed myself in preparations for the impending Prelims of 1994. I focused intensely on improving my general studies and essay writing, areas where I had fallen short.

The air was thick with anticipation as I awaited the final verdict. On the evening of 22 June 1995, a jubilant uproar erupted within the walls of my college hostel: I had clinched the twenty-sixth rank in the CSE 1994. The euphoria was electrifying. With the sweet taste of success still lingering, I soon found myself aboard a Haryana Roadways bus, embarking on a dream voyage to the prestigious Lal Bahadur Shastri National Academy of Administration (LBSNAA) in the enchanting town of Mussoorie.

Over the years, the UPSC has implemented significant changes in the exam pattern, further intensifying this already formidable challenge. The introduction of the Civil Services Aptitude Test (CSAT) in the Prelims and an ethics paper in the Mains has added complexity to the process. While the optional subjects have been reduced from two to one, there has been a corresponding increase in the number of essays to be written and a paper on ethics has been added. Additionally, the liberalization of the Indian economy has opened a plethora of diverse and attractive career opportunities for the youth. However, despite these changes and the availability of alternative paths, the allure of the UPSC's Civil Services Examination has grown and the competition has intensified.

In 2023, an astonishing 10,16,850 candidates applied for the CSE, with 5,92,141 taking the Prelims. From this vast pool, only 14,624 candidates advanced to the second stage. Just 2855 demonstrated the fortitude to conquer the Mains, earning a coveted call for the Personality Test. Ultimately, a mere 1016 candidates reached the pinnacle, with only 180 securing recommendations for the IAS.

What drives these individuals to embrace this gruelling challenge with an incredibly low success rate? The answer lies in the allure of the IAS—a profession that offers unparalleled opportunities to work in diverse fields, face myriad challenges and experience the excitement and fulfilment of public service. The aura of authority, respect and influence associated with the IAS transforms the CSE into a national passion. Aspirants willingly immerse themselves in this daunting challenge, fuelled by the fervent desire to one day proudly declare, 'Maa, I have become a collector.'

Unveiling Mount UPSC

The formidable CSE consists of three rigorous stages: the Civil Services Preliminary Examination (Prelims), the Civil Services Main Written Examination (Mains) and the Personality Test (Interview). The marathon commences with the publication of an advertisement by UPSC in February each year, inviting applications for the Prelims. The exam is marked by intense competition, with a success rate of less than 1 per cent. An outline of the exam is shown in the figure below:

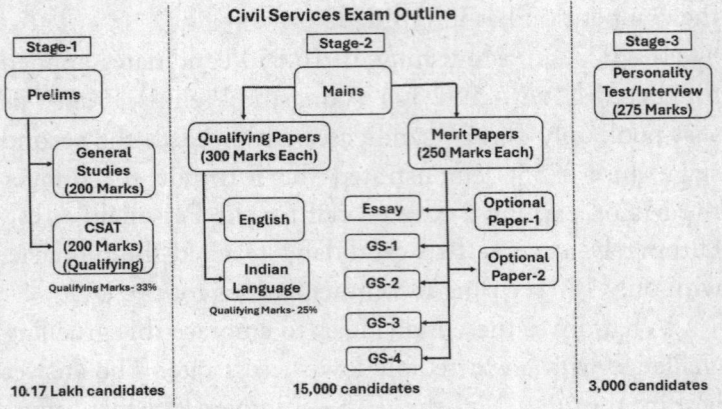

The Prelims comprises two compulsory, objective-type papers, each lasting two hours and carrying 200 marks. General Studies–1 (GS–1) covers a range of topics, including current events, Indian history, geography, polity, economy, environment and general science. Negative marking applies, deducting one-third of the marks for each incorrect answer. The GS–2 or CSAT paper is qualifying, requiring candidates to score at least 33 per cent marks. It assesses comprehension, logical reasoning, decision-making, general mental ability and basic numeracy.

The Prelims serve as a screening test for shortlisting candidates eligible to apply for the Mains. Marks obtained in Prelims are not considered for determining the final order of merit. The number of candidates selected is approximately twelve to thirteen times the total number of vacancies.

The Mains exam is descriptive, assessing a candidate's depth of understanding, analytical thinking and writing skills. It expects candidates to articulate their views on socio-economic goals with conceptual clarity and flawless organization.

The Mains examination encompasses nine papers, with two—English and one Indian language—serving as qualifying assessments. Candidates select their Indian language from those listed in the Eighth Schedule to the Constitution. Each of these compulsory papers, set at a matriculation or equivalent standard, carries a maximum of 300 marks. Candidates must secure a minimum of 25 per cent marks in each to pass. The compulsory papers are immensely important because the UPSC disregards scores from the remaining seven papers if a candidate fails to meet the qualifying criteria in the compulsory papers.

The remaining seven papers (Paper-I to Paper-VII) are each valued at 250 marks and contribute to the final ranking. These papers are:

- Essay
- General Studies–I: Indian heritage and culture, history and geography of the world and society
- General Studies–II: governance, Constitution, polity, social justice and international relations
- General Studies–III: technology, economic development, biodiversity, environment, security and disaster management
- General Studies–IV: ethics, integrity and aptitude
- Optional Subject–1
- Optional Subject–2

Candidates may choose any one of the optional subjects from amongst the list of subjects provided by UPSC. The duration of each paper is three hours.

The culmination of the CSE journey is the Interview/ Personality Test, a pivotal phase carrying 275 marks. Typically, the number of candidates summoned for interviews is approximately twice the number of vacancies for the year's exam. During this stage, candidates face a board tasked with assessing their mental acumen, personal suitability and leadership potential for a career in public service.

The arduous journey spanning fifteen months is fraught with uncertainty, intense pressure and occasional frustration. Candidates confront social, physical and economic hurdles, making sacrifices and taking risks along the way. For months on end, aspirants immerse themselves in rigorous study, sacrificing personal and social pursuits. While some achieve success swiftly, others endure repeated setbacks before tasting victory. Each triumphant candidate's journey is a tale of dreams, struggles, failures, unwavering determination and eventual triumph.

This book tells the captivating life journeys of seven remarkable individuals who, over the past five years, have conquered the formidable Mount UPSC to join the prestigious IAS. It also throws light on the labyrinthine challenges these heroes encountered and the ingenious strategies they employed to navigate each phase of this rigorous examination. Each narrative stands as a testament to the power of hard work, dedication and unwavering self-belief.

Our Seven Heroes

Minnu P.M., a junior clerk in Kerala police, fought a relentless five-year battle to conquer the formidable Mount UPSC. Minnu faced immense challenges after her father tragically passed away while she was in Class 12. Married off early, she juggled the responsibilities of a two-year-old child, household duties and a demanding job. Estranged from the world of studies for years, Minnu's journey was nothing short of heroic. Despite failing the Prelims thrice and stumbling at the interview stage once, her unyielding spirit never faltered.

Satyam Gandhi, a twenty-one-year-old from a quaint village in Bihar's Samastipur district, triumphed over adversity to hit the bull's eye on his very first attempt. After failing the IIT–JEE and facing rejection from the National Defence Academy, Satyam's grit and determination shone through. Knowing his parents were borrowing at exorbitant rates to fund his studies, Satyam began his preparations in the final year of graduation. Enduring poor food, financial hardships, taunts from professors, illness and Covid-19, he studied fourteen hours a day according to a well-conceived study plan and secured the tenth rank in CSE-2020.

Bharat Singh's journey from the servants' quarters of IAS officers to becoming one of the latter himself is profoundly inspiring. His struggle began early when his parents moved him from a Hindi-medium government school to an elite English-medium school in Class 6. He endured a gruelling four-hour daily commute and overcame inferiority complexes and isolation to become a mechanical engineer. Bharat then made a monumental decision: leaving an attractive job at Tata Motors, sacrificing newfound status and respect to pursue his IAS dreams. Over four years, he faced a series of failures, financial strain and mental trials to emerge victorious.

Lavish Ordia, a graduate of IIT Bombay, lived a luxurious life in Houston, USA. He enjoyed a comfy apartment, a high-priced SUV, business class travel and a generous salary. However, the call of the IAS was stronger than corporate glitter. Leaving behind these comforts, he moved to a shared, non-AC room in a hostel in Delhi. With smart planning, a rigorous study schedule and strict adherence to targets, Lavish secured eighteenth rank in his maiden attempt.

Life plunged into darkness for **Anjali Sharma**, the daughter of a factory worker in Sikkim, when she lost her eyesight in Class 10. Yet, this loss made her vision for the UPSC crystal clear. Unfamiliar with aids for the visually impaired, Anjali fought all odds and began preparing for the CSE immediately after her graduation, relying solely on self-study through YouTube. Even though she grappled with poor-quality scribes, lack of proper reading material, pressing health issues and repeated failures, her sheer determination and hard work helped her realize her dream.

Waseem Ahmad Bhat, the son of a beekeeper from Anantnag, Jammu and Kashmir, was once fascinated by engineering. The visit of young Kashmiri IAS officers, Shah Faesal and Athar Amir, to his college, inspired him to pursue the IAS dream. Rejecting attractive job offers, Waseem moved to Old Rajinder Nagar, Delhi, the Mecca for IAS aspirants. His meticulous note-making, refined writing style and intense fourteen-hour study sessions paid off when he secured the seventh rank in CSE-2022.

Shruti Sharma, a humble girl next door, transformed into an emblem of hope and inspiration for millions when she topped the CSE-2021. Hailing from a quaint village in Bijnor, Uttar Pradesh, her journey is a poignant rollercoaster of perseverance and resolve. From mistakenly selecting the wrong exam medium to fearing failure in the Prelims and grappling with a less-than-ideal interview, Shruti's path was anything but smooth. Her struggle was supported by her mother and beloved amma, whose sacrifices and encouragement lit her way.

The final chapter of the book, titled 'Becoming an IAS Officer: The Success Mantras', offers a comprehensive guide to conquering Mount UPSC, building on the inspiring stories of seven young achievers.

These captivating life stories of the seven individuals with diverse background and challenges will not only inspire and motivate millions of civil services aspirants but will also provide them invaluable guidance to conquer the formidable Mount UPSC and achieve their IAS dream.

Ms. Minnu P M, IAS

Chapter 1

Clerk to Collector: A Mother's Journey

An Angel in Police Uniform

For Minnu P.M., a young junior clerk, this August morning in Kerala's Thiruvananthapuram was not out of the ordinary. The state was in the thick of the monsoon—there was the rhythmic patter of raindrops and skies were lighted by low-hanging clouds. The air carried the heady fragrance of damp earth.

But Minnu did not pay much attention to all this. She was draped in a cream saree with a thick golden border and her focus was on Suryakant Panda (name changed), the additional director general of police, as she stood attentively listening to what he had to say.

Minnu had invested the previous evening preparing a crucial note and letter for the ministry of home affairs. The work kept her in her office until late, inviting displeasure from her in-laws. As Panda meticulously perused the contents, a sense of satisfaction illuminated his face, and he readily signed the letter.

'Why are you squandering your life as a clerk? You should consider writing the CSE and becoming an officer,' Panda suggested with a smile as he pushed the thick file towards Minnu.

Panda's smile and comment brought Minnu a wave of relief. It vindicated the hours of hard work that she had put into the job the night before. While it wasn't the first time she had received praise for the quality of her work, it was different this time. Panda's words stirred a unique set of emotions within Minnu, an elation shrouded by a shadow of doubt.

'I don't think I can do it, sir,' Minnu stammered. The path he suggested seemed too distant and too unrealistic to fathom.

'Why not? You are young, intelligent and hardworking, a post-graduate and a rank holder in the university. I have seen your excellent notes on files,' Panda said with conviction.

'But sir, this exam is extremely tough and takes years to prepare. I don't think I stand a chance,' Minnu said hesitantly.

'*Mol* [daughter], don't underestimate your potential. I will sanction leave to prepare for the exam,' Panda was serious.

'I will seriously consider it. Thank you, sir,' Minnu couldn't bring herself to argue further. She quickly gathered her file from Panda's desk and left his chamber, her heart racing.

In those thirty steps that she took from Panda's chamber to her section, Minnu found herself in a different world. Panda's words had shaken off the thick layer of dust that had settled on her long-lost dream of becoming an IAS officer. To test the waters, she had even appeared in the CSE-2012 Prelims exam.

A Child in the Police Headquarters

In a twist of fate, Minnu had become a junior clerk at the police headquarters. She had got this job under the 'death in harness' rule after her father, a constable in the Kerala police, passed away in 2007. Initially dismissed by colleagues for her compassionate appointment, Minnu proved her worth through hard work and dedication, earning praise from senior IPS officers and envy from peers.

Upon returning to her section, Minnu eased into her chair to regain her composure. She placed her head gently on the cool surface of her desk, shutting her eyes and taking slow, deliberate breaths. She fondly recalled the staff meeting that Panda had called on his inaugural day a few months back. He asked everyone to introduce themselves and outline their roles.

'What's a child doing here?' Panda quipped with a smile when it was Minnu's turn. Her youthful appearance made her look younger than her actual age. It sparked a ripple of light laughter throughout the room.

'Sir, I am Minnu P.M., a postgraduate in biochemistry from Kerala University. I handle weaponry and construction,' a shy Minnu replied.

After the meeting, Panda had thrown her a challenging task. 'Minnu, I need comprehensive statistics on all ongoing construction projects and detailed information about weaponry in the Kerala police. When can you provide that?'

Caught off guard, Minnu hesitated, glancing at her immediate boss, Shyam Sharma (name changed), assistant inspector general of police.

'Sir, we'll have the details ready by tomorrow,' Sharma came to Minnu's rescue.

'I want them today. There is no tomorrow,' Panda said sternly.

'Yes, sir. I will compile the details today,' Minnu replied, surprised by her own determination.

It was a daunting task, but Minnu, accustomed to challenging deadlines set by IPS officers, rushed to compile the needed information. Hours of relentless effort paid off and she prepared a comprehensive note. Anxious that Panda might leave without acknowledging her hard work, she hurried to his office, only to find him in a meeting. Determined, she waited in the nearby section.

Deep in conversation with the superintendent, her attention was abruptly seized by an irate voice. 'Minnu, why are you here? What happened to the note I asked you to prepare this morning?' She quickly turned to find Panda entering the room.

'Sir, it's ready,' Minnu said, her voice trembling slightly as she gestured towards the folder she clutched tightly in her hands.

'Really? Let's take a look,' Panda, who had anticipated an apology from Minnu for missing the target, was surprised by her response.

Upon reading the note, Panda's stern countenance melted into genuine delight. He hadn't anticipated such a thorough and analytical note from a young clerk. 'This is excellent,' Panda complimented, visibly impressed.

Emotional Tempest

With her eyes closed, Minnu reflected on her past interactions with Panda and the thought he had planted. She had always felt her true calling was beyond a clerk's role. However, life had pulled her into the duties of marriage. Her dream lay buried under daily obligations: caring for her husband and in-laws, managing her job, running the household and raising her young son.

Can I truly achieve this? Would I even stand a chance against the younger aspirants? Will Joshy, her husband, support the idea? How would amma and appa react? There were more questions than answers.

As she meandered through these thoughts, a familiar voice broke through her reverie. 'Minnu, is everything alright? Did Panda sir reprimand you?' Her colleague leaned in from the adjacent desk.

'No, *chechi* [elder sister], Panda sir profusely complimented my work. He is genuinely concerned about my career development and suggested I write the CSE and become an officer,' Minnu said, a smile lighting up her face.

Her colleague's worried expression transformed into an encouraging smile. She supported Panda's advice. 'Absolutely *ente sukha petal* [my sweet angel], you should give it a serious consideration,' she said, giving Minnu's shoulder a congratulatory pat.

Minnu's heart was brimming with eagerness to share Panda's advice with her husband. As she prepared to leave the office at 5 p.m., her cousin Didhish, who also served in the Kerala police, appeared. Overjoyed to see him, Minnu exclaimed, 'Didhish, I need to discuss something crucial.

Joshy is waiting for me downstairs. Let's go to our favourite tea spot.'

Joshy, Minnu's caring husband, worked as a technician at the Vikram Sarabhai Space Centre (VSSC) in Thiruvananthapuram. Minnu affectionately called him *chettan*.

'Chettan, before we head home, let's stop at *Manaveeyam-Veedihi*. It's been such an eventful day and I'm excited to share it,' Minnu said, her voice quivering with enthusiasm as she fastened her helmet and settled on the pillion seat of Joshy's bike. Dadish followed closely behind.

A Lot Can Happen Over a Cup of Tea

Manaveeyam-Veedihi, the city's cultural corridor, is renowned for its artworks, cultural performances and eating joints. The trio settled into their cherished spot. As steaming cups graced their table, Minnu passionately recounted her day—the meeting with Panda, his unexpected advice about CSE preparation and the appreciation from other IPS officers. With a playful chuckle, she asked, 'What do you both think? Should I give the CSE a shot?' Her inquiry carried a mix of emotions.

'Why not? I know you deserve so much more. I remember that before Jeremiah was born, we visited a coaching academy for CSE guidance. We dropped the idea because amma wanted you to have a child,' Joshy replied promptly, his eyes filled with appreciation for his wife.

Minnu felt elated at Joshy's words, but the excitement was soon overshadowed by a wave of apprehension.

'But I have the huge responsibility of nurturing a two-year-old child. To chase my dreams, I cannot, even for a moment, think about neglecting him,' Minnu's maternal instincts recoiled.

'Even now, you spend a lot of time in office and Joshy's parents happily look after him. They'd be willing to share more if you convince them,' Didhish chimed in.

Minnu remained anxious and uncertain, her voice reflecting her inner turmoil. 'It's an incredibly challenging three-stage exam. Even after years of hard work, I might stumble at the very first hurdle,' she shared her deepest fears.

However, Minnu wasn't alone in this maze of apprehension. All IAS aspirants grapple with similar uncertainties, given the alarmingly low success rate of 0.01 per cent.

Joshy steadfastly encouraged Minnu, recognizing the significant sacrifices she had made. Marrying early without establishing her career and postponing her CSE aspirations to prioritize family weighed heavily on him. He was determined to support her aspirations.

'Minnu, you've got nearly a year until the next Prelims. Take leave and immerse yourself in preparation. I'm confident you can achieve it,' Joshy reassured her, with Didhish nodding in agreement.

Minnu and Joshy headed home. The support of Joshy's parents was crucial for this challenging journey. At supper, while relishing his appam with stew, Joshy narrated the day's events to his parents, highlighting the recognition Minnu's work received from senior IPS officers and her aspiration to tackle the CSE.

Minnu, her appetite waning, nervously awaited their response.

'Mol, is this something you truly desire? Have you taken the time to contemplate it thoroughly?' Joshy's father asked, pausing his meal to delve into the sudden revelation.

'It's been my ambition since college, Appa. I even attempted it once during my post-graduation,' Minnu responded respectfully, her eyes reflecting her determination.

'Appa, Minnu has always excelled academically. She married young and this clerical job doesn't do her qualifications justice,' Joshy interjected, steering the conversation to avoid his father's immediate rejection.

'This is an incredibly challenging exam, and she'll need extended leave to prepare. How will you manage financially?' Joshy's father inquired, understanding the exam's rigour.

'Appa, the leave will be a few months. We might face temporary financial challenges, but we can manage with our savings. If it doesn't work out, she can return to her job,' Joshy presented passionately.

'If she's that determined, let her pursue her dreams. I believe in Minnu's potential. We'll take care of the house and our *muthe* [pearl],' her mother-in-law, who had been eating quietly, declared with a supportive smile. Joshy's parents affectionately called Jeremiah muthe.

Minnu's heart swelled with joy, her admiration for Joshy's mother evident. While she had reservations, she knew her mother-in-law valued women's education and empowerment and would support her decision.

Entry into the Gold Smelter

Since childhood, Minnu had been curious, hardworking and bright. Throughout her school and college years, she triumphed in various quiz, essay and elocution competitions. Her father, Paul Raj, stressed the importance of staying informed about the world. Despite his modest income, he bought her newspapers, books and magazines, fostering a love for reading. While her peers discussed textbook topics, Minnu gravitated towards global current events, prompting friends to say, 'You will become a collector one day.'

However, fate took an unexpected turn, and she became a clerk instead of a collector. Her dream of becoming an IAS officer became a wistful echo, buried beneath daily obligations.

That night, Minnu tossed and turned, her mind ablaze with thoughts of scaling Mount UPSC. Re-entering the study mode and acquiring the vast knowledge needed was impossible without joining a coaching academy and committing her time fully.

The following morning, she took a leap of faith and applied for a three-month leave from her job. Later that day, accompanied by Joshy, Minnu visited a private coaching academy. It was a modest institute catering to a diverse spectrum of students pursuing various competitive exams. The academy's director agreed to admit Minnu but demanded a fee of Rs 25,000. Despite Joshy's willingness to secure a loan from his workplace, Minnu insisted on mortgaging her gold bangles.

With newfound enthusiasm, Minnu devised a meticulous timetable and re-entered the realm of education, attending classes at the academy from 8 a.m. to 8 p.m. daily. Having been distanced from academic studies for a while, she laid a solid foundation with National Council of Educational Research & Training (NCERT) books, starting from Class 6 onwards and gradually transitioning to more advanced texts.

Minnu's passion for history, geography, economics and political science propelled her forward in her exam preparation. This love for humanities had sparked in high school, but her parents envisioned her as an engineer or doctor. One evening on their terrace, a heated argument ensued, but ultimately, her parents prevailed despite her supportive grandmother's intercession.

Minnu diligently read two newspaper dailies every day, absorbing vital information, taking copious notes and preserving editorials, important news pieces and captivating photographs in her notes register.

A significant challenge was the CSAT. Minnu analysed her strengths and weaknesses. English comprehension emerged as her strong suit while she struggled with mathematics. So, she decided to focus on the former, but it wasn't enough to get her through. She then worked on her reasoning and fundamental mathematics skills to help her sail through.

Minnu's diligence and hard work began to instil her with growing confidence. Time flew by and before she knew it, the formidable challenge of the Prelims arrived in August 2016. However, to the disappointment of Joshy and his family, Minnu couldn't surmount this first hurdle. She remained unfazed by the setback.

'It was a close call. I've qualified in the CSAT, and I got good marks in general studies. I'll definitely clinch it in my next attempt,' she declared with a contented smile, her determination unshaken.

Towards the end of that year, Minnu embarked on a pilgrimage to the Holy Land with Joshy and his parents, broadening her horizons beyond Kerala. The Holy Land, roughly corresponding to the modern states of Israel and Palestine, ignited a new spark within her, fuelling her aspirations to become an IAS officer and explore the beauty of the wider world.

'I need a reputable coaching academy to guide me on this arduous journey,' she thought, her resolve strengthening with each passing day.

A Divine Blessing

Shortly after her return from the Holy Land, Minnu received a divine gift through her friend, Sherin (name changed). 'Didi, I've got some exciting news for you,' Sherin exclaimed, waving a newspaper advertisement. 'Chennai's famous IAS Academy is opening a branch right here in Thiruvananthapuram.'

Minnu's eyes lit up with anticipation, having heard glowing praises for this academy. However, a cloud of uncertainty momentarily dimmed her joy. 'But Sherin, it's a big institute and I may not be able to afford their fee,' she said, her enthusiasm waning.

Sherin quickly allayed Minnu's concerns. 'Didi, read carefully. They are starting with a 'test series' that's quite affordable. They're even providing a reading room.'

Despite Sherin's reassurance, Minnu harboured worries about the financial burden. After dinner, she shared her concerns with Joshy. 'Don't worry, Minnu. Jesus has arranged the money, too. I received some pay arrears today,' he said with a broad smile, bringing a big sense of relief to Minnu.

Minnu enrolled in the test series at the Academy on 1 December 2016, kicking off her rigorous preparations for the upcoming Prelims exam. She dedicated herself to her studies every day after returning from the office, often studying until the early morning hours. Weekends and holidays were fully committed to her preparations.

Unlike her past study routines, Minnu's approach this time went beyond mere reading. She diligently tackled test series from the academy, previous years' question papers and questions posted on websites of various coaching institutes. At the peak of her preparation, Minnu devoted an impressive ten to eleven hours daily to her studies.

But the persistent feeling of being unable to spend quality time with her son gnawed at her. She yearned for the simple joys of telling him bedtime stories, feeding him, playing with him after returning home and attending his playschool events. She longed for those precious moments that seemed to slip through her fingers.

Amid the sacrifices, Minnu found solace in her improving performance with each round of the test. Over time, she consistently earned high marks, often securing the top position in the test series, boosting her confidence. Joshy was her strong pillar of support: providing emotional and financial assistance, shouldering family responsibilities, caring for their child, shielding Minnu from societal pressures and acting as her cheerleader during moments of stress and self-doubt.

'Chettan, I've meticulously cross-checked my answers with the answer key. I'm confident that I will clear the

Prelims,' Minnu shared with Joshy, her excitement palpable, after the 2017 Prelims exam.

Minnu's prediction turned out to be spot on when she found her roll number among the list of successful candidates shortlisted for the Mains. The entire Joshy family erupted in joy.

A Wild-Card Entry Wins Hearts

The dawn of the next day brought the reality of a more formidable challenge—the Mains exam. Although Minnu harboured a deep love for geography and had chosen it as her optional subject, she hadn't delved into it since high school.

'Chettan, in the Mains, I have to write long answers requiring diverse and profound knowledge of the subject. I also need to practice answer-writing under the guidance of a skilled tutor,' she confided in Joshy while stirring their morning coffee, her face etched with concern.

'Don't worry, Minnu, we'll find a reputable academy for your preparations,' Joshy tried to assuage her anxiety, gently patting her.

After thorough exploration, Minnu and Joshy zeroed in on an academy in Thiruvananthapuram. A fellow aspirant had sung praises about the institute's stellar geography faculty.

Upon visiting the academy, Minnu and Joshy were welcomed by one of its co-founders. Despite his welcoming demeanour, he didn't mince words about the challenge ahead. 'You haven't studied geography since college and there are only three months left for the Mains exam. Covering the syllabus will be extremely difficult,' he cautioned, casting a shadow of disappointment over Minnu and Joshy.

However, a glimmer of hope emerged when he suggested, 'I may consider taking you after testing your answer-writing skills.'

Minnu attended an answer-writing session that very day. Impressed by her articulate writing style, the faculty agreed to admit her. To cover the extensive syllabus, they recommended a demanding schedule—two daily sessions from 6 a.m. to 8 a.m. and 4.30 p.m. to 6.30 p.m.

The new routine posed challenges not only for Minnu but also for Joshy, who had the responsibility of dropping her off at the academy before heading to work and returning to pick her up in the evening. Minnu remained at the academy throughout the day, utilizing the institute's reading room between her geography sessions.

Minnu devised a comprehensive strategy to navigate the diverse array of subjects and papers in the Mains exam. Among the two qualifying language papers, English posed no difficulties. However, she needed to rekindle her grasp of Malayalam, which she hadn't studied since school. Her mother, a Malayalam teacher, took on the responsibility of teaching her and evaluating her answers.

For general studies, Minnu began with topics she had not covered for the Prelims exam. To overcome her limited attention span, she adopted a mixed approach, dedicating time each day to study all papers.

For her optional subject, Minnu adopted a strategic approach. In the first paper, she decided to focus on answering as many questions as possible from human geography, which she relished as compared to the other part, physical geography. The second paper centred on Indian geography, where UPSC posed more generic questions. Minnu cleverly applied the theoretical concepts from the first paper to enrich her answers in the second paper.

She disabled all her social media accounts, ceased chatting with friends, skipped social functions, stopped dining out and momentarily forgot about her office commitments. Just as Arjuna, in the Mahabharata legend, focused solely on the eye of the bird he was asked to strike, Minnu's gaze was fixated solely on her Mains exam, rendering the rest of the world temporarily invisible to her.

Her relentless hard work bore fruit as Minnu cleared the Mains exam. It was a momentous occasion for Minnu and her family, and the celebration continued for hours.

'Amma, I can't believe that I have made it to the interview stage. It's like a wild-card entry reaching the final of a grand slam,' Minnu shared with her mother-in-law, radiating pride.

Braving the Tsunami

That night, the absence of her father weighed heavily on Minnu's heart. She was deeply attached to him and still wondered why he left them so soon. He was her hero, the epitome of strength and security.

'If he were alive today, he would have been brimming with pride and joy', Minnu thought. A storm of emotions brewed inside her, its waves breaking in her eyes. Memories of June 2007, when her father's battle with depression ended tragically, flooded her mind.

On a day when Minnu was honoured for her academic excellence by their church, she excitedly planned a shopping trip with her father. Little did she know it would be their last.

'I will go to the doctor and get a medical certificate,' Paul Raj said as he dropped Minnu home. However, he didn't return, leaving the family extremely worried. The next day brought the devastating news of his passing, leaving the family shattered. Amidst their grief, whispers and taunts haunted Minnu, blaming her for her father's death.

Walking down the street, Minnu couldn't escape from the hurtful whispers: 'Look, she's the girl who has caused her father's death.' At the bus stop, heartless taunts from youngsters added to her torment. 'Who will take care of you now? Come and live with us,' they jeered.

But amidst the storm, Minnu found solace in her grandmother's steadfast support and her uncle John's comforting presence. Their love shielded her from the harshness of the world.

As Minnu's graduation neared, discussions about her marriage filled the air. Concerned about the gossip surrounding Minnu, her family felt marrying her off quickly would protect her. Minnu, too, longed for an escape from the house that had haunted her since her father's passing. So, in 2011, when a marriage proposal from Joshy came her way, Minnu accepted without much contemplation.

A Christmas Gift

After Paul Raj's passing while in the Kerala government's service, the 'death in harness' rule provided an opportunity for one member of his family to secure a Group-C government job. They family nominated Minnu for the position. Guided by her uncle, John, she initiated the application process.

'Which job would you like to apply for, Minnu? Police constable or clerk?' John asked, reviewing the options.

Minnu pondered, her father's memory lingering. 'Being a constable demands physical strength and irregular hours,' she reflected.

John nodded, 'True, but clerk positions have a long waitlist. Constable jobs often have more immediate openings.'

Concerned about rigorous police training, Minnu hesitated, 'I'll wait for the clerk's position and focus on my studies.'

With a playful jab, John teased, 'I know, you're too lazy for the police force.'

Thus, Minnu's name joined the long list of hopefuls for appointment on compassionate grounds. However, the list moved at a snail's pace and the process seemed interminable. With each passing month, Minnu started losing hope. Joshy consistently motivated her, assuring her that the job letter would soon be in her hands.

In September 2012, Minnu completed her post-graduation in biochemistry, securing the second rank in the university. Finally, in the first week of December, the long-awaited offer letter for a clerk's job in Kerala police arrived. Minnu was asked to report to police headquarters (PHQ) on 26 December 2012.

On that day, Minnu's heart swelled with emotions as she remembered her father. Her mother, too, had tears in her eyes. Minnu rose early, visited the church and prepared for her first day in office.

'You're lucky. You've been assigned to the PHQ itself. Go to room number 121 on the first floor to complete the paperwork,' one of the elderly ladies at the PHQ reception informed her.

Minnu's heart leaped with joy. Her deepest desire was to be posted in or near Thiruvananthapuram. For the next three years, Minnu devoted herself wholeheartedly to her work at the PHQ. It seemed like her path was set until Panda's advice changed the course of her journey.

The Elusive Summit

Returning to March 2018.

Following a day of celebration upon the announcement of the CSE-2017 Mains exam results, Minnu enthusiastically prepared for the interview. To confront the ultimate challenge, she, accompanied by Joshy, boarded the Kerala Express to New Delhi.

On the day of the interview, Minnu awoke earlier than usual. Due to anxiety, she couldn't eat breakfast. She hastily reviewed her profile and accomplishments and perused the day's newspaper. Boarding an auto with Joshy from the Kerala House, where they had been staying, they made their way to Dholpur House, the imposing UPSC office at Shahjahan Road.

The grandeur of Dholpur House left Minnu in awe. Following security checks, she entered a spacious waiting hall, filled with fellow aspirants. A UPSC officer briefed them on the interview procedure before wishing them luck and departing.

Minnu, consumed by anxiety, kept mostly to herself, exchanging limited interactions with other aspirants. After a lengthy wait, her turn finally arrived just before lunch.

As she entered, the chairperson of the board greeted her, acknowledging the late hour. 'We're nearing lunchtime, so let's keep this brief. Please start with a self-introduction,' he said.

Summoning a smile, Minnu began recounting her journey. The chairperson listened attentively, but the next question caught her off guard. 'Is there something you'd like to add that isn't mentioned in your Detailed Application Form (DAF)?' He inquired.

Fumbling for an answer, Minnu struggled. 'Sir, there's nothing more. I'm a reader and a traveller,' she stammered.

'But that's already in your DAF; there's no need to repeat it,' He stated, increasing Minnu's nervousness. The interview delved into her work and academic choices, with questions about Kerala police's authority to issue arms licences and her decision to select geography as her optional subject, despite having a biology background.

'Having lived in Thiruvananthapuram for a long time, have you ever considered moving out of the city?' one of the board members asked.

Minnu found the questions random; not many were focused on the topics she had prepared for meticulously from her DAF. The interview lasted less than fifteen minutes, leaving Minnu feeling disheartened.

After the interview, she meticulously analysed her performance and identified several weaknesses: her body language betrayed apprehensions, erosion of confidence due to negative feedback in mock interviews in Kerala, a dip in self-belief upon seeing aspirants from across the country in Delhi and a tendency to respond to every question, whether she knew the answer or not.

Plummeting Dreams

On the brisk morning of 27 April 2018, Minnu battled a storm of nerves. Rumours flew through a Telegram app group about the imminent release of results. She found it challenging to concentrate on her work and repeatedly checked her phone. Finally, in the evening, a PDF containing the names of successful candidates appeared. With bated breath, Minnu scanned the list, her heart sinking as her name eluded her grasp.

The disappointment was palpable, casting a shadow over the dinner table where her family gathered, tears clouding their eyes. But amid the gloom, Minnu remained resilient, trying to console them. 'Please don't be so upset. Isn't it a significant achievement that I made it to the interview stage. My name will definitely be on the list next year,' she assured them.

However, the heavens had decided to test her determination and mental strength further. The period of anxiety leading up to the results, followed by the disappointment of her failure, left her in no shape to adequately prepare for the next Prelims, scheduled just two weeks later.

Despite not performing well in Prelims-2018, Minnu was hopeful that she would sail through to the Mains stage. However, she was dumbfounded when she didn't find her name in the list of candidates shortlisted for the Mains exam. When the marks were published, she found that although she had scored well in general studies, she couldn't qualify in the CSAT.

Struggling under the weight of disappointment and fear, Minnu found herself paralyzed, unable to face her colleagues after the setback. The daunting prospect of returning to the office kept her confined at home. Despite Joshy's earnest efforts, Minnu remained ensnared in the tendrils of despair.

But Joshy's staunch support gently nudged her back into the fray. Reluctantly, Minnu returned to the office, bracing herself for the judgemental gazes of her colleagues. Yet, with each passing day, she found the strength to rise above their taunts, a testament to her indomitable spirit.

She mustered the strength to apply for leave and confront the Prelims-2019. However, fate dealt her another cruel blow as CSAT thwarted her aspirations once again.

Pandemic Makes Life Beautiful

On 12 February 2020, Minnu saw an advertisement from UPSC for the CSE-2020 exam. The sight of it stirred a mix of emotions within her—excitement, sadness, hope and despair. She left her workplace and made a photocopy of the advertisement. Sitting in the car, she showed it to Joshy.

'Should I take the chance? What if I fail again?' Minnu asked, tears in her eyes.

'Success is only a matter of time, Minnu. Take leave and prepare diligently. Consider this attempt for me,' Joshy reassured her, gently holding her hand.

'I've already missed out on so much, including precious moments of Doodle (Jeremiah) growing up. I can't keep gambling indefinitely. This will be my last try,' she declared firmly.

The next morning, Minnu started her preparations with renewed determination. However, her progress was halted by the onset of the Covid-19 pandemic. To curb the spread of the virus, the Kerala government ordered the closure of coaching institutes on 8 March 2020 and the exam was indefinitely postponed.

Confined to their home like billions of others, Minnu reevaluated the worth of many aspects of her life. Her husband, Joshy, became the most significant revelation.

'I used to believe our marriage worked because we saw each other less. But I was wrong. During the lockdown, we were always together. We cooked side by side, watched television, talked for hours and enjoyed each other's company. I have truly understood Joshy now,' Minnu confessed to her best friend during a Zoom call.

Joshy's friends often questioned his support for Minnu's IAS exam pursuit.

'How will you handle it when your wife becomes an IAS officer? You're just a technician. You'll be several ranks below her. She'll be riding in a car, living in a bungalow, wielding significant power,' they inquired.

One day, Joshy asked Minnu playfully, 'After you clear your exam and become an IAS officer, will you still go on a bike ride with me?'

Minnu laughed heartily and hugged him. 'I'll just change my profession, but I won't become a different person. I'll always treasure a bike ride with you,' she replied.

A Gift from the Coaching Academy

During the Covid-19 pandemic, Minnu studied with her best friend Aswathy (name changed) on Zoom. One day, Aswathy asked, 'Minnu, did you know our coaching academy owns a flat near the academy? Why don't you ask the centre in charge to let us stay there to prepare for the exam? You are their top performer in the test series, and they might agree if you request them.'

Minnu's eyes lit up at the idea, but then dimmed at the thought of leaving her son and husband for months. She contemplated not pursuing it. However, Joshy, who overheard the conversation, convinced her. 'You will be able to concentrate on your studies better if you shift with Aswathy,' he told her. The next day, Minnu talked to the centre in charge, who readily consented.

As Minnu packed her bags, excitement coursed through her veins. Yet, as the moment drew near to leave, a tidal wave of sorrow crashed over her. The mere thought of being separated from her son and Joshy for months gripped her heart in an unrelenting vice.

That night, as darkness enveloped her room, sleep eluded Minnu like a distant memory. Instead, her mind became a gallery of memories, each frame adorned with the radiant smiles of her son and the comforting presence of Joshy. Tears silently streamed down her cheeks.

The next morning, after breakfast, Minnu placed her suitcase in the car's trunk. Her son clung to her; his arms wrapped tightly around her neck. She kissed him, reassured him of daily video calls, promised she would return soon and then, hiding her tears, she sat in the car. The pressure to conquer Mount UPSC had now intensified.

As they stepped into the apartment, Minnu and Aswathy immersed themselves in studies with renewed vigour. To save time, they cooked once every two days and cleaned the apartment once a week. Amidst the intense preparation, daily calls to their families became a lifeline.

The Prelims exam finally took place on 4 October 2020. Minnu, though well-prepared, couldn't shake off the fear of the CSAT. 'Chettan, I am confident about general studies, but the fear of not qualifying in the CSAT haunts me,' she confided in Joshy on their way to the exam centre.

'I have a trick that will make you pass the CSAT. But I will tell you after the general studies paper,' Joshy reassured her with a smile.

Joshy had noticed a pattern in Minnu's previous attempts. After the general studies paper and before CSAT, she would sit in the car with her phone and the question paper, trying to confirm her answers. Discovering some incorrect answers soured her mood and sapped her confidence before the CSAT.

After Minnu completed the general studies paper, Joshy decisively withheld the question paper and her phone. 'This is the trick to clear the CSAT that I was mentioning earlier. You won't get your phone and the question paper back until you complete your CSAT,' he insisted.

The result was a well-deserved victory over the CSAT, propelling her to the next round.

The Final Battle

Without waiting for the Prelims results, Minnu and Aswathy started preparing for the Mains. Minnu analysed her performance in the last Mains exam she took in 2017. She worked on her weak areas, participated in test series for each paper and indulged in intense answer-writing practice. She effectively used evaluators' feedback to refine her responses.

The hard work paid off, as both Minnu and Aswathy successfully cleared the Mains exams.

Recognizing the limitations of interview coaching in Thiruvananthapuram, Minnu decided to spend a month in Delhi with Aswathy. The time in Delhi was filled with mock interviews that greatly boosted Minnu's confidence.

Minnu and Aswathy also conducted mock interviews with each other. After Aswathy's interview, Minnu's mother joined her in Delhi. Mock interviews with her mother provided Minnu with valuable feedback on her composure and articulation.

On the eve of her interview, Minnu sought guidance from Panda, the IPS officer who had motivated her to write the exam. His advice was simple yet profound: 'Talk to the board very freely, just like you are talking to me. You are good, just be yourself.' These words bolstered Minnu's confidence.

On 21 September 2021, draped in a beautiful green saree, Minnu returned to the UPSC central hall for her Personality Test (Interview). Her Interview was scheduled for the post-lunch session. Calm and composed, she exchanged friendly banter with fellow aspirants while awaiting her turn. The messenger arrived at 5.30 p.m. to guide her into the interview room.

As she entered the room, a board member casually mentioned, 'My granddaughter's name is also Meenu,' eliciting light laughter and warm smiles. This light-hearted moment put Minnu at ease, and she responded with a warm smile.

The board's questions covered various aspects of her DAF, including biochemistry, geography and her police force experiences. They also asked about her travels, the states she had visited and her experiences in foreign countries. While the questions were probing, they weren't overwhelming.

Leaving the grand Dholpur House, Minnu reflected on her performance. 'This will either turn out very well or extremely poorly. However, this will undoubtedly be my final one. I hereby conclude my UPSC journey,' she thought.

The Ascent of the Queen

On 24 September 2021, Minnu stepped into her office, feeling the anticipation in the air. WhatsApp and Telegram buzzed with news of the imminent release of the CSE-2020 results. Unable to focus, Minnu constantly checked her phone. Amid this tension, Minnu received a call from Joshy around 11 a.m.

'Minnu, your second Covid-19 vaccine shot is scheduled today at VSCC. Can you come, or should I pick you up?' Joshy inquired.

Nervous, Minnu replied, '*Pranayini* [sweetheart], I can't take the bus today. People say the result will be declared. I'm extremely nervous. Please pick me up.'

Joshy reassured her, 'Minnu, I am coming right away. Just relax; you will make it this time.' His words comforted her.

After her vaccination, Joshy offered to drive her back to the office, but wanting to be with Joshy, she declined. 'Chettan, I'm very stressed. Let's take the second half off and head to the beach,' she suggested.

Understanding her anxiety, Joshy readily agreed. They drove to the beach, but the heat kept them inside the car. Minnu's stress led to a flurry of comfort food demands, which Joshy happily met.

As the day progressed, Minnu's anxiety persisted. Suddenly, she declared, 'Chettan, I want to meet Aswathy. Let's pick her up and come back to the beach.'

They headed to Aswathy's place and returned to the beach. The tension grew with the flood of messages about the result. Finally, around 7 p.m., pictures of the result sheets appeared on Telegram.

Silently praying, with hearts racing, Minnu and Aswathy downloaded the pictures and scrolled through them, fingers trembling. A triumphant shout broke the silence: 'Congratulations, Minnu, you've done it! It's serial number 150,' Aswathy exclaimed. Overjoyed, Joshy cheered, 'Minnu, your hard work has paid off. I am so happy and proud!'

Minnu verified her name and roll number. The tension melted away, leaving a radiant smile and tears of happiness in her eyes. However, her eyes remained fixed on the list, searching for Aswathy's name, yearning to celebrate their success together.

They scrolled through the list repeatedly. But Aswathy's name was missing. The joy of Minnu's success was bittersweet without her dear friend's selection. Their five-year journey had been full of highs and lows; celebrating alone felt incomplete.

A Star Is Born

On Aswathy's insistence, they dropped her home. Minnu's phone buzzed incessantly, and Joshy was managing the calls. Minnu, with her eyes closed, felt a sense of emptiness; the success had not fully sunk in. She thought it was a dream and asked Joshy more than once to pinch her, needing confirmation that it was indeed a reality.

'Minnu, your geography sir from the coaching academy is on the line,' Joshy said, extending the phone towards her. Minnu felt a surge of happiness.

'Congratulations, Minnu, you have made all of us proud,' his warm words flowed through the phone, filling her with a sense of accomplishment.

'Please come to the academy right away,' he told her.

Without much thought, they made their way to the academy, where the faculty was waiting at the gate to receive her.

'Thank you so much sir,' Minnu expressed her gratitude to her geography teacher and mentor amidst the tears streaming down her cheeks.

Inside the academy, Minnu was met with a delightful surprise. The academy founder had organized a gathering to celebrate her achievement, including a prominent minister. A throng of media personnel had also assembled to capture the moment, their cameras flashing in a whirlwind of activity. In the mere minutes following the results, Minnu had been thrust into the spotlight, her newfound stardom sweeping her off her feet.

Joshy was overjoyed as he observed the scene, feeling as if he, too, had become an IAS officer. He reminisced about Minnu's relentless toil and the countless sacrifices she had made over the last six years. His eyes became moist as he recalled Minnu's pain of living away from their child.

After an hour, amidst the whirlwind of interviews with countless journalists, Minnu spotted her husband standing quietly in a corner. Joshy was looking at her with unmistakable pride and a beaming smile. The bustling chaos around Minnu momentarily faded and a tidal wave of love and gratitude surged within her as she locked eyes with her husband. In his gaze, she recognized the same pride and support that her father displayed whenever she achieved success in her younger days.

The clock read 10.30 p.m. when Minnu and Joshy finally returned home. Their son and parents welcomed them, their eyes brimming with tears of joy. The house was abuzz with the presence of relatives and media personnel.

On seeing his parents, Jeremiah ran towards them and embraced Minnu. He had been fielding questions from the media about his mother's struggle and success. By now, he knew that his mother had done something really big. Minnu's mother, her voice filled with emotion, said, 'I wish your father was alive to celebrate with us today,' as she held Minnu close in a heartfelt hug.

Minnu's heart swelled with a mixture of joy and pride, not just for her own achievement but for her family's resilience. Amidst the celebration, she couldn't help but remember the hardships her mother had endured after her father's passing, igniting a whirlwind of emotions she had long suppressed.

The Coastal Girl Gasps in the Himalayas

The next two months whisked by in a whirlwind of celebrations, interviews and reunions. On 30 November 2021, Minnu prepared to catch her flight to Delhi. She had spent the past few days shopping for the extensive list of items required by the Lal Bahadur Shastri National Academy of Administration (LBSNAA), Mussoorie. As Joshy loaded her luggage into the car's trunk, Aswathy arrived with a bouquet of flowers. She enveloped Minnu in a heartfelt hug, extending her best wishes. Minnu was overwhelmed with emotions. 'I'll eagerly anticipate seeing you in the academy as an officer trainee next year,' she said, wrapping Aswathy in a warm embrace.

On 1 December 2021, Minnu, accompanied by Mithun, another successful candidate, boarded a taxi from New Delhi to Mussoorie. When she arrived, the picturesque hill station left her in awe. The first glimpse of the LBSNAA unleashed a tempest of emotions and the six years of her struggle played like a vivid reel in her mind. She fondly recalled the brief conversation she had with Panda on that fateful day which changed the course of her life.

Soon, Minnu found herself in her designated room in the Narmada hostel. As she stepped in, a warm and friendly face welcomed her with an illuminating smile. 'Welcome, Minnu. I've been looking forward to meeting you,' said her roommate, who had been selected for the Indian Information Service. Minnu smiled and embraced her.

'You are elder to me. I will address you as "*akka*", which means elder sister in Tamil,' she said.

With grace and warmth, Minnu replied, 'I would love to be your akka.'

The first day passed by meeting other officers who had joined the LBSNAA that day. In the evening, they went to the mess to have their dinner. Minnu felt breathless while climbing up from the hostel. She could hardly eat as she was tired, had a headache and didn't like the food. But she was happy to meet so many young and cheerful officers, highly elated to have achieved their long-cherished dream.

Mussoorie's harsh climate was a far cry from the warmth Minnu was accustomed to. Initially, her ill health and an outbreak of Covid-19 kept Minnu confined to her hostel room. However, her world at the academy began to brighten by Republic Day 2022. She started connecting with her peers, attending events and savouring every moment. It felt like a return to her college days.

Learning the Ropes in District Training

During her Foundation Course, when Minnu received her cadre allocation, the news brought a blend of surprise and contentment. Maharashtra, her second choice, was to become her new home. After a brief round of training at the Yashwantarao Chavan Academy of Development Administration (YASHADA) in Pune, Minnu and her colleagues were taken on a 'Maharashtra darshan' to familiarize them with this vibrant state.

Thereafter, she was allocated Washim district for her training, where she was warmly welcomed by the collector, Shanmugarajan S., who proved to be a remarkable mentor.

Minnu embraced the local culture and made efforts to learn Marathi. Her attempts at speaking the language in broken yet sincere sentences brought smiles to the faces of her staff and the local people.

After her attachments to various government offices, Minnu was entrusted with the responsibility of chief officer, municipal council, Washim. Two weeks into her role, Minnu was summoned by Shanmugarajan.

'The city is plagued by encroachments. The streets have become hardly recognizable, causing immense inconvenience to the people. Take up a drive immediately to remove these encroachments.' Shanmugarajan got straight to the point.

Minnu felt a surge of unease; the thought of dismantling encroachments meant that many people would lose their homes and their livelihoods. She was also concerned about potential damage to her soft and friendly public image. Trying to appeal to the humanitarian aspect, she said, 'But sir, it will cause great hardships to thousands of people and result in the loss of livelihood for many families.'

Shanmugarajan, however, remained resolute. 'These are illegal structures that have encroached upon the right of way. Consider the plight of many more who endure hardship due to these encroachments,' he said sternly.

Minnu mustered some courage to find a way to avoid taking up the drive, 'I agree sir. But there are dense permanent and semi-permanent structures. This will be an extremely formidable task which should be handled by a regular chief officer,' she pleaded.

The collector remained firm, 'I understand that it will be a daunting operation. However, it's young officers like you who can handle such onerous and complex tasks without fear or favour. It will also be an invaluable experience for you and help you in tackling tougher challenges in your future assignments,' he tried to motivate her.

'I will provide you with all the support you need for this drive. Start preparations immediately and I expect it to be completed in two weeks,' he ordered.

With clear directives from the collector and a determination to alleviate the inconveniences faced by citizens due to encroachments, Minnu transitioned from being the amicable face of the community to a formidable force.

Challenges emerged, with the most immediate being the legal battle. A staggering 150 cases were filed against her and the collector in the district court. Undeterred, Minnu met with the principal district judge. Following her compelling argument, all the petitions were summarily dismissed.

However, more challenges awaited, primarily in the form of political pressure from local leaders. On the day of the drive, a massive crowd gathered, shouting slogans and some even pelted stones. But Minnu responded assertively and defused potentially volatile situations.

When the encroachments were finally removed, Minnu was surprised to witness the city's transformation. The people of Washim also couldn't believe their eyes.

For the first time, they truly grasped their city's inherent beauty. The wide streets and beautiful fountains, once lost to encroachments, revealed a city that had been thoughtfully and beautifully planned.

As Minnu left Washim upon the completion of her district training in August 2022, a sizable crowd gathered at the circuit house to bid her farewell. Her driver and PSO's family had brought packed lunch for her journey. Minnu felt a surge of emotion. After expressing her gratitude, she settled into her car, embarking on a journey to a new district, ready to face a new set of challenges.

* * *

Key Takeaways from Minnu's Story

1. **Don't Bury Your IAS Dream:** Many women in India give up on their IAS dreams after marriage or motherhood. Minnu's journey shows that with determination, you can achieve your IAS dream while balancing your familial responsibilities and other formidable challenges both at home and at work.

2. **Age is Just a Number:** You can start your journey to realize your IAS dream at any age within the range prescribed by UPSC. Don't be disheartened by the thought of competing with younger aspirants. With hard work and a disciplined study schedule, you can bridge any gap. Use your age and life experiences as assets, not hindrances.

3. **Embrace Failures as Stepping Stones:** Failures in the CSE are common and should be seen as learning experiences. Failing in the Prelims after clearing all other stages also happens. Don't be disheartened. Use failures as weapons to strengthen your resolve, fuel your determination and leap higher in your next attempt.

4. **Take CSAT Seriously:** The CSAT might be a qualifying paper, but it is crucial. Every year, many aspirants see their IAS dreams shattered despite performing well in general studies. Analyse your strengths and weaknesses and invest your time in CSAT accordingly. Relax before CSAT, don't

dwell on your GS performance and approach it with a calm and focused mind.

5. **Don't Fear Competition or Feel Inferior:** Don't be afraid of the competition or feel inferior to aspirants from Delhi or other metropolitan cities. Your hard work, discipline and perseverance matter most. Compete with yourself, continuously improve and don't let an inferiority complex hold you back.

6. **Be Calm, Confident and Honest in the Interview:** The Interview is not just a test of your knowledge but a reflection of your personality. Face it with confidence, honesty and a calm demeanour. Don't be afraid to admit when you don't know an answer. The board appreciates honesty as much as knowledge. Approach your Interview as a conversation, be yourself and let your genuine personality shine through.

Chapter 2

Hitting the Bull's Eye at the First Attempt

Regar Pura Erupts in Jubilant Screams

24 September 2021. Warm sunset hues filled the streets of Regar Pura in central Delhi's Karol Bagh and it was a kaleidoscope of colours and sounds. Local cafes and roadside eateries were buzzing with music and the lively chatter of the crowd.

Once a hub of leather factories, Regar Pura has undergone a remarkable metamorphosis into a bustling neighbourhood and is today teeming with shops and paying guest (PG) accommodations. Reasonably priced lodging and proximity to many known coaching institutes has turned Regar Pura into a sought-after destination for civil service aspirants.

At around 6.45 p.m. that evening, a nondescript four-storeyed building in the congested neighbourhood was pierced by a crescendo of jubilant screams. A tempest of emotions emanated from its ground floor.

Intrigued by the sudden commotion, three boys residing on the same floor rushed to the epicentre of the uproar. It was a small room inhabited by a young recluse named Satyam Gandhi. He had moved into the building a year-and-a-half ago and was known for his rare appearances outside the confines of his abode.

Driven by a sense of urgency, one of the boys pushed the door. Surprisingly, it swung open effortlessly. What greeted them inside was a captivating scene. A compact fifty square-foot space bursting at the seams with books, newspapers and magazines. The clutter adorned every available surface—the table, floor and even the bed.

Amidst this chaos, they saw Satyam Gandhi in the throes of euphoria. He was jumping on his bed with childlike exuberance, his voice a mix of shouts and sobs. 'I have done it! I can't believe that I've done it in my first attempt!' he screamed.

Overwhelmed by curiosity, one of the boys asked, 'Bro, what has happened?'

A little embarrassed at the sudden entry of the trio, Satyam broke into a beaming smile. 'I have cracked the CSE. I have got tenth rank in my first attempt,' he shared, intermittently wiping his tears of joy away with trembling hands.

The boys had some idea that Satyam was preparing for the CSE. They had witnessed his dedication, observing him always confined to his room. However, the enormity of Satyam's achievement took them by surprise. They did not anticipate that their young neighbour would crack CSE with a top rank.

'That's incredible bro, we are so proud of you,' the boys exclaimed in unison, with a tinge of disbelief in their voices. They extended hearty handshakes, warm hugs and sincere congratulations before settling down in whatever little space they found. Satyam got busy with his phone, incessantly buzzing with congratulatory messages. The small room amplified the volume, allowing the troika to overhear the conversations.

'Papa, I have cleared the UPSC. I have got tenth rank', they heard Satyam say over a phone call, elated with joy.

'*Arre wah, beta!* I had full confidence in you,' said his father, with immense pride in his voice.

'*Suniye ji, aapka beta IAS ban gaya hai* [Listen, your son has become an IAS officer],' Satyam's father informed his wife, who was busy in the kitchen. She hastily abandoned her cooking and snatched the phone from her husband's hand.

'Maa, God has answered your prayers,' Satyam shared, tears streaming down his face as soon as he heard his mother's voice.

The boys could hear Satyam's mother crying with happiness and gratitude. After a moment, she composed herself and said, 'Lord Shiva has blessed us today. Well done beta, you have made us so proud.'

In the interim, Natansh, one of Satyam's college friends, arrived with a small cake. As Satyam ceremoniously cut the cake, they playfully smeared it on Satyam's face before savouring a piece each.

'Let's go out and celebrate,' Natansh suggested.

However, Satyam had no money to throw a lavish party. Undeterred, they strolled down to a humble tea stall in the nearby Guru Gobind Singh market in Karol Bagh. The modest celebration of a grand success culminated with the comforting warmth of tea and *ladoos*.

The First Gandhi of Dighra

Satyam hailed from a small village named Dighra in the Samastipur district of Bihar. His father, Akhilesh Kumar, served as an assistant in the sugarcane department at the nearby Rajendra Agricultural University in Pusa. Satyam's mother, Manju Devi, skilfully managed their home.

In his early years, Satyam achieved a unique distinction—he became the first person in his village to be adorned with the title 'Gandhi'. How did that happen?

Amidst school breaks and their parents' pilgrimage to Devghar, Satyam and his brother Shivam spent time with their *mamaji*, Prem Ranjan, and *mamiji*, Sidhi, in Muzaffarpur.

'Satyam is such a very quiet child. He embodies non-violence, much like Gandhiji, and joyfully shares his favourite toys and candies,' Sidhi remarked one evening.

'I agree. He happily eats whatever you give him, even if it's bitter gourd,' Prem Ranjan added with a smile, glancing at Satyam engrossed in playing in a corner of the room.

'So, I've begun calling him Gandhi, our Gandhi baba,' Sidhi chuckled.

And so, Satyam became Satyam Gandhi. His father accepted the title so fondly that when he filled out the admission form for the Kendriya Vidyalaya at Rajendra University in 2005, he officially changed his son's name from Satyam Kumar to Satyam Gandhi.

Satyam, too, cherished the 'Gandhi' surname. In a school fancy dress competition, he gleefully dressed up as Mahatma Gandhi.

Satyam was the favourite grandchild of Sachidanand Rai, a respected figure in his village. Rai had retired from the post of assistant at Rajendra University. Every evening, the neighbourhood children would assemble at Sachidanand's house, and he would assist them in their studies. He also told them captivating stories and anecdotes.

'When the television arrived in our village, people thought that someone was sitting inside it and talking,' he shared, laughter dancing in his eyes.

'And when someone brought a torch for the first time, people thought it would burn their hands and were afraid to touch it,' he smiled, recalling another delightful anecdote.

Satyam's grandfather handed him a page of the newspaper every day, nurturing an early love for reading. The stories of collectors touring villages and resolving local issues intrigued Satyam, sparking a curiosity about the identity of these influential figures. One evening, unable to contain his curiosity, he turned to his *dadaji* and asked about them.

'Beta, a collector is the head of the government in a district. Only IAS officers can become collectors,' dadaji explained, as Satyam listened intently.

With a hopeful glint in his eyes, dadaji added, 'We have such a big family. I hope one of my grandchildren will become an IAS officer.'

'Dadaji, I will fulfil your wish and become a collector one day,' Satyam declared, his eyes shining with determination and a promise.

From that moment, the aspiration to become an IAS officer burned in Satyam's heart. There was an urgency as his dadaji was already 85 years old.

The Grind Polishes the Diamond

The sun would barely kiss the horizon when the day began for Satyam's parents in their modest one-room dwelling in Dighra. Manju Devi would cook food and gently wake Satyam and his brother Shivam, sleeping in their covered little balcony.

Akhilesh would ready their humble mode of transportation—an aging bicycle adorned with two towels tied around its top tube. These towels doubled as seats for Satyam and Shivam. There was a daily battle for the coveted front position. At 6.30 a.m. sharp, their five-km journey from the village to the school would unfold.

Satyam was a bright and enthusiastic student. His passion for debates, general knowledge competitions and science exhibitions painted a vivid picture of his intellect. In Class 10, his model showcasing the climate change in Pusa earned him a spot at the national-level Children's Science Congress.

In adolescence, people often have multiple career dreams. Besides his fascination with becoming an IAS officer, Satyam was also captivated by the armed forces, particularly the Indian Air Force (IAF). He dreamed of soaring high in a fighter aircraft, performing daring manoeuvres. Through his research on the Internet, he learned that securing a high rank in the National Defence

Academy (NDA) examination after Class 12 was the gateway to joining the IAF.

When the Class 10 results were announced, the entire family was engulfed with joy. Satyam's perfect 10/10 GPA prompted a celebratory feast of 'halwa'. Amidst the joy, Akhilesh Kumar envisioned his son becoming an engineer, a dream shared by many parents.

'Manjuji, you will see your son become an engineer soon,' Akhilesh Kumar proclaimed with delight, savouring the warmth of the halwa.

'But Papa, I love humanities and want to pursue the Arts stream,' Satyam expressed reluctantly, taken aback by the unexpected announcement.

'No, you must pursue science subjects. Only those who struggle with their grades or lack dedication opt for humanities,' Akhilesh frowned disapprovingly.

While Akhilesh Kumar's decision and its delivery may seem stern and unreasonable, it mirrors a prevailing reality in many parts of India, where children often bear the weight of academic choices imposed by their parents.

Satyam opted for the science stream. Later, when he was in Class 12, he was forced yet again by his father to take the Joint Entrance Examination (JEE) for admission to the Indian Institutes of Technology (IIT). Lacking interest in engineering and without adequate preparation, he unsurprisingly secured a rank with six digits, resembling a telephone number.

However, unfazed by this, Satyam had his gaze fixed on Delhi University.

A Dream Shatters

On a calm September evening of 2017, within the 17-Services Selection Board (SSB) campus in Cariappa Colony, Bengaluru, a storm brewed in the hearts of forty young boys. Aged between eighteen and twenty years, they had gathered with dreams of joining the NDA and getting commissioned into the armed forces.

The air was charged with the collective yearning for success. Seated attentively in the conference room, they eagerly awaited the result declaration with a blend of tension and fervent hope. In the past seven days, they had been subjected to an unrelenting barrage of tests and interviews designed to assess their psychological attributes, intelligence, physical fitness, creative thinking, communication finesse and leadership potential.

The tension multiplied as the president of the SSB entered, clutching a crucial piece of paper. Everyone rose to their feet to welcome him.

'Good evening, boys. I sense the anxiety in this room. How shall I unveil the results—randomly or in the sequential order of chest numbers?' he inquired.

'Randomly, sir!' came a resounding voice vote.

'Very well, boys. Listen carefully. The candidates who have earned the recommendation are chest numbers thirty-nine, five, eleven and twenty-eight.'

The announcement of 'chest number eleven' resonated like sweet music in young Satyam's ears. For a fleeting moment, disbelief seized him—had he truly conquered the SSB in his inaugural attempt? But soon, he soared on cloud nine. His dream of joining the IAF and becoming a pilot may now come true.

With the dawn of the next day, the four chosen candidates were in the Command Hospital in Bengaluru for their comprehensive medical examinations. Spanning five exhaustive days, these examinations meticulously scrutinized the candidates' medical parameters and fitness.

The climactic day of the medical examination was reserved for the scrutiny of eyes. Satyam, brimming with confidence, was convinced his eyesight would pass with flying colours. He was eager to board the train and rush back to his village, where celebrations awaited with his family. In his mind, he was already visualizing himself clad in a uniform, navigating the boundless blue skies in a fighter jet, executing a breathtaking array of manoeuvres.

The day started with the examination of eyesight, a hurdle that Satyam effortlessly cleared. Following this, he found himself ushered into a dimly lit room for the mysterious 'lantern test'. Surrounded by LED lights of varying hues, he confidently called out each colour for the examiner. However, the hearty laughter of the other three candidates left him puzzled. 'Why are they laughing?' he wondered.

'Alright, Satyam, let's move on to another test. We call it the Ishihara test,' the doctor announced. They moved to the adjoining room, where the doctor handed Satyam a book. Each page of the book was a mosaic of dense dots.

'Look closely at each page and tell me the number written on it,' instructed the doctor.

Satyam diligently flipped through the pages, attempting to decipher the hidden numbers. 'Sir, I can't see any number on any of the pages. There are just dots,' he confessed, a visible cloud of confusion shrouding his expression.

The doctor delivered a devastating blow. 'You are not fit to join the armed forces,' he declared.

Satyam couldn't fathom the words. 'What's he saying? Why is he saying that?' His mind raced, grappling with the sudden and unexpected turn of events.

'Sir, please don't say that. I am perfectly fine. If there is any minor problem, I will get it treated,' he pleaded desperately, his voice choked with tears and anxiety.

'You are colour-blind, Satyam. You can't differentiate between different colours,' he delivered the news to an anxious Satyam.

'Sir, I will get it treated. There must be some medicine or surgery available,' Satyam pleaded, desperation etched in his voice.

'Unfortunately, it's a genetic condition and there is no cure for it. It is just bad luck,' the doctor tried to offer a semblance of comfort to Satyam.

That night, Satyam's tears flowed freely. 'Why did this happen to me? Where am I in fault here?' he pondered.

Gradually, the weight of realization bore down on Satyam. The doors to the armed forces were now firmly closed for him. In the echo of that bitter truth, a quiet resolve took root within him.

'There's only one door left to uplift my family and secure a decent life. Perhaps, this is God's indication that my destiny lies not in the armed forces but in the IAS,' he whispered to himself.

Discovery of a Role Model

Satyam had enrolled for a BA (honours) in political science at Delhi University's Dyal Singh College. Towards the end of his first year, he stumbled upon an enticing announcement on the college notice board: an unpaid summer internship in the office of the collector, Ranchi. He applied promptly and was overjoyed to receive a message of his selection a few days later.

Stepping into the collector's office, he found himself amidst a cohort of twelve interns. An orientation session, graced by collector Mahimapat Ray, awaited them. For Satyam, this marked the first encounter with a collector in the flesh, filling him with an exhilarating mix of thrill and curiosity.

Ray impressed him with his remarkable intellect and dynamism. He meticulously laid out his expectations for the interns: study the implementation of the government's rural development schemes and compile a report on their impact.

Each intern was assigned a specific block, and Satyam was allotted Silli block, nestled on the border with West Bengal. Here, he spent a month-and-a-half entrenched in the day-to-day operations of the Block Development Officer (BDO). Beyond the evaluation of scheme impacts, Satyam participated in a unique project, 'Leader of Light'. It aimed at empowering women Self-Help Groups (SHGs) by teaching them how to assemble solar lamps.

Satyam drew profound gratification from this experience. The diversity and impactful nature of the work of an IAS officer, as he experienced during his internship, ignited a deeper passion in him for the job.

On the closing day of the internship, Ray hosted a dinner in his expansive bungalow for the interns. In an atmosphere of camaraderie, he encouraged everyone to share their experiences. Satyam had discovered a role model in Ray.

A *Barsati* in Lajpat Nagar

Satyam's initial sojourn in the Delhi NCR led him to his mamaji's house in Sector 62, Noida. Coming from a quaint village, he was awestruck by the towering buildings, giant metro rails and throngs of people in Delhi. However, within a few months, he realized that commuting from Noida to Dyal Singh College was neither sustainable nor cost-effective, consuming over three hours each day.

As his second year began, Satyam started searching for accommodation closer to his college. After meticulous research, he settled on a place in Lajpat Nagar with a monthly rent of Rs 7000. His first home in Delhi was a modest barsati, a small tin-roofed structure perched on the terrace of a building. Unable to afford a bed, he settled for a mattress and a small gas stove for cooking.

Yet, culinary challenges loomed large. Dining out was prohibitively expensive, with a meal costing Rs 100. To cut costs, Satyam began skipping meals, a sacrifice that took a toll on his health. By the end of his second year, his weight had plummeted from 65 kg to a mere 52 kg.

The adversity only fuelled his determination to pursue IAS, with the goal of putting an end to his family's hardships. He conducted extensive research to grasp the requirements of the CSE and the most effective preparation strategies. Reading *The Hindu* newspaper became a daily ritual.

In college, Satyam discovered invaluable mentors in Kamal Nayan Chaubay and Prakash. However, he also encountered numerous faculty members who attempted to dissuade him, some advising him to pursue a career in academics instead.

Undeterred, Satyam stood firm in his resolve. From his second year of graduation, he dual-focused on both his academic studies and CSE preparation. This early commitment laid the groundwork for the formidable journey he was about to undertake.

Mounting Family Debt Compels an Early Start

The burden of his father borrowing money to finance his expenses at an exorbitant interest rate from a local moneylender, Battukdev, haunted Satyam persistently. Fuelled by this financial challenge, he resolved to expedite his journey to scale Mount UPSC in the final year of his graduation. Starting his serious preparations in April 2019 for the CSE Prelims-2020, he enrolled in a popular coaching academy in Karol Bagh. However, the daily commute from Lajpat Nagar consumed precious time, prompting Satyam to bid farewell to his modest barsati.

His search for accommodation culminated in a small room in Regar Pura. This minuscule 10-ft by 5-ft space in a four-storeyed building, barely accommodated a single bed, a small study table and a chair. With no almirah, Satyam resorted to stacking his books on the floor and bed. Apart from the comparatively lower rent, the room's greatest advantage lay in its proximity from his coaching centre.

Due to the precarious financial situation of his family, Satyam had capped his monthly budget at Rs 12,000, including the room rent of Rs 8000. It severely constrained his food budget, compelling him to opt for a modest tiffin service of two daily meals at Rs 65 per meal.

With coaching classes scheduled from 5.30 p.m. to 7.30 p.m., Satyam initially attempted to balance college in the morning and coaching in the evening. However, the taxing routine left him with minimal time for CSE preparations. The expense of commuting to college added to his financial strain, too. So, he made the tough decision to attend college only for tests and submission of assignments.

Satyam's approach earned the ire of many of his teachers who disapproved of his sporadic attendance. Their taunts, such as calling him 'collector sahab' when he did attend, aimed to embarrass Satyam. Some faculty members attempted to humiliate him by asking particularly difficult questions in class and mocking him when he couldn't answer.

However, these humiliations only strengthened Satyam's resolve. He redoubled his efforts, studied harder and sequestered himself in his room to focus entirely on his studies.

Time Management Tricks

Satyam's approach to time management became a defining feature of his exam preparations. Each night, before retiring, he meticulously scrutinized the day, logging every minute spent on various activities. He would document this analysis on a sheet of paper, enabling him to assess time wastage, gradually instilling a greater sense of discipline. Within two months, this practice became second nature to him, resulting in an increase in the duration devoted to his studies.

Even during his commute to college, Satyam utilized his time fruitfully by carrying reading material, studying in the metro rail and during classes. He arrived early for coaching classes to secure a spot in the front row. Though other aspirants engaged in casual conversations while standing in line, Satyam utilized this time to study his notes.

Satyam astutely recognized that many classes at the coaching academy were not productive, and he could cover these topics in one third of the time in self-study. Despite having paid a substantial fee of Rs 1.6 lakh, equating to Rs 500 per class, he courageously prioritised his time over monetary considerations. So, he attended only the sessions covering the topics he found to be challenging.

Understanding the time-consuming allure of social media, reels and short videos, Satyam deactivated all his social media accounts. These included his beloved Instagram, where he showcased his photography skills. This allowed him to maintain sharp focus on his studies.

Satyam made a deliberate choice to distance himself from most of his friends, recognizing the significant time commitment involved. Upholding the principle of not squandering time at any cost, he believed that true friends would understand a temporary disconnection.

He maintained contact with only two friends, Harsh and Natansh. While Natansh was his college friend, Satyam had met Harsh at the coaching centre. He could reach out to Harsh even at odd hours to clarify doubts and grasp economic concepts.

A Master Strategist

Before embarking on his preparation journey, Satyam conducted extensive research, watched videos of IAS toppers and read their blogs and answer sheets. One crucial lesson he learnt was the importance of multiple revisions of books and notes. Additionally, he realized the significance of selectively reading from an optimum number of resources.

Satyam demonstrated a remarkable ability to plan the trajectory of his preparations over a six-month period. He broke down his targets into weekly and daily goals, encompassing the number of pages or chapters to be covered. He firmly believed that mere hours of study without specific targets would not lead to success. Instead, one must strive to achieve daily objectives.

During the initial few months, Satyam covered all subjects daily, making a concerted effort to meet his everyday targets before going to bed. In the event of any lapses, he reserved Sunday as a strategic day to bridge any gaps. Adherence to this rigorous strategy and hard work enabled him to revise each subject multiple times before the Prelims.

Moreover, Satyam carefully analysed topics to discern which ones carried a higher likelihood of featuring in the exam. He observed that some aspirants invested substantial time and effort for subjects like world history or post-Independence history, which yielded disproportionately low returns. In contrast, focusing on subjects like polity, medieval history, economics and geography, known for easier and a higher question frequency, offered a more strategic use of limited study time.

Another key element of his strategy was the segregation of coaching study and self-study. Satyam believed that reviewing the day's coaching material at home was counterproductive. Instead, he adopted an inverse approach, studying the upcoming coaching topics in advance. This allowed him to clarify doubts and gain a deeper understanding during the coaching sessions.

To stay updated with current affairs, Satyam followed a routine of reading *The Hindu* in the morning and the *Indian Express* before bedtime. While he initially read the entire newspapers, he later became more selective in his approach. Recognizing the approaching mental exhaustion during the Mains exam period, Satyam stressed the importance of pushing one's comfort zone well in advance.

Implementing what he referred to as the 'adaptation formula' or 'prepare-test-identify-weaknesses-prepare', Satyam systematically worked on removing his weaknesses. He concentrated on the areas where he had scored lower. For topics where mistakes were recurrent, he delved into the basics to pinpoint and rectify the root causes of his errors.

However, he wisely avoided a common mistake made by many aspirants—taking mock tests too early in their preparation journey. Instead, he focused on building a solid foundation of knowledge before testing himself.

Integrated Approach Advantage

Satyam followed an integrated approach and carefully blended his Prelims and Mains preparation. He believed that a robust Prelims groundwork forms the cornerstone for Mains success.

For Mains, the basic books don't suffice. Understanding this limitation, Satyam read supplementary materials such as the Yellow Book from Vajiram and the Value Added Material from Vision IAS. To enhance the quality of his notes, he simultaneously read from two books, placing one on each side and crafting integrated notes for each topic. Although time-consuming, this technique significantly enriched the depth of his study.

In September 2020, Satyam took a careful look at the UPSC Mains syllabus. He transcribed it onto A-4 sheets and pasted them prominently in front of his study table. This gave him a comprehensive overview of the topics and helped him in studying only the relevant topics.

Initially, he used bound registers for taking notes. However, Satyam soon recognized the impracticality of adding notes to them as his preparations advanced. Consequently, he transitioned to creating notes on loose A-4 sheets. It gave him more flexibility in accommodating notes from the evolving nature of study material from newspapers and magazines.

Covid-19 Derailment

In March 2020, an unwelcome and dreaded guest, Covid-19, knocked at India's doors. Having read about the havoc the virus wreaked in other countries, Satyam understood the potential seriousness. By 15 March 2020, with only ten reported cases in Delhi, he sensed the situation might worsen. Alone and anxious, he booked a train ticket and hastily packed his books in two huge bags. The next day he left for his village, without vacating his PG room, assuming the situation would be under control shortly. His brother Shivam, who was studying in Chandigarh, also accompanied him.

Satyam and Shivam alighted swiftly at Pusa, laden with heavy bags filled with books. As they were contemplating how to transport the bags outside the platform, two policemen rushed towards them, instilling fear in the brothers.

'What are you carrying in these heavy bags? Open them immediately,' one of the cops ordered.

'Sir, there are books inside, nothing else. You may see,' Shivam said, opening the chain of one of the bags.

However, the cops remained unsatisfied. 'We are not fools. Take out all the books and show us. I am sure you are carrying liquor beneath them,' one of them said sternly.

Given the complete prohibition in Bihar and with incidents of liquor smuggling not uncommon, the cops were strongly suspicious that the two young boys were attempting to exploit the situation for personal gain.

Satyam and Shivam found themselves unpacking every book from their bags for the sceptical cops.

Due to the pandemic, the Prelims exam, initially scheduled for 30 May 2020, got postponed to 4 October 2020. Considering the widespread lockdown and uncertainty, UPSC allowed candidates to change their examination centres. Given the circumstances, Satyam opted to change his centre from Delhi to Patna.

However, Satyam soon realized that studying at home was challenging. So, in July 2020, amidst the ongoing

Covid-19 pandemic, he took a grave risk and returned to Delhi. The extended preparation time due to the pandemic turned out to be a blessing in disguise, allowing him to create comprehensive notes and cover previously untouched topics.

However, his resolve was soon put to the test. As the exam approached, Satyam developed a high fever, reaching 104 degrees on 30 September 2020. Despite the severity of his illness, going to the hospital was not an option, as it would disrupt his studies. Instead, he chose to manage his symptoms by taking paracetamol and multivitamins purchased from the local chemist.

Given that his exam centre was in Patna and with no option to change the location available now, Satyam decided to travel to Patna by train, even with a high fever. After the exam, he meticulously compared his answers with the answer key released by the coaching institutes, instilling confidence that he would qualify for the Mains. After a brief two-day break, he resumed his preparations for the Mains exam.

Overcoming the Second Hurdle

In the initial month following the Prelims, Satyam prepared notes for the remaining topics, investing at least twelve hours a day in his studies. With meticulous planning, he struck a fine balance between the study of various subjects and answer-writing practice.

However, a formidable financial hurdle surfaced again. Satyam wanted to purchase test series for the general studies and ethics papers. Additionally, he wanted to enrol in a crash course for political science and international relations. This required about Rs 1 lakh, which would have been a huge financial burden for his family.

One day, as Satyam appeared visibly distressed in the coaching class, his friend Harsh encouraged him to share his concerns. Harsh hailed from an affluent family and had always been a source of motivation for Satyam owing to his humility, dedication and disdain for wasted time.

Later that day, Satyam received a call from Harsh's father, extending a generous offer to fund Satyam's fee for the test series and the crash course. Grateful yet hesitant, Satyam initially declined but, upon persistent insistence, accepted with the promise of repaying the money. The test series proved invaluable for enhancing his answer-writing skills.

For the essay paper, Satyam delved into Durushetty's book, titled *Fundamentals of Essay and Answer Writing*, supplementing it with insights from news, other books and coaching notes. Initially concerned about potential language barriers, he was happy to discover that, with a good flow and a depth of knowledge, even modest English could yield good marks. Through consistent practice, elaborate readings, meticulous analysis of evaluators' feedback and targeted improvement efforts, Satyam enhanced his English proficiency, too. He also accumulated a repertoire of versatile quotes for incorporation into his essays.

For the ethics paper, Satyam based his preparation on the material and guidance obtained from newspapers, toppers' videos, test series and value-added material of a coaching centre. To add real-world context, he meticulously collected real-life examples.

Recognizing the pivotal role of legible handwriting and efficient speed in the exam, Satyam devoted attention to cultivating both. Advice of past toppers that leaving no question unanswered and finishing within the stipulated time frame significantly increases the likelihood of Mains success echoed constantly in his mind.

Initially, Satyam overlooked his optional subject, political science and international relations, postponing engagement until November. Believing he could grasp the subject solely through book readings, he adopted a casual approach and didn't prepare notes. However, the harsh reality hit him hard when he appeared in the first mock test. Recognizing the gravity of his oversight, he swiftly downloaded copious notes and books from libgen. is, blending them with notes of a famous coaching teacher, and prepared a comprehensive set of personal notes.

The Nervous Breakdown

Satyam was immersed in an intense study regime, dedicating a rigorous over twelve hours a day to his preparation. Initially, he adhered to a standard sleep schedule, wrapping up his studies at 11 p.m. However, he soon recognized the tranquillity of the night hours and their conducive environment for focus. So, he dismissed the idea of adhering to a fixed 'Brahma-muhurat' and transitioned to an unconventional routine—studying throughout the night, sleeping at 8 a.m. and waking up at 3 p.m.

Aware of the limited financial resources available to his family, Satyam felt the weight of the ticking clock and the limited number of attempts he could make. As the Mains exams drew near, the vastness of the syllabus and the lingering untouched topics induced a mounting sense of pressure and anxiety. The culmination of these factors triggered a nervous breakdown on 29 December 2020, just days before the Mains exam.

As per his daily routine, he called home around 9 p.m. that day. As his mom picked up, Satyam started crying loudly. His mom got very worried. 'What happened beta, please stop crying and tell me?' she asked.

'Maa, I am sorry. I know you have taken loads of loans to fund my coaching, but I won't be able to clear the exam this time. Let me prepare harder and try next time. I am just twenty-one years old and I have so many attempts left,' he said, crying inconsolably.

His mom was supportive as usual. 'I understand, beta. You have made us proud by clearing the Prelims in the first attempt. You don't need to worry about money. Calm down, take your time and try next year,' she said. Satyam's father also supported her.

Satyam kept the phone down after talking to his parents for a while. It gave him a lot of strength and renewed his resolve to become an IAS officer in his first attempt. So, he returned to his books and studied until 8 a.m. Then he switched off his phone and went to sleep.

When he got up at 3 p.m. and switched on his phone, he got scared to see sixty missed calls from his parents. He immediately called home and as he said hello, he heard his mom's voice, which was a mix of sobs, cries and screams.

'Where were you, Satyam? Why was your phone not reachable? Are you fine, beta? We were extremely worried after talking to you last night. We fully understand your situation and we are okay if you don't write the exam. But don't think negatively or harm yourself,' she said in one breath.

Satyam had a tough time explaining to his parents that he was perfectly fine and it's usual for him to get up at 3 p.m.

Satyam felt very guilty, but he also felt blessed that his family cared so much about him. He realized that the dream of becoming an IAS officer was not solely his but belonged to the entire family.

To combat his loneliness and depression, Satyam started going to a nearby library. He was happy to see people around and liked the changed environment. He tweaked his schedule and adopted a cycle of sleeping for four hours and studying for six hours. From the Prelims to the Mains, he had decided not to get a haircut. His hair had grown long. None of his college friends could have recognized the fat, long-haired, bearded Satyam.

The Admit Card Saga

It was 7 January 2021, the day of the essay writing paper, the first of the Mains exam. Satyam had studied until the early morning and when he got up, it was 7 a.m. He hurriedly got ready and looked for his admit card and Aadhaar card, which were to be presented for inspection in the examination hall. But he couldn't locate them. He desperately searched the entire room, looking everywhere, searching the piles of books on the table, on the floor and on the bed. He had saved copies of both documents on his phone, but unfortunately, phones were not allowed inside the examination hall.

In a state of panic, he came out of the room. It was the peak of Delhi winter with biting cold. Dense fog enveloped the surroundings. He ran to the nearby Karol Bagh market to download and print the documents, but all the shops were closed. He called many shop owners on the mobile numbers written on the shop signboards and begged them to help him. But none of them heeded his pleadings. Helpless and frustrated, he sat on the pavement and started crying. The weight of his dreams and the pressure of the moment overwhelmed him, and tears streamed down his face in the cold foggy morning.

Suddenly, he looked at his watch and realized that it was 8 a.m. Entry inside the examination hall was scheduled to start within half an hour. In a state of desperation, he composed himself, hailed an auto and decided to go to his examination centre. On the way, he kept praying to God for a miracle.

Thankfully, his prayers were answered and as an exception, the centre in-charge allowed him to take the phone inside, show his documents to the invigilator and deposit the phone back. However, the morning's events had taken a significant toll on his concentration. He forgot all the quotes and anecdotes that he had worked hard to remember for the essay paper. Many facts, figures and details were also erased from his memory. However, he managed to complete both essays.

Nevertheless, in the subsequent general studies and optional subject exams, he performed well and left no question unanswered. After the exams concluded, Satyam felt confident and estimated a 90 per cent chance of clearing the Mains exam.

A Dance on the Road

After completing the Mains exam, Satyam decided to prioritize his health. He incorporated jogging and gym sessions into his daily routine. He visited his family and embarked on a couple of treks, too.

On 24 March 2021, his coaching academy's Telegram group was simmering with messages anticipating release of the Mains exam results. After waiting anxiously for the whole day, Satyam decided to hit the gym. Midway through his workout, he glanced at his phone and his heart skipped a beat. Someone had posted a PDF containing the Mains result.

Quickly exiting the gym, he swiftly downloaded the PDF and used the search function to find his roll number. On spotting his roll number, excitement overcame him, and he erupted into spontaneous joy. Dancing and jumping on the road outside the gym, he threw his fists in the air, shouting with exuberance. Onlookers inside the gym, observing him through the expansive glass windows, were left in awe, trying to fathom the extraordinary moment unfolding before them.

In the midst of his jubilation, Satyam suddenly became aware that he was in a public space, surrounded by a growing audience appreciating his impromptu celebration. Feeling a sense of embarrassment, he quickly retreated into the gym, where curious onlookers gathered around him, eager to understand the reason behind his streetside revelry.

As he shared the news, disbelief and surprise rippled through the crowd. Some of them, fellow civil service aspirants who had struggled through multiple attempts at the Prelims without success, couldn't conceal their astonishment. One of them, voicing the collective sentiment, remarked, 'You look like a first-year college student. How could you clear such a tough exam?'

The Rebirth

Amid the excitement of his upcoming interview on 31 May 2021, Satyam's world was disrupted by the unwelcome return of the Covid-19 pandemic. This time, its Delta variant wreaked havoc across India. On 10 April 2021, Satyam was gripped by fever and a persistent cough. He decided to get tested, only to be met with the distressing revelation that he had contracted Covid-19.

Delhi was facing a grim situation. Securing a hospital bed had become next to impossible and oxygen was in critically short supply. The thought of succumbing to the virus alone in his cramped room haunted Satyam. Determined to seek medical assistance, he made his way to the Dr Ram Manohar Lohia (RML) Hospital.

Upon arrival, he was greeted by a dreadful scene—a queue of ambulances, patients relying on oxygen support and the distressing sight of bodies being transported in plastic bags. Undeterred, Satyam, alarmed and anxious, redirected his steps to the nearby B.L. Kapoor Hospital. However, the situation there mirrored the one he had just left. Nevertheless, he braved the circumstances, enduring a lengthy wait before finally seizing an opportunity to approach a doctor in the corridor.

In a desperate plea, he begged to be admitted, emphasizing his vulnerable state and the fact that he was all alone. The doctor's response, however, was callous laughter. 'You are young and seem to be fine. Don't you see that there are hundreds of serious patients who need a bed much more than you,' he said and walked away.

Defeated but undeterred, Satyam retraced his steps to his room. On the way, he bought a handful of medications based on a prescription circulating on WhatsApp—paracetamol, zinc, azithromycin, multivitamins and a pulse oximeter. He took the medication regularly and monitored his oxygen levels. His anxiety soared when the oxygen saturation dropped to 88 on the third day. The fear of a further decline haunted him, but thankfully, it didn't go down any further.

Despite this reprieve, Satyam found himself in the throes of physical agony, battling breathing difficulties and grappling with the heavy weight of isolation and fear. His desolate surroundings echoed with the incessant sirens of ambulances, amplifying his sense of solitude. His parents and brother were extremely worried about him.

His modest tiffin service had stopped, too, worrying him more. Faced with the existential challenge, a stroke of recollection brought forth his small gas stove from the days in Lajpat Nagar barsati. With a spark of hope, he cleaned the stove and rejoiced at its revival. Gathering some rice from a nearby grocery shop, he managed to cook a meagre meal.

Satyam survived the tumultuous ordeal as the fever gradually subsided. The sense of survival was akin to a rebirth. Yet, an unsettling tightness lingered in his chest. In pursuit of a conducive environment for recovery, Satyam sought refuge in Noida, residing with his mamaji's family. However, the aftermath of the illness rendered him bedridden for three months. Fortunately, due to the pandemic, his Interview that was originally scheduled in May was postponed to 1 September 2021. The respite allowed Satyam space for recovery as well as time to prepare for the Interview.

Satyam prepared for the potential questions that might arise from his Detailed Application Form (DAF). In a bid to bolster his confidence for the Interview and enhance his proficiency in English, he appeared in numerous online and offline mock tests. He also watched mock interviews of past years' toppers on YouTube, particularly of those who had secured more than 200 marks in their Interview. To enhance his linguistic skills, he watched English dramas and read fiction and non-fiction books.

Positive reviews in mock Interviews bolstered his confidence. The interviewers also asked to minimize his eyebrow movement and hand gestures, adopt a softer and more polite tone and maintain an upright posture akin to an army officer. However, balancing the need for improvement with the risk of forgetting answers, Satyam opted for measured changes in his approach.

A Rare Compliment

The Interview call also meant a significant financial burden for Satyam. To meet the demands of the occasion, he had to buy a new shirt, suit, tie and a pair of shoes costing a staggering Rs 10,000. This necessitated additional borrowing from Battukdev at an exorbitant interest rate.

On the auspicious day of 1 September 2021, at approximately 11 a.m., Satyam adorned himself in a suit and tie. Donned with a face shield, mask and gloves, he beheld his reflection in the mirror. A chuckle escaped him at the sight of his appearance, resembling someone geared up for entry into a nuclear reactor. Following a moment of prayer and seeking blessings from his mamaji and mamiji, Satyam embarked on the journey to the UPSC building for his Interview scheduled in the post-lunch session.

When Satyam entered the central hall of the UPSC building, he found himself among fifty or sixty other aspirants seated in different rows. The atmosphere was palpable, different from the mock Interviews he had experienced. The Interview room was different, too. Unlike the expansive halls equipped with cameras, this room resembled a typical government office, with a small space hosting five individuals seated around a table in a horseshoe configuration. Initially taken aback, he had the fleeting thought that he might have walked into the wrong room.

The newspapers had published the quarterly GDP data in the morning. Expecting questions on economics, one of his weak areas, Satyam was worried. To his surprise, no such questions were asked.

When Satyam stepped into the Interview room, the chairman gestured for him to remove his face-shield. Thereafter, he requested Satyam to introduce himself. This led to a series of questions revolving around his DAF. The panel explored his experiences at the SSB for the NDA.

The atmosphere lightened momentarily when one of them inquired, 'Which Pusa are you from? The original in Bihar or the duplicate in Delhi?' His response sparked a few chuckles.

Thereafter, the interview delved into the developmental challenges faced by Bihar and Jharkhand. His role as the president of the photography society in college took centre stage, with the panel delving into the qualities he acquired and the initiatives he spearheaded. The discussion seamlessly extended to the future of films in India.

Given Satyam's mention of reading science fiction as a hobby, one of the members inquired about the state of the space sector in India, questioning why it's not more advanced. The conversation seamlessly transitioned to speculative ground as they explored the potential real-world manifestation of a movie storyline in the future.

Shifting gears, the discussion turned to the 'vocal about local' approach advocated by the Prime Minister. The interview delved further into the comparative development status of India and China. One of the panel members appeared dissatisfied with Satyam's answers, visibly displaying a lack of contentment. Despite Satyam's attempts to establish eye contact, the member continued to gaze out of the window, creating an air of uncertainty. Satyam perceived this as a potential test of his psychological resilience. Meanwhile, a lady seated at the end of one side attentively observed his composure and speaking style.

The Interview left Satyam in a state of ambiguity regarding its overall success or failure. However, as he exited the interview room, a board member who had earlier posed questions about the development of Bihar and Jharkhand, offered an unexpected compliment, stating, 'You have done very well.'

Such positive feedback from board members is uncommon. It provided Satyam with a sense of happiness and boosted confidence as he entered the suspenseful phase of awaiting the results.

Bags Packed: Mussoorie or Dighra?

Satyam knew that his family was financially strained and unable to continue funding his living and coaching expenses in Delhi. With each passing day, the expenditures and loan from Battukdev were mounting. The guilt of burdening his parents with high-interest loans weighed heavily on Satyam. Faced with this financial crunch, he resolved to make a choice: either go to the LBSNAA in Mussoorie for induction in the IAS or return to his village, Dighra, to study for the next attempt.

On 24 September 2021, Satyam was very nervous as the UPSC was poised to announce the results. Messages inundated WhatsApp and Telegram, creating an overwhelming atmosphere. Succumbing to the mounting stress, Satyam halted his studies at 3 p.m. The tension peaked at 6.15 p.m., when a PDF file surfaced on Telegram.

Determined to witness the result first hand, Satyam downloaded the PDF, activated flight mode on his phone, offered a silent prayer and began reading names from the top rank. To his astonishment, he spotted his name on the very first page. Overwhelmed with disbelief, he double-checked the roll number, confirming the match. Still wary, he entertained the thought of a prank, switched on his phone and was greeted by a flood of congratulatory messages, dispelling any lingering doubts.

As the realization sunk in, he recognized that he had not only altered the trajectory of his own life but had also transformed the fortunes of his family. The fulfilment of his dadaji's wish and the realization of his parents' dream brought immeasurable joy.

Meanwhile, media personnel descended upon Satyam's home in Dighra. In his absence, his parents gracefully handled their inquiries. Intriguingly, parents of prospective brides seeking an IAS groom also gathered. Watching one news video, Satyam couldn't help but be amused as his mother ceremoniously applied a 'tilak' to his photograph. The winds of change were undeniably sweeping through his life.

The Star Comes Home

Becoming an IAS officer with such a high rank was a momentous occasion in Bihar, drawing a multitude of well-wishers to Satyam's home. However, seeking a quiet reunion with his family, he discreetly booked his train ticket for 19 October 2021. Despite expressing his desire for a low-key return, the reality that awaited him was quite different.

Upon disembarking at the railway station, he was greeted not only by his parents and brother but also by a sizeable crowd eager to garland him. A convoy of vehicles, including a car specially decorated with flowers, awaited him outside the station. The platform buzzed with excitement as he found himself draped in a cascade of floral tributes.

When he arrived in his village, the grandeur of the welcome overwhelmed him. An elaborate welcome gate decked the village's entrance, with similar structures on every street he traversed. Welcome posters featuring his pictures adorned the village. Flower petals cascaded upon him, creating a festive atmosphere. The entire village was immersed in celebration, bringing immense joy to his parents and his dadaji.

Although Satyam wasn't fond of the extravagant display, his mother comforted him, emphasizing the village's love for him. 'Beta, don't be angry. It's the villagers' way of expressing their love for you. You've become a role model for society now. Don't give them a chance to think you've become arrogant,' she advised.

A public function unfolded outside his home, attracting prominent residents of the village. Speeches were delivered and Satyam, though fatigued by the end of the day, was called upon to share his thoughts.

After a few days, he was filled with joy to receive an invitation to his school as the chief guest. Just three years ago, he used to stand in line to welcome the district magistrate and other dignitaries during the school's annual day and sports day, listening to their speeches. Now, he was the chief guest, experiencing the same kind of welcome from the students. It was a remarkable and gratifying feeling.

During his stay in the village, Satyam was constantly surrounded by people. Numerous affluent individuals arrived, bringing marriage proposals for their daughters. His parents marvelled at the sight of people arriving in lavish cars bearing large boxes of dry fruits and sweets. A queue of relatives, some of whom had never spoken to them before, formed outside their home.

Satyam was initially confident of getting the Bihar cadre. However, his hopes were dashed when he learned through the WhatsApp group that two candidates, ranked one and seven, were also from Bihar, leaving him with no chance.

When the cadre allocations were disclosed, Satyam received the Maharashtra cadre, causing disappointment not only to his family but also to the entire village. The enthusiasm in the marriage market waned and the warmth from many people dissipated.

Transformation of a Bookworm

At LBSNAA, Satyam transformed into a fitness enthusiast. After classes, he would rush to the riding ground, dedicating one-and-a-half hours to learn horse riding. Following this, he would hit the gym, engage in sports and go for running in the mornings. During weekends, he embarked on treks with his close friends.

Despite his reputation for consuming large quantities of food, Satyam managed to shed five kg due to his rigorous routine, bringing his weight down from 72 kg to 67 kg. Though he harboured a desire to learn swimming, the experience of feeling breathless and overwhelmed in the water led him to reluctantly give up on that particular endeavour.

In contrast, his roommate Abhishek had a completely different routine. While Satyam returned from morning physical training, Abhishek would still be sound asleep.

Satyam, in an effort to rouse him, would prepare and offer toothbrush and toothpaste at 8.55 a.m., coaxing him out of bed with the reminder, 'Bro, please get up. You'll get a memorandum asking for an explanation if you're late to the 9 a.m. class.'

Addressing Child Marriages in Dhule

Satyam was allocated Dhule district of Maharashtra for district training under the guidance of Jalaj Sharma, an IAS officer of the 2014 batch. Sharma had a demeanour akin to a coconut—tough on the outside but with a compassionate core, always supportive of his probationers. Initially, Satyam grappled with understanding the language used in meetings, but he gradually acclimated.

Another concern lingered in Satyam's mind—he was quite young. He contemplated how he would manage older subordinates. To his surprise, these concerns proved unfounded as he adeptly handled independent charges as the block development officer (BDO), tehsildar and sub-divisional magistrate (SDM).

He also learned the art of handling telephone calls from politicians and navigating the pressures associated with the political executive and leaders, all while managing to avoid political interference.

Dhule, being a part of the tribal belt, presented its own set of challenges. Child marriages were prevalent, constituting 40 per cent of all marriages. Satyam dedicated considerable effort to combat child marriages in Dhule. He went on numerous trips to tribal villages, aiming to educate communities about the detrimental effects of child marriages on their daughters' health. He also proactively utilized the 1098 toll-free number, raising awareness about its significance. Moreover, he orchestrated numerous raids at marriage venues just before the ceremonies were solemnized.

During these interventions, Satyam encountered a profound disparity between his perspective and that of the local populace. Poverty and limited access to education had shaped their outlook, with many unaware that marrying off a fifteen-year-old girl was illegal. For them, it seemed like a means to secure a breadwinner for the girl and ensure her well-being.

Satyam recognized the need to comprehend their viewpoint, acknowledging that policies and laws alone couldn't effect change. Convincing people on the ground, employing language and perspectives they understand, is a challenging but essential approach to bring about the desired social change.

***

Key Takeaways from Satyam's Story

1. **Achieving Top Rank in Your First Attempt is Possible**: It's entirely possible to conquer Mount UPSC and secure a top rank on your very first attempt. By following a well-crafted strategy, maintaining a disciplined routine, adhering to deadlines and dedicating yourself fully, you can achieve success right after graduation.

2. **Turn Setbacks into Stepping Stones for Success**: Don't let setbacks and failures discourage you. When one door closes, another opens, often leading to greater opportunities. Use failures as catalysts to strengthen your resolve, renew your efforts and refocus on your target. Each setback is a lesson, propelling you closer to hitting the bull's eye next time.

3. **Stay Organized to Reduce Exam Day Stress**: Keep all necessary documents for the examination hall ready and easily accessible. Misplacing these items on the morning of the exam creates unnecessary stress and diverts your focus, impacting your performance. Prepare everything the night before, ensuring a calm and composed start to your exam day, allowing you to concentrate fully on the task at hand.

4. **Master Time Management**: Manage your time meticulously. Keeping a log of your daily activities helps you adapt to a rigorous schedule, instilling

discipline and preventing unproductive use of time. Immersing yourself fully in studies, limiting conversations with friends and reducing social media time will enhance your productivity.

5. **Don't Neglect Your Optional Subject**: Don't neglect your optional subject, even if it's the same one you studied in college. The syllabus, recommended books and examiners' expectations differ. High score in your optional subject is crucial not only for your overall success but also for securing your desired service and cadre.

6. **Stay Focused Despite Taunts and Humiliation**: Don't be discouraged by taunts and attempts to humiliate you. Many people might feel jealous even at the thought of your success. Maintain your focus and concentration and let your success be the best response to their negativity.

Chapter 3

Leap from Servants' Quarters to Bungalow

'I Will Live in a Bungalow One Day'

On a cold December morning in 2001, a grand bungalow in Delhi's Civil Lines became the stage for a heart-wrenching confrontation. Officials from the public works department (PWD) were engaged in a heated argument with the residents of the servants' quarters located right behind the bungalow. A small crowd of onlookers had gathered at the gate.

Until recently, the stately residence had belonged to P.V. Jayakrishnan, the chief secretary of Delhi. The three families living in the servants' quarters attached to the bungalow had just bid a tearful farewell to Mr and Mrs Jayakrishnan. Among them was Uma, who now found herself the spokesperson for their collective anxiety.

Uma, along with her husband Tikam Singh and their children, eight-year-old Dolly and six-year-old Bharat, had called this place home for the past six years. Tikam worked in a shop in Kamla Nagar. Bharat was born in these very quarters. Now, the PWD officials, led by an assistant engineer, were adamant about their eviction, citing the vacancy of the main bungalow.

Protesting their eviction, Uma implored, 'Sir, why are you forcing us to vacate the quarters? We have been living here for so many years.'

'We can't allow people to live in the servants' quarters if the bungalow is unoccupied,' the assistant engineer said sternly.

Ganga, another occupant, stepped forward, her eyes pleading. 'Sir, please have mercy. Where will we go with our young children in this harsh winter?'

The engineer's response was cutting, 'Do we need to tell you a hundred times? Rules do not allow you to stay here any longer.'

Desperation deepened in Uma's voice as she made one last attempt with folded hands. 'Sir, the new chief secretary will be moving in soon and we will all serve him. It's a matter of only a few days. Please allow us to stay.'

The assistant engineer's tone was final. 'We have already told you it's not possible. So, don't waste our time and move your stuff out by tomorrow. Else we will be forced to throw it out,' he declared, pushing Uma aside as he walked out with his team.

The three families were left in a state of shock. Winter was at its peak and they had no alternative shelter. Finding a room in the servants' quarters of nearby bungalows seemed impossible on such short notice. With meagre incomes, even renting a room in the nearby slum was financially daunting. Sleep eluded them that night.

Determined, Uma decided to make one more fervent appeal to the PWD officials the next day. But her pleas fell on deaf ears. This time, the officials arrived with police and labourers and mercilessly threw their belongings out.

As she packed their modest belongings into a rickshaw, Uma's heart ached with a mix of despair and defiance. Leaving the bungalow premises, she clutched her children close, the sting of her abrupt displacement and the harsh treatment by the PWD officials burning in her mind. Tears streamed down her face as she made a silent, determined vow, 'My children will become officers, and I will live in a bungalow one day.'

Struggle for Survival

In desperation, Uma turned to her elder brother, Rajesh Chauhan, a driver in the Delhi Jal Board (DJB). Rajesh was residing with his wife and two daughters in one-room quarters at the DJB's Chandrawal water works nearby. Despite their cramped space, facing adversity, he extended a helping hand.

Rajesh's modest house was a tight fit for both families. Uma and Tikam soon realized the discomfort Rajesh's family was facing. So, they insisted on moving to a small hut (barsati) on the roof of the house.

Their barsati was hardly an 80-sq-ft space with bare walls and a low, leaking tin roof. Although extremely uncomfortable and providing no protection from the sun or rain, they had no other option but to stay there for a year. Their quest for a home reached fruition when they secured a place in the servants' quarters of the bungalow of an IAS officer nearby.

Life became more manageable in their new, more spacious abode, where Uma found employment as domestic help. However, this respite proved fleeting as circumstances forced them to leave their new home within a year. Uma then secured a job in one of Delhi Transco's flats on the adjacent Shyam Nath Marg, prompting the family to relocate to servants' quarters attached to the flat.

The new complex resembled a small colony, with 14 servants' quarters in a row, two attached to each flat. Tikam's younger brother Amar Singh's family also lived in one of the quarters. Dolly and Bharat were happy as their school was just across the road and there were many children of their age to play with.

However, Uma and Tikam soon realized that the colony's environment was not conducive to their children's development. The other children played constantly and used foul language. Apprehensive about Dolly and Bharat's future, they prohibited them from playing with the other kids. Whenever Uma and Tikam went out, they locked their children inside. Poor Dolly and Bharat felt horrible watching their friends play from their small window.

There was no cable connection in their home, so the only TV channel available for Dolly and Bharat was Doordarshan. Moreover, when the school exams approached, Uma would disconnect the television's power supply and antenna wire and wrap it in a bedsheet.

A Life-Changing Opportunity

One evening in 2003, Tikam returned from work with a box of sweets, his face beaming with excitement. 'I have got a peon's job at the Sanskriti School in Chanakyapuri,' he announced, his eyes glimmering with pride as he opened the box.

'But Chanakyapuri is quite far. Will it not be difficult for you to commute daily?' Uma expressed her concern.

'It's a prestigious school, Uma. The children of IAS officers, army officers and ministers study there. Plus, the pay is significantly higher,' Tikam assured her, hoping to ease her worries.

Uma couldn't help but dream aloud, 'I hope one day Dolly and Bharat will also study in Sanskriti School.'

Sometimes, wishes uttered with earnest hearts find their way directly to the Divine, where they are carefully heard and ultimately granted.

Two years later, Tikam returned home one evening, his face radiating with joy. As Uma offered him water, he couldn't contain his excitement. 'There's a life-changing opportunity for Bharat. He can study at Sanskriti School,' he shared, his eyes twinkling with hope.

Uma was overjoyed but curious. 'But how is that possible? Isn't Sanskriti School reserved for children of senior IAS and civil service officers?' she asked.

'Thanks to the Right to Education Act, schools are now required to admit some children from poor families as well. Sanskriti School will soon organize a test and preference will be given to the children of the school staff,' Tikam explained, anticipating her question.

However, financial worries clouded Uma's initial elation. 'The school fees will be steep and there will be additional expenses for books and uniforms,' she fretted.

'Don't worry. Students from poor families like ours will have their fees waived. Moreover, the school will also provide books and uniforms free of charge,' Tikam reassured her.

Bharat, who had been silently listening to the conversation, was overwhelmed with a mix of emotions. While he was thrilled at the prospect of attending Sanskriti School, leaving behind his friends at the government school tugged at his heartstrings.

A few days later, Bharat found himself at Sanskriti School, sitting for the entrance exam for Class 6. Alongside a handful of other hopefuls, he awaited the outcome with bated breath. The next evening, Tikam returned home with a new school bag brimming with books and a set of crisp uniform.

With tears of joy in his eyes, he proudly announced that Bharat had been admitted to Sanskriti School.

For parents from such a humble background, there could be no greater source of pride and happiness than knowing their child would now study alongside the children of top-notch bureaucrats and politicians.

An Assimilation Nightmare

Bharat's life took a dramatic turn the very next day. He never imagined that he would be thrust into a relentless grind testing his academic mettle, physical endurance, social acceptance and emotional fortitude.

The first formidable task was the daily struggle to reach school. In the predawn darkness, Uma would rouse him at 4.30 a.m., a time when most children were still cradled in the comforting arms of sleep. With Tikam needing to report an hour before classes commenced, young Bharat had no choice but to accompany him. Boarding three crowded Delhi Transport Corporation (DTC) buses in succession, their journey commenced at 5 a.m.

The day extended beyond the final bell. With Tikam's working hours spreading until 4 p.m., Bharat found himself compelled to wait. They endured the crowded DTC buses on the return journey, which stretched his fatigue to the limit. They would reach home only by 6 p.m. Immediately after, Bharat had to rush for tuition classes, concluding at 8 p.m. Sometimes, Dolly had to catch him at the bus stop to hand over a tiffin so that he could go straight for the tuition. By the day's end, exhaustion left no room for play or conversations with friends.

Bharat's inaugural day at the new school proved to be a bewildering ordeal, making it clear that assimilation would be a daunting task. Instructions during the morning assembly were issued in English, leaving Bharat grappling with comprehension. Seeking assistance proved futile, as the replies, too, were veiled in the same language.

Classroom dynamics presented another formidable challenge. Bharat, alongside four other Economically Weaker Section (EWS) students—Pankaj, Sushil, Heena and Gurmeet—found themselves isolated. The affluence of their peers created an insurmountable divide. The elite group taunted and mocked them for their oily hair, thick layer of collyrium, weak English and perceived inferiority.

Bharat, thin and underweight, also became an easy target for bullying.

The educational chasm between Sanskriti School and his previous government school became glaringly apparent. Despite being a topper in his old school, he struggled to keep up. Communication hurdles escalated, especially with teachers delivering instructions in English. Oral exams filled Bharat with fear as he struggled to articulate responses in English.

To help, the school organized parallel classes for EWS students. Here, Ashiya ma'am became Bharat's mentor and guide, assisting him in improving his English and gradually restoring his confidence.

Despite tireless efforts, Bharat struggled to secure good marks in exams. To shield himself from reprimand and his parents from disappointment, he began concealing his grades. However, during parent–teacher meetings, Tikam would inevitably discover Bharat's performance, leading to scoldings and occasional slaps. Bharat yearned to return to his old school. This discontentment seeped into his self-esteem, fostering an inferiority complex.

The initial three years in Sanskriti School proved nightmarish for Bharat. However, as he entered Class 9, a semblance of stability began to emerge. Breaking through barriers, he started integrating with the 'elite group'. Though most of the other EWS students couldn't withstand the pressure and dropped out, Bharat managed to hang on.

A Timely Wake-Up Call

In Sanskriti School, Bharat was introduced to the world of elite civil services. His classmates often shared stories of their parents in these prestigious roles. This planted a seed in Bharat's mind—cracking the civil service examination could alleviate his family's struggles and elevate their social status.

In the Class 10 exams, Bharat performed well, scoring a CGPA of 8.8 out of 10. For Class 11, he chose conventional subjects—physics, chemistry, mathematics, English and computer science. Following his classmates' trend, he persuaded his parents to arrange a whopping Rs 1 lakh for IIT-JEE coaching. However, he became casual in his studies.

His attitude shifted towards achieving the bare minimum marks. He developed the habit of bunking classes and roaming around the campus with a friend. This was a recipe for academic disaster, which struck soon. Bharat failed in three subjects in the Class 12 pre-board exams. Tikam, furious and ashamed, scolded him upon reaching home.

'You have spoiled my reputation in the school. I felt ashamed when the principal called me to her chamber in the afternoon and scolded me. She threatened to throw you out of the school because you will spoil its result,' he said.

Uma, equally upset, took Bharat to four different temples the next morning, searching for solace.

This wake-up call jolted Bharat into action. For the next four months, he immersed himself in rigorous study. His hard work reflected in his Class 12 marks, where he scored 88 per cent in his best four subjects. Moreover, although he couldn't taste success in the IIT-JEE exam, he managed to secure a good rank in the All-India Engineering Entrance Exam (AIEEE), earning admission to Delhi Technological University (DTU). Tikam and Uma's happiness was boundless.

In DTU, Bharat chose mechanical engineering, guided by his fascination with cars. He found added satisfaction in knowing that mechanical engineering was one of the optional subjects for the CSE. The seed of civil services planted in his mind at Sanskriti School was subconsciously taking root.

Team India in Hong Kong

In the bustling corridors of DTU, Bharat savoured a newfound equality. Here, there was no elitism, no EWS tag to weigh him down and no one knew his family background. His father's gift of a mobile phone and a monthly allowance of Rs 1500 added to the thrill of this freedom.

Bharat's imagination was captured by DTU's car teams. While team Solaris worked on solar-powered vehicles, team Defianz Racing researched high-speed cars. However, the most coveted was the Centre for Advanced Studies and Research in Automobile Engineering (CASRAE), popularly known as the biodiesel lab. This innovation hub explored alternate fuels and advanced braking systems.

But a tough entrance test shattered Bharat's dream of joining his ideal lab. Disheartened but not defeated, he stumbled upon a design competition focused on aids for visually impaired persons. The prospect of representing India in the world championship in Hong Kong ignited a spark within him to win the competition. Bharat assembled a team from students of other disciplines comprising Ashish, Gautam and Mohammed Zubair. Together, they created 'Netra', a smart walking stick.

Netra boasted a range of features: a light detection sensor that activated an LED light in the dark, an ultrasound sensor that alerted if the user approached an object, an emergency button equipped with a SIM card to send distress messages and GPS coordinates to select phone numbers when the emergency button was pressed. They also developed an Android app to display such notifications and track the sender's location.

Their invention's success was immediate. Winning the national competition secured their ticket to the world championship organized by the Institution of Mechanical Engineers (IMechE) in September 2013. Defeating the team from the Indian Institute of Technology (IIT) Delhi in the national competition was the cherry on top. At just eighteen, the thrill of standing on an international stage was unmatched.

In Hong Kong, 'Team India' showcased Netra to global acclaim. Judges praised its features, affordability and user-friendly design. The visually impaired individuals who interacted with the invention expressed their appreciation and heartfelt gratitude. Securing the position of second runners-up and winning a cash award of £100 was a huge triumph for Team India. The boys' joy was further amplified by an invitation to an exquisite dinner hosted by the chief executive of Hong Kong for the winning teams.

Low-Scoring Boy Gets High Placement

Bharat's victory in Hong Kong opened the doors of the much sought after biodiesel lab of DTU for him. He developed a keen interest in research and spent long hours in the lab. His dedication led to the publication of two research papers in reputed international journals: one on regenerative braking and another on hydrogen as an alternative fuel.

The professor at the biodiesel lab challenged Bharat and his friend Amya Kak to run a ten-year-old petrol generator on hydrogen. Enthusiastically accepting the task, the duo toiled for three months making effective use of the limited funds provided for this purpose. One evening, their efforts paid off as the generator roared to life on hydrogen, a triumph that echoed through the lab.

However, the focus on research took a toll on Bharat's academic performance. His aggregate marks after the second year were just 58 per cent. When he saw the placement records of his seniors, he realized he needed at least 65 per cent to even sit for placement tests. Determined to improve, Bharat poured his heart into his studies, lifting his aggregate to 66 per cent just in time.

Placements began on 1 August 2015. Bharat faced a series of rejections due to his sub-70 per cent aggregate marks. In cases where he was allowed to appear, he failed the written tests. By 15 September 2015, he had no job offer. However, a glimmer of hope remained as Tata Motors was yet to come. On 16 September 2015, Bharat cleared the written test for Tata Motors. The interview was easier, focusing on his research projects.

Despite his low marks and being in the bottom 10 per cent of his class, Bharat secured a job at Tata Motors, surprising his classmates and faculty. His work in the biodiesel lab and his published papers played a crucial role in his placement.

Bharat was deployed in Tata Motors' operations in Delhi. Although he had a keen interest in research and regretted not being posted in the Pune-based Engineering Research Centre, he didn't know that fate had different plans for him.

A Monumental Decision

Securing a position at Tata Motors lifted a significant weight off Bharat's shoulders. With his joining date almost a year away, he found himself with ample time to explore other avenues. A silent yearning for something grander lingered. The dormant dream of civil services, nurtured in the bungalows of IAS officers and in Sanskriti School, rekindled its flame.

However, Bharat was shrouded in self-doubt and muted ambition and dared not speak his desire aloud. He quietly started researching about CSE on Google and YouTube. He learned that the NCERT books were the starting point for the CSE preparations. So, he began studying them clandestinely.

In August 2016, Bharat joined Tata Motors in Mumbai, entering the corporate world. After a week, he was sent to Lucknow for training. Away from the cocoon of home, with a monthly income of Rs 45,000, he succumbed to the allure of heavy smoking, blissfully unaware of the impending storm.

One night, in a lonely Tata Motors guest house in Lucknow, in the cold grip of December, he woke up at 4.30 a.m. with a severe bout of coughing. There was blood in his sputum too. Bharat got scared that he had developed a serious disease, and tears welled up in his eyes. A cascade of existential questions flooded his mind. The fragility of life confronted him: 'What legacy will I leave behind? What of my family, with no money, no house, father on the brink of retirement and sister waiting to be married?' The realization struck hard.

In that moment of vulnerability, two life-altering decisions were born. First, the solemn vow to quit smoking. Second, a pledge to embrace the formidable challenge of summiting Mount UPSC with utmost sincerity. Bharat considered it the much-needed lifeline to lift his family from the shackles of financial instability and gain respect in society.

The wheels of Bharat's life kept turning. After completing training in Lucknow, Bharat was posted in the Rohini Depot of DTC. His job was to supervise a bus maintenance team. Bharat enjoyed his work as it was the first time people were reporting to him and looked up to him for guidance. The mechanical hum of bus maintenance accompanied the quiet turning of NCERT book pages as Bharat tried to balance the demands of work and dream-chasing. He applied for the CSE 2017.

Facing a hectic work schedule, erratic shifts and a six-day work week, Bharat found it challenging to dedicate sufficient time to CSE preparation. He appeared in the Prelims exam on 18 June 2017 but didn't perform well.

Over a simple lunch in a nearby park after general studies (GS) and before the CSAT paper, Tikam inquired, 'How did the exam go?'

'Papa, I don't think I'll pass this time. To crack it, I need to leave my job and prepare full-time,' Bharat expressed his honest opinion.

The air thickened with the gravity of his suggestion. Tata's secure job, the family's newfound financial stability and the whispers of societal respect were all at stake. However, Tikam, boldly bestowed his blessing upon Bharat's dreams. 'Don't worry about the job. Prepare with full commitment, put your heart into it and do it,' he said.

Bharat was pleasantly surprised. 'I promise, Papa, I will not disappoint you,' Bharat said, having made the monumental decision to quit his coveted job.

The next day, driven by the fire of his dreams, Bharat tendered his resignation.

Two Cardinal Mistakes

Bharat harboured a desperate desire to enrol in a prestigious coaching institute for GS. But his aspirations were shattered by the exorbitant fee of over Rs 1.5 lakh. However, when one door closes, another opens—if you sincerely wish.

Bharat decided to seek guidance from Rajat, his senior at Tata Motors, who had left his job a year prior to pursue the IAS dream. Rajat had enrolled in a prestigious coaching institute in Delhi for GS that provided recorded lectures. Appreciating Bharat's financial strain, Rajat extended a lifeline, 'Bring a hard disk and copy all the lectures from my laptop,' he generously offered.

Bharat stood in stunned disbelief; the sheer magnanimity of Rajat's offer seemed too good to be true. The next morning, he hurried to Rajat's home, eager to seize this unexpected opportunity. With gratitude in his heart, Bharat downloaded all the lectures.

The next challenge was the selection of an optional subject. Amidst the labyrinth of choices, Bharat selected geography. He saw it as the most technically intriguing among the social sciences. Its syllabus intertwined with scientific concepts like conduction, convection, wind temperature, atmospheric pressure and precipitation—familiar ground from his previous studies.

Being a novice in geography, Bharat enrolled in a three-and-a-half-month coaching programme. He attended classes with newfound seriousness. Positioned at the front rows, he absorbed every lecture, determined not to miss a single class.

Bharat soon realized that concentrating on studies at home was an uphill battle. So, he joined a private library in Karol Bagh. It was essentially an air-conditioned reading room furnished with study tables and chairs.

With the rising sun, Bharat embarked on his daily journey, commencing at 7 a.m. The early hours were devoted to absorbing the news during his commute. On the journey back on the Delhi Metro around 9 p.m., he revised from his notes.

The day preceding the Prelims exam, Bharat was a bundle of nerves. Anxiety gripped him so tightly that he managed a mere two hours of sleep. The stakes were towering over him, having left his prestigious job at Tata Motors a year ago. The savings from his salary were dwindling rapidly, intensifying the urgency to clear the exam that year. Failure would translate into another year of waiting and toiling.

The exam went off well and as Bharat cross-referenced his answers with the keys provided by coaching institutes, a wave of confidence swept over him. Without wasting time, he plunged into preparation for the Mains exam.

However, in his Mains preparations, he committed a cardinal mistake by wasting a month reading post-Independence history and world history, from which the proportion of questions asked was very low. Another mistake was over-reliance on coaching notes for geography and not reading standard textbooks. After the Mains, he was overwhelmed by a thick cloud of fear that he had not performed well in the Mains.

A Tapestry of Triumph and Tragedy

Disheartened, Bharat lingered in demotivation, idling away at home for a month. However, Bharat couldn't believe his eyes when he saw the Mains result. He had cleared this hurdle and was called for the Interview. Bharat's Interview was scheduled for 8 March 2019.

On the fateful morning, he awoke early. While he readied himself, Uma was fervently praying for his success since the wee hours. Amidst the predawn quietude, Tikam, his father, imparted his blessings before departing for work at 5.30 a.m. After a light breakfast and seeking his mother's blessings, Bharat hailed an autorickshaw, embarking on a journey to the renowned Dholpur House.

The journey to the Interview room was more than a physical commute; it was a pilgrimage of aspirations. His nerves tingled with anxiety as he stepped into the interview room. The first question, akin to many mock interviews he had endured, centred around his name—a query for which he was well-prepared.

However, the subsequent salvo from the chairman shifted gears unexpectedly. 'Is there a common name for

Shahrukh Khan in the movies?' The inquiry, seemingly unrelated to his preparation, caught Bharat off guard. Undeterred, the chairman pressed on, delving into the intriguing world of cinema. 'Why do actors often keep the same name in movies? Could it be due to superstition?' he quizzed. Then, a curveball—'What used to be the common name of Manoj Kumar in the movies and why?'

In the days following his interview, as Bharat anxiously awaited outcome of his efforts, the death of his grandmother cast a sombre shadow over his family. Amidst the heavy pall of grief, the announcement of results added another layer of disappointment; Bharat's name was conspicuously absent from the list.

Uma and Tikam, though undoubtedly disappointed, shielded Bharat from their own feelings. 'You have done very well by reaching the Interview stage in your first serious attempt. Try again and the next time, you will definitely become an IAS officer,' they assured him.

Nonetheless, the relentless rhythm of the UPSC calendar provides no respite to an aspirant. Within days, the next Prelims exam loomed on the horizon, leaving no room for tears. Bharat was compelled to shift his focus back to the study desk.

The stakes had escalated, and the challenges intensified. But so had Bharat's resolve.

Casting a Wide Net

The CSE Prelims-2019 results once again ignited a spark of hope for a bright future in Bharat's eyes. Simultaneously, UPSC revealed the marks of CSE Mains-2018. A low score in geography, his optional subject, had shattered his IAS dream. Determined not to be defeated again, Bharat devoted more time to the subject, meticulously studying from the recommended books and notes from prominent coaching classes.

However, despite his best efforts, he couldn't register a satisfactory performance in the geography optional papers in Mains-2019, too. Consequently, the uncertainty of success loomed over him. So, he decided to cast his net wider and applied for the Madhya Pradesh Provincial Civil Service (MPPCS) exam. Many IAS aspirants reluctantly embrace such fallback options. However, the MPPCS exam presented its own set of challenges, including state-specific questions.

In his relentless pursuit of a decent job and a respectful life, Bharat also wrote the exam for assistant commandant in the Central Armed Police Forces (CAPF). News of his triumph in the written exam was fleeting as a rigorous physical challenge awaited him. It involved a 100-metres race in less than sixteen seconds, an 800-m sprint under three minutes and forty-five seconds, a 3.5-m-long jump and a 4.5-m shot-put throw.

The requirements were more daunting for Bharat as the sedentary lifestyle due to CSE preparations had transformed him into a 100-kg mass. He was not only overweight but lacked the stamina demanded by these tests. However, the true strength of character comes to the fore in such challenging circumstances.

Undeterred, Bharat embarked on a herculean journey, shedding 15 kg in a mere twenty-five days. He was fit and bubbling with energy on the day of the physical tests.

The tracks witnessed his resurgence, and the shot-put pit celebrated his determination, but alas, the elusive long jump proved to be his Achilles' heel. He pulled a muscle in his very first attempt and failed to qualify.

Bharat's downward slide touched another low. He wrote the exam for a Grade-B officer in the Reserve Bank of India (RBI) but failed in this exam, too. In the spate of failures, Bharat also sought refuge in the low-ranked Staff Selection Commission's Common Graduate Level Exam. However, due to an innocuous oversight, he forgot to fill out its main form and couldn't download his admit card. It plunged him into the abyss of his lowest point.

As his dreams seemed to slip further away with each passing day, Bharat started questioning his decision to leave a lucrative job at Tata Motors. While he had invested three years in the pursuit of the IAS dream, his friends had climbed the corporate ladder, their MBA degrees opening doors to high-paying jobs.

One day, the weight of his struggles became too much to bear. In a moment of vulnerability, Bharat broke down in front of his mother. Through tears and quiet sobs, Uma listened, her heart breaking for her son. She placed a reassuring hand on his shoulder and said, 'Bharat, your journey is not over. Believe in yourself. Your dream is still within reach.'

A Desperate Job Hunt

In the crucible of uncertainty, Bharat found himself standing at the crossroads of necessity and aspiration. Wrestling with his internal turmoil, he pondered, 'If I secure a job in a company, I won't be able to prepare for the CSE. I need to earn but still need to have time for preparations.'

After much contemplation, he decided to explore a content developer's job in a coaching institute. 'It would allow me to both earn a living and prepare for the CSE,' he thought. Armed with determination, he sent applications to twenty-five coaching institutes. However, disappointment struck again as none of the institutes responded to his inquiries.

Undeterred, Bharat took to the streets of Karol Bagh, the bustling heart of coaching institutes. Every door seemed to close as he revealed his purpose. Amidst the sea of disappointment, Bharat stepped into a modest institute named Maluka IAS. Lachhan Singh Maluka, a bearded sardar in his mid-thirties, looked at the visibly hassled and frustrated young man, his shirt dampened by the sweat of relentless pursuit.

'Sir, I want to talk to you,' Bharat uttered, anticipating one more humiliation. Surprisingly, Maluka didn't turn him away; instead, he extended a seat and a glass of water.

As Bharat drained the glass in one gulp, he revealed the story etched in the lines of his weary face. 'Sir, I have cleared Prelims twice, including this year. I am looking for a content developer's job,' he confided in Maluka.

Hope flickered as Maluka inquired about Bharat's optional subject. However, his next sentence cast a thick shadow over Bharat's hopes.

'Unfortunately, our institute is not that big, and I already have three people for content creation,' Maluka declared.

Yet, in the very next sentence, Maluka offered an olive branch. 'But I have an opening for a geography teacher.

Would you be able to teach? I will pay you Rs 1600 for a two-and-a-half-hour class,' he offered.

In a heartbeat, Bharat accepted, his heart swelling with gratitude. The offer not only promised financial respite but also an opportunity to deepen his knowledge of geography. Maluka's words instantly breathed life into Bharat's sagging confidence.

The Rebound

Destiny had another cruel twist in store for Bharat. On 14 January 2020, dark clouds enveloped him again as he failed to clear the CSE Mains-2019. Although the breakup of marks was yet to be revealed, Bharat was convinced that his optional subject, geography, had betrayed him again. So, he made a bold decision to change his optional subject to political science and international relations for CSE-2020.

In the wake of the Covid-19 pandemic and countrywide lockdown in March 2020, the CSE Prelims were postponed. This seemingly bleak period provided Bharat with a golden opportunity to study his new optional subject. He armed himself with the notes of a renowned teacher and bought standard books recommended for the subject.

However, low on confidence, Bharat also applied for the post of assistant commandant in the Indian Coast Guard and assistant manager in the National Bank for Agriculture and Rural Development (NABARD). The call for the Service Selection Board (SSB) for recruitment in the Coast Guard arrived soon and Bharat cleared its first stage comfortably. He also cleared the screening test for NABARD.

The months of September and October 2020 brought both challenges and opportunities for a triumphant rebound as the NABARD exam, the second round of Coast Guard SSB and the CSE-2020 Prelims were scheduled in succession.

The Coast Guard SSB was the first in the row and Bharat emerged triumphant. But Bharat didn't feel the surge of happiness that fellow selected candidates displayed when the result was announced. It wasn't surprising, as getting into the Indian Coast Guard was never his dream. Bharat also cleared CSE prelims and conquered the hurdle of the NABARD Mains exam.

However, success was a fleeting wisp, dancing on the edge of every challenge. The Coast Guard asked Bharat to join on 26 December 2020, while his CSE Mains was scheduled from 10 January 2021. His earnest pleas for leave to write the CSE Mains fell on deaf ears, forcing Bharat to boldly decline the Coast Guard job. Once again, he sacrificed certainty in pursuit of an uncertain dream. His parents, pillars of staunch support, stood by him in this audacious choice.

Soon thereafter, the final result of the NABARD exam was declared, and Bharat's name was on the list of successful candidates. On 23 March 2021, Bharat stepped into the NABARD training institute in Lucknow, ending his three-year tumultuous journey without a job. After a week of training, he was posted in the regional office in Shimla.

A Graveyard of UPSC Dreams

Yet, fate's quill continued to write Bharat's story. The CSE Mains results, unveiled the day after he joined NABARD, announced his success. Excitement surged through his veins. However, the euphoria was soon replaced by the bitter reality of inherent jealousy that permeated NABARD.

An officer revealed the disdain for civil service aspirants within the organization. NABARD and RBI, he claimed, were graveyards of UPSC dreams, as almost every officer here had unsuccessfully tried their luck in CSE. In a deliberate attempt to ensure failure, the mere hint of someone preparing for the CSE led to an avalanche of work.

The apprehensions soon turned out to be true. Envious seniors targeted him, overburdening him with work to thwart his journey towards conquering the final frontier of the CSE. He was posted in the supervision department, renowned for its technical intricacies and tailored for those with Chartered Accountant qualifications. Bharat found himself engulfed in the arduous tasks of inspecting and auditing the accounts of Regional Rural Banks and Regional Cooperative Banks. Unjust scoldings and unwarranted humiliations became the norm, a bitter concoction served without rhyme or reason.

Amidst this storm, Bharat clung to a glimmer of hope, immersing himself in his preparations whenever he could carve out some time. He sensed the urgency of the ticking clock, knowing that this could be his last attempt to scale the formidable Mount UPSC.

A Taste of UPSC's Disdain for Coaching Institutes

In his second attempt at the Personality Test, Bharat encountered an unexpected and formidable challenge. When he had initially filled out his DAF–1, Bharat was employed part-time at the Maluka IAS and he duly noted this in his application. However, he was unable to update the DAF after securing a position at NABARD due to the lack of any such update facility.

Considering his current role at NABARD, Bharat anticipated questions related to banking, insurance and the financial sector in the interview. He had diligently prepared for such queries, thinking, 'Even if the board asks questions about my engagements with coaching, I will make a mention of my current position at NABARD and redirect the conversation.' However, as the saying goes, 'Man proposes, God disposes.' Things didn't go Bharat's way.

The board, staunchly against the coaching culture, launched a relentless barrage of questions at Bharat, aiming squarely at his previous involvement with a coaching institute. The chairperson fired the first salvo, challenging Bharat's perspective on the socio–economic divide: 'Do you think whatever is happening between haves and have-nots is good?' she asked.

Another volley followed: 'Do you think coaching centres are doing the right thing?' The chairperson expressed UPSC's concern, asserting, 'UPSC wants a student to read 200 pages on a topic, but you guys compress it into a *kunji* of 20 pages. Do you think this is fair?' The onslaught continued. Despite his attempts to clarify that he no longer worked in a coaching institute, the board persisted.

Bharat faced the barrage with confidence, standing his ground against the board's disapproval of coaching institutes. He articulated his thoughts on the role of coaching centres, emphasizing that while they provided guidance, the onus was on the students to delve deeper into the subjects. His calm demeanour and rational responses gradually shifted the line of questioning. The board started delving into Bharat's hobbies and he heaved a sigh of relief. Surprisingly, there were no queries about his current role in NABARD or the financial sector.

Loud Cries in the Parking Area

On the chilly evening of 24 September 2021, Bharat found himself in a packed conference room at NABARD's Shimla office, accompanied by his assistant, Rohan. Bharat struggled to concentrate, earning a scolding from his boss. There were strong rumours circulating that UPSC was on the verge of declaring the CSE–2020 result. Someone had even shared a photo of the UPSC notice board being cleaned.

Bharat had confided in Rohan, who, in turn, was also gearing up for the next CSE. Their camaraderie had grown stronger over time. As Bharat's engagement in the meeting concluded around 6 p.m., Rohan offered to drop him home. 'Sir, I'll quickly grab the car keys from my room upstairs and meet you in the parking lot,' Rohan proposed.

While awaiting Rohan, Bharat opened the Telegram App on his phone and his heart skipped a beat. Someone had posted a PDF file containing the CSE–2020 result. With bated breath, Bharat began searching for his name. He froze for a moment as he spotted the name 'Bharat Singh'. At that very moment, his phone rang in a divine coincidence. It was the customary evening call from his mother, Uma. Like clockwork, she checked on his well-being daily and reminded him of the groceries to pick up on his way home.

Bharat had always harboured the dream that when he would get selected in the IAS, his mother would be the first to hear the news. God fulfilled his wish that day. She called him right at the very moment he laid eyes on the result. Overwhelmed with emotion, Bharat couldn't contain his tears, openly weeping in the parking lot. Unmindful of the world around him, he cared little about the possible judgement from the parking area guard or onlookers.

'Maa, your son is now an IAS officer,' Bharat announced, delivering the news with an unexpected jolt of joy.

Ecstatic, Uma couldn't contain her excitement and promptly shouted, '*Dolly ke papa, Bharat select ho gaya, jaldi aao* [Dolly's father, Bharat has been selected, come here fast],' her jubilation accompanied by tears of joy.

In the midst of this emotional whirlwind, Rohan rushed to the scene. Having seen the result on the Telegram app, he exclaimed, 'Congratulations, sir! You made it!' With uncontainable excitement, Rohan enveloped Bharat in a bear hug, lifting him in the air while Bharat was still immersed in conversation with his family.

Born in a New World

Bharat concluded the phone call with his family. Yet, he remained standing in the parking area in a daze, uncertain of his next move. However, a profound sense of relief washed over him—he would no longer be required to navigate the treacherous cycle of the CSE. Mount UPSC had been scaled.

'Sir, the meeting of senior officers is still in progress. Let's head upstairs and share the news,' Rohan's voice broke his chain of thoughts. Bharat's mind was still a whirlwind and he mechanically followed Rohan. Before entering the conference room, Bharat detoured to the washroom, splashing water on his face to regain composure.

Meanwhile, Rohan had informed Sanjay, the peon stationed outside the conference room, about Bharat's selection. Sanjay, usually draped in an air of superiority as the personal staff of the chief general manager (CGM), seldom acknowledged greetings from assistant managers like Bharat. However, on this extraordinary day, as Bharat approached, Sanjay almost dived to Bharat's feet, offering hearty congratulations.

Still in a daze, Bharat accepted Sanjay's greetings and entered the conference room with Rohan by his side. Rohan made a beeline for the CGM, who was presiding over the meeting. 'Sir, Bharat sir has been selected,' he informed the CGM, momentarily disregarding the wide hierarchical disparity between their ranks.

'Selected where?' the CGM frowned, visibly irked by the abrupt interruption of the meeting by a subordinate clerk. 'In IAS, sir. The result was declared a few minutes ago,' Rohan replied, gesturing towards Bharat, who stood quietly behind him.

The CGM promptly rose from his seat, extending a congratulatory handshake to Bharat. Other officers in the room followed suit, offering their good wishes. Even Bharat's DGM, who had previously denied Bharat leave for Interview preparation and occasionally subjected him to harassment, extended congratulations with a sheepish smile, saying, 'Bhai, if I come to meet you, will you give me an appointment and offer a seat?' The room echoed with laughter.

Within moments of announcement of result by the UPSC, Bharat felt as if he was born into a new world.

Reality Refuses to Sink In

Unlike most successful candidates, Bharat and his parents opted for a subdued celebration. They chose to keep the joyous news under wraps, revealing it only to a select few. Committed to his work at NABARD, Bharat continued his routine and delayed his visit to Delhi. Upon his arrival twenty days later, his mother performed an aarti and a modest cake-cutting ceremony marked the intimate celebrations.

Despite seeing his name on the list multiple times, the reality of success eluded Bharat for an extended period. He grappled with the surreal notion that perhaps it was a dream. Fearing that the achievement could be snatched away, he urged his parents to keep it a secret until he formally joined the LBSNAA.

Bharat also made a conscious decision to defy the popular trend of delivering a topper's talk at coaching academies. However, indebted to Maluka for his support during challenging times, Bharat couldn't decline his request.

As he walked from the staff room to the lecture hall, memories of the starkly contrasting circumstances a year ago flooded Bharat's mind. In 2020, having faced the disappointment of failing to clear the Mains, he traversed the same ten steps with his head hanging low, each step laden with the weight of humiliation. Anxious about potential questions regarding his result, he avoided eye contact with his students.

However, the scenario had undergone a complete transformation this time. Accompanied by Maluka, a jubilant and proud Bharat walked the same distance with an elevated chest, eager to share his joy. Maluka honoured him with a bouquet of flowers and Bharat spoke passionately to his students for an hour-and-a-half.

The Cadre Conundrum

Around 7 p.m. on 14 March 2022, Bharat found himself alone in his room at LBSNAA's Kaveri hostel. His roommate had headed to the mess for an early dinner. Having just returned from a leisurely stroll along the famous Mall Road with his close friends, Bharat was looking forward to reuniting with them in the officers' lounge an hour later.

The excitement in the air of LBSNAA was palpable as the Foundation Course was set to conclude on 17 March 2022. Bharat was eager to relish the last moments with his friends. Many of them would soon depart for their respective training academies after completing this shared course designed for multiple civil services.

Suddenly, a shout echoed through the corridor, 'Cadre allocation has been published!'

Cadre allocation carried significant weight, as it meant an IAS officer would need to learn the local language and dedicate a substantial portion of their career to the allocated cadre. Bharat grabbed his phone immediately and opened WhatsApp, where a PDF posted in his batch's group awaited him.

Based on his preference and rank, Bharat was expecting the Andhra Pradesh cadre. However, as his eyes scanned the document in search of his name, he found that he had been allotted the West Bengal cadre. Bharat was lost in thought, his reverie broken by the buzzing of his phone. It was his friend and batchmate Rahul Reddy, an IPS officer. Reddy congratulated Bharat on the cadre allotment.

'Reddy, I am a bit confused. I was expecting Andhra Pradesh,' Bharat responded.

Reddy calmly reasoned with him, 'Who lives in Andhra Pradesh from your family? Do you know Telugu? Do you know anyone influential there?'

Bharat, pondering over Reddy's questions, replied, 'No.'

'Then what difference does it make if you serve in West Bengal or Andhra Pradesh?' Reddy's words sounded logical.

Reddy's advice brought a smile to Bharat's face. Both states were equally distant from Delhi, requiring him to learn the local language in either case. In the grand scheme of things, the difference between West Bengal and Andhra Pradesh seemed inconsequential.

Learning the Ropes in Gangasagar Mela

After completing the IAS Professional Course, Phase-1, at LBSNAA, district training provided an expansive learning ground to Bharat. He was assigned to South 24 Parganas district where he was attached with various offices and also held the charge of the BDO as a part of his training.

However, the experience which was truly amazing and which he relished the most was being part of the team which organized the renowned Gangasagar Mela on Sagar Island. The team was led by the district magistrate.

This grand mela is the largest pilgrimage for people from eastern Uttar Pradesh, Bihar, Jharkhand and Chhattisgarh. On Makar Sankranti, millions of pilgrims converge to take a sacred dip at the confluence of the River Ganga and the Bay of Bengal.

Besides the huge crowd, organizing the Gangasagar Mela posed a unique challenge due to its location on a confined island measuring a mere 280 sq. km. Bharat was assigned the critical role of crowd monitoring, leveraging surveillance cameras to ensure order. His responsibilities also required intricate coordination with diverse stakeholders. It provided him the opportunity to understand the role of various central and state government functionaries.

Bharat learned the protocol work as he coordinated visits of numerous dignitaries to the mela. His responsibilities provided him the opportunity to master the finesse of media interactions as well. Through this multifaceted experience, he also learnt the complex dynamics at play in such high-profile events. Interaction with local people on a continuous basis honed his Bengali language speaking skills, further deepening his connection with the community.

Bharat's journey added a poignant chapter when his parents, Tikam and Uma, visited him in Kolkata. Uma's eyes sparkled with pride as they entered Bharat's bungalow. Her silent tears spoke volumes, echoing the stark contrast to a moment two decades ago, when she faced eviction from a similar bungalow.

Bharat's success had not only uplifted his own life but also redeemed the struggles of his family, turning past hardships into a story of triumph and resilience.

A Rousing Welcome by the Alma Mater

On 27 July 2023, excitement and nervousness intertwined within Bharat as he set foot inside Sanskriti School for the first time since his graduation in 2012. The occasion was the school's twenty-fifth foundation day.

To inspire the current crop of students, the school had organized a panel discussion on the challenges and aspirations of a career in the civil services. Bharat decided to bring his mother along, who had been his unwavering pillar of support. Little did he anticipate the heartfelt reception that awaited him.

As Bharat entered the school, he was awed at the sight of the entire campus adorned with banners proudly welcoming him. To the teachers and students who had known him as perhaps not the most serious student, Bharat was now the embodiment of success.

Surrounded by a sea of eager faces, Bharat found himself at the centre of attention. Students, teachers and staff members approached him with enthusiasm, eager to capture the moment with selfies. The corridors echoed with whispers of awe and admiration.

As Bharat stepped into the staff room, he was greeted with an outpouring of warmth from his teachers. Overjoyed, he began to share the intricate chapters of his post-school journey.

'Next time I will come to the Gangasagar Mela and sit in your red beacon-adorned car,' Nita Ganguli, one of his teachers, teased.

Joining in the banter, Sharavasti ma'am and Manisha Choubey ma'am playfully declared their intentions to visit Kolkata, asserting their rebellious plans to ignore traffic lights and park in no-parking zones. Bharat relished every moment of the light-hearted interaction. Gratitude filled his heart as he personally thanked Ruchi Saigal ma'am, the English teacher whose red pen had meticulously corrected his essays.

Seated beside Bharat, his parents' radiant smile became a canvas of pride and joy. Amidst the laughter and shared memories, Tikam's colleagues seized the opportunity to express their awe. 'I will take a selfie and show it to my son. He will get huge motivation from your achievements,' one of them exclaimed.

Thereafter, Bharat made his way to the auditorium, which pulsated with an eager audience of students and teachers. Seated in the front row, Bharat's parents brimmed with pride, their eyes fixed on their son.

'Sanskriti School holds a very special place in my life,' Bharat began, 'Not only because I studied here, but because my father has dedicated the last twenty years of his life working in this institution,' his voice carrying weight of his emotions.

Bharat continued, 'After joining Sanskriti School in Class 6, I discovered there is another life worth exploring, another realm where one can strive for success.' The audience hung on every word, captivated by his journey.

Addressing students from EWS, Bharat's words resonated with profound sincerity, 'You may feel equal while wearing the school uniform, but as soon as you step outside, you encounter a significant gap. Bridge that gap through hard work and accomplishments,' he said, prompting a resounding applause that echoed through the auditorium.

As the session concluded, a wave of pride and joy engulfed Bharat. Teachers gathered to congratulate not only him but also Uma and Tikam. There was a competition among students and teachers to get clicked with him. In that moment, Bharat recalled the unwavering support his parents provided during times of his repeated setbacks.

Bharat felt profoundly blessed and hugged his parents, the sense of gratitude and achievement radiating through his embrace.

* * *

Key Takeaways from Bharat's Story

1. **A Family's Journey:** Scaling Mount UPSC is not just the struggle of the candidate but the entire family. Bharat's parents, despite their precarious financial situation and other pressing needs, encouraged him to take risks and supported him through his lows. They were the anchors that kept him grounded and focused on his goal.

2. **Iron Will is Essential:** Cracking the CSE is a game of nerves, requiring an iron will. Failures, depression, uncertainty and darkness are all part of the journey. Those who sail through the thick and thin ultimately unlock the gates of LBSNAA to join the IAS.

3. **Judicious Use of Time:** The CSE journey is a race against time. A vast syllabus must be covered in a short period. It's critical to analyse past years' question papers to identify the frequency of questions asked on each topic. Candidates must invest their time wisely, focusing on topics based on the likelihood of questions being asked.

4. **Careful Selection of Optional Subject:** The optional subject can make or break your CSE journey. Don't select it based on a cursory Internet search. Consider diverse aspects like your interest in the subject, its syllabus, availability of study material, scoring potential and overlap with GS papers before making a choice.

5. **Beyond Notes:** Solely relying on someone else's notes is a recipe for failure. Apart from notes, candidates must read syllabus topics from standard books to gain a deeper understanding and enrich their answers.

Chapter 4

Lost Vision but Not Sight

A Dark Gorge

On a December afternoon in 2011, Anjali's voice trembled with uncertainty as she navigated the darkness in the hushed confines of a hospital room in Patna.

'Papa, where are you? It's dark, please switch on the light,' she implored. As she struggled to sit up in bed, her mind raced to grasp the fragments of memory before she had slipped into unconsciousness.

Anjali was born in 1997 in the rustic Vyaspur village in Samastipur district of Bihar. In 2008, she moved to the serene hills of Sikkim with her parents, Ashok and Sanju Sharma, sister Swati and brother Sanskar. Anjali was admitted to the Kendriya Vidyalaya at Tadong in Gangtok. Her father worked in a medicine factory, while her mother was a homemaker.

Life was beautiful for the academically brilliant Anjali until the onset of relentless headaches. Initially dismissed with a pill, the pain intensified with each passing day until it became unbearable. A futile visit to the nearby dispensary only heralded the storm to come.

After a few days, agony struck like a thunderbolt. Anjali was writhing in pain and was vomiting repeatedly. Her parents hailed a taxi and hightailed it to the nearest hospital in Kalimpong. That two-hour ride was like something out of a horror flick. But somehow, they made it there. Anjali lost consciousness as a nurse was piercing a cannula in her vein.

For six agonizing days, Ashok and Sanju waited with bated breath, their hearts teetering on the edge of despair. They had brought Anjali from Kalimpong to Siliguri and then to Patna for treatment. She was semiconscious and was unable to comprehend anything.

Anjali's plea for light drew her parents closer with hearts pounding in fearful anticipation. 'I'm right here, Anjali,' Ashok said, his voice thick with emotion. But as Anjali couldn't see a thing, confusion only deepened. 'Why are you not switching the light on,' Anjali repeated, her tone tinged with frustration.

'Beta, there's enough light in the room. Try to open your eyes properly,' Sanju urged, her voice trembling with fear.

Anjali's brow furrowed in confusion as she attempted to follow her parent's instructions. 'Papa, don't joke. It's dark. Please give me my phone. I will switch on its torch if there is a power cut,' she insisted, visibly irritated now.

Anjali's words struck like a dagger to Ashok's heart. His mind whirled with thoughts as he struggled to comprehend what was happening. Panic surged through him like a wave as he bolted from the room in search of help, leaving Sanju to hold her daughter in a tender embrace.

'Sister, please help us!' Sanju cried out, her voice a desperate plea echoing through the corridors.

Minutes stretched into eternities as they waited for the doctor's arrival. He finally appeared with a nurse in tow. As the doctor carefully examined Anjali, his expression slowly turned grave, telling Anjali's parents everything they feared to know.

'It looks like Anjali has lost her vision. It could be temporary, or it may be permanent. I can't say,' the doctor admitted. A gut-wrenching mix of shock, disbelief and heartbreak washed over Anjali's parents.

Tears streamed down Anjali's cheeks. She felt her world crumbling around her like a house of cards. 'I can't see. I can't see anything,' she whispered, her voice a raw expression of grief.

The family was plunged into a darkness deeper than what they had ever known.

A Divine Intervention

The doctors' primary concern was to save Anjali's life as her condition was deteriorating rapidly. Signs of paralysis had begun to manifest in her hands. So, they referred her to the All-India Institute of Medical Sciences (AIIMS) in New Delhi.

The physicians at AIIMS became Anjali's guardian angels. They diagnosed her illness as tuberculous meningitis, or brain TB and successfully halted its progression. While they managed to prevent the paralysis of her limbs, the damage to her optic nerve made the loss of her eyesight irreversible. She had 95 per cent visual disability and could only see very blurred, black and white difference from a very close distance.

The loss of her vision cast a dark shadow over Anjali's spirit, robbing her of the vibrant life she once knew. The colours of the world disappeared and the realization that she may never see again struck her like a blow to the chest. Confined to her home, she grappled with waves of despair.

Slowly, with the steadfast support of her family, Anjali began to navigate this new reality. She learned to move cautiously through her home. Many a times, her attempts at independence ended in injuries, frustration and tears. Yet, she refused to give up.

Even in that gloomy state, her thirst for knowledge remained unquenchable. She would plead for her books, tears streaming down her face. Witnessing her struggle brought sorrow to her parents and sister.

Amidst the darkness, after six months, a ray of light pierced through the gloom one morning. Sanju was assisting Anjali with her breakfast as Ashok prepared for his office in the adjoining room when his phone rang. It was Sumit, Anjali's social sciences teacher.

As Ashok finished the telecon, he rushed to Anjali's room. 'Anjali beta, congratulations. You've passed the Class 10 exam!' he exclaimed, brimming with pride. Anjali was in complete disbelief. 'How could I pass the exam without even sitting for the final exam?' she wondered.

'I believe God has some plans for you,' Ashok said, his voice filled with joy. He explained that, fortunately, the CBSE had discontinued the board exam for Class 10 from that year. Instead, the final exams were conducted within the school itself, with weightage given to students' performance in internal assessments. Anjali's exceptional performance in the half-yearly exams and assignments was enough to secure her promotion to the next grade.

There were tears of happiness all around. The phone call was a divine intervention, a glimmer of hope amidst the darkness. With newfound determination coursing through her veins, Anjali decided that she will return to school. 'I may have lost my eyesight, but my mind, intellect and senses are intact and functioning. I will utilize them to their fullest extent,' she thought to herself.

Anjali had always loved her studies and knew she excelled at them. Despite her devastating loss of vision, she felt a powerful will to overcome it. Moreover, she had understood that her passion for learning was not just a personal drive but a crucial path to survival and a life of dignity. However, it took a full year for Anjali to fully recover from her illness and adapt to living without eyesight.

Many of their relatives tried to dissuade Ashok from sending his blind daughter to school citing security and safety issues. But Ashok was firm in his decision.

A Surprising Topper

The first week of July 2013 marked the dawn of a new chapter in Anjali's life. Gripping her father's hand tightly, she stepped back into the corridors of her school. As she entered her classroom, she was enveloped in a wave of warmth and affection from her teachers and classmates. In that moment, she felt a stirring in her soul, as if she were being reborn.

Anjali found herself placed in the junior batch of Class 11; her classmates having progressed during her absence. Before she lost her eyesight, Anjali wanted to become an engineer or a scientist. Her dream was to invent new things to help the poor. However, she had to opt for humanities as it was almost impossible to study maths and science just based on listening.

Despite this setback, she approached her studies with steadfast determination. In class, she absorbed every lecture with meticulous attention, etching the lessons into her mind. Upon returning home, she relied on her Papa and Swati to read the lessons to her. Sanju also helped her with Hindi classes.

Anjali used to feel sad when her classmates went out to play during physical education classes. She would either keep sitting in her seat, thinking or write something on the blackboard in big font size to revise whatever was taught in class.

When the first unit test arrived, Anjali resolved to write it herself. However, despite her best efforts, she could neither read the questions properly nor write their answers. Frustration threatened to overwhelm her and tears stained her answer sheet. Soon, her teacher stepped in, offering comfort and a solution. She gave her a fresh answer sheet and called a Class 9 girl to act as Anjali's scribe.

'Anjali, she will read out the questions and write the answers for you. I will give you extra time,' she told Anjali.

Days later, when the result of the first unit test in political science was announced, it marked a transformation for Anjali. Her heart swelled with pride as she received a standing ovation from her teacher and her classmates for scoring the highest marks. Her stellar performance instilled a newfound sense of confidence within her. Her parents, too, were overwhelmed with joy at her success.

Over the next two years, Anjali dedicated herself wholeheartedly to her studies, with her family members, including her brother Sanskar, tirelessly reading lessons to her for hours on end. Her teachers and classmates continued to offer their solid support. Her hard work and determination culminated in a moment of triumph when Anjali emerged as the top scorer in her school in Class 12 board exams. The accolades poured in, including a commendation from the Union ministry of education.

Accompanied by her father, Anjali visited her school to collect her marksheet. She also went to the staffroom, where she was greeted with warm congratulations from her teachers.

'Keep working hard child. You have the potential to become an IAS officer one day,' her class teacher said, embracing Anjali in a warm hug.

Anjali had no idea about IAS or UPSC then, but her words planted a seed of ambition in her mind. Sumit sir urged Ashok to send Anjali to Delhi University for her graduation, explaining the opportunities and facilities she would get there.

'In my long career, I have not seen such a bright and determined student,' he told Anjali's proud father.

However, the prospect of attending DU left Anjali and her parents apprehensive. 'How will she survive there alone? Who will read out the lessons for her?' they wondered.

Countless Falls and Numerous Victories

A month later, Anjali found herself at the Government College in Gangtok, seeking admission in the BA programme. The lady at the admission counter couldn't hide her surprise at seeing a blind girl applying and tried to dissuade her.

'The campus is spread out and classrooms are at different levels. How will you manage?' she questioned sceptically.

'I will manage, ma'am,' Anjali replied with steadfast determination.

'The attendance policy is strict here, requiring 75 per cent attendance,' the lady continued, hoping to deter her in some way.

'I've overcome many challenges already, ma'am. I'm sure I can handle this one, too,' Anjali responded with a broad smile.

With her admission guaranteed based on her Class 12 marks, Anjali's passion for geography led her to choose it for BA (honours). However, the geography professor refused her admission.

'Sir, why can't I pursue geography when I've scored one of the highest marks in the state?' Anjali questioned, her tone tinged with rebellion.

'My dear, this course involves a lot of practical work. It would be extremely challenging for you to handle,' he explained kindly.

Consulting her mentor Sumit sir, Anjali decided on English (honours), a subject which her family could read to her. Anjali also opted for sociology and geography without practicals, as her minors.

An era of intense struggle dawned as Anjali navigated the unfamiliar college environment. She often stumbled, fell and got up, tears mingling with occasional trickles of blood. But she refused to let these setbacks shatter her determination.

Anjali was the first visually impaired student at her college. She often sparked surprise and unsolicited advice. Some teachers even suggested special school, while others recommended that she use a cane. However, Anjali remained resolute in her choices.

Commuting was no less daunting. Her college was an hour's drive away, adding to the complexity. To navigate this, a family member would assist her in boarding a bus or taxi. Upon arrival at the college, Anjali would seek assistance from the people around to reach her class. For the return journey, she relied on classmates to help secure transportation.

At times, the taxi would break down on the way, or Anjali would inadvertently disembark at the wrong location, necessitating her to solicit help in hailing another cab. In the midst of these challenges, Anjali and her parents felt fortunate to be in Sikkim, where the environment was safe and people were remarkably helpful.

Rejecting the use of a cane or divulging her disability, Anjali chose to blend in seamlessly with her peers. She adamantly declined to learn Braille. From outward appearances, no one could discern that she was blind. One day, in the market near her college, Anjali walked hand-in-hand with her friends. When a lady inquired why they were assisting her, rather than revealing her visual impairment,

Anjali bashfully replied that she was experiencing pain in one of her legs.

Gradually, she found her place in the college community, her ears becoming her eyes. Other students began to recognize her and willingly offered their assistance. She memorized the keypad of her old Nokia phone, using it to communicate despite occasional mishaps.

Gliding Her Way Through YouTube

The Internet and smartphone revolution have brought about many changes across the world. They ushered in a revolutionary change in Anjali's life, too, when on 29 March 2016, her father presented her with a smartphone.

This device had become a necessity for her college studies, as notes and vital information were exchanged through WhatsApp groups. Anjali's siblings, Swati and Sanskar, enthusiastically taught her how to use various features of the phone and different apps with voice commands. Anjali especially loved YouTube.

Initially, Anjali delighted in the simple pleasure of listening to music on YouTube. However, after a few days, a newfound sense of purpose emerged within her. Her hidden ambition began to surface as she recalled her class teacher's words affirming her potential to become an IAS officer. Intrigued by the idea, she started listening to toppers' talks, seminars, articles and videos on how to become an IAS officer.

As days turned into weeks, Anjali meticulously gathered information on UPSC's CSE, the number of papers and the syllabus of each. She methodically compiled a list of essential books. Moreover, she sought out audio and video lessons on topics in the CSE syllabus.

Anjali synchronized her college studies with the rigorous demands of the CSE. She approached every lecture and assignment with the CSE syllabus in mind, facilitating a seamless alignment between her academic pursuits and her aspirations. She also began selecting her optional papers in college based on their relevance to the CSE.

Yet, amidst her determination, Anjali found herself plagued by doubt and insecurity. The profiles of IAS toppers, hailing from prestigious institutions like IIT, AIIMS, DU and JNU, cast a daunting shadow over her aspirations.

'Do I stand a chance competing with them?' she wondered. In remote Sikkim, lacking the resources and guidance of top-tier coaching institutes, Anjali felt the weight of her limitations pressing upon her. The absence of a mentor who had successfully navigated the path to the IAS only amplified her uncertainty.

Thick, dark clouds of doubt shroud many IAS aspirants, especially those from rural backgrounds and remote parts of the country. Those who successfully ward off these doubts emerge victorious. Will Anjali be bogged down by these doubts or rise above them?

A Monumental Decision

In June 2018, Anjali stood at a crossroads, her heart torn between two divergent paths. As she boarded the bus bound for her college to enrol in the master's programme, a tempest of emotions raged within her.

'Do I truly want to pursue a postgraduate degree?' she pondered, the weight of uncertainty pressing upon her shoulders. The prospect of daily attendance at college loomed large, threatening to consume the precious time she needed for her CSE preparation. Doubt gnawed at her resolve, as questions swirled like a relentless tempest in her mind.

'How will I manage? Would a master's degree enhance my career prospects, or would it merely divert me from the ultimate goal?' she wondered.

As the bus rolled towards her college, Anjali's resolve solidified like a mountain peak amidst the tumultuous sea of her thoughts. Upon reaching the college gates, instead of applying for admission, she gathered her certificates and with steady steps, retraced her path, boarding the bus homeward bound.

Dialling her father's number, Anjali's voice trembled as she uttered the words that would seal her fate. 'Papa, I've made a decision. I won't be enrolling in college. Instead, I'll devote myself to becoming an IAS officer.'

Silence lingered on the line, pregnant with the weight of expectation. Then, like a beacon of firm support, her father's voice cut through the airwaves, a bastion of reassurance in the stormy sea of uncertainty.

'I believe in you, Anjali,' he replied, his words a lifeline of affirmation. 'Whatever path you choose, I stand by you, wholeheartedly.'

An Eye-Opening Conversation

Despite her determination to scale Mount UPSC, Anjali knew she needed to arm herself with knowledge before embarking on her journey. From one of the coaching institutes, she got the contact number of Guddi Jha, a blind girl who was preparing for CSE. Guddi was studying at JNU in Delhi. Intrigued and eager to learn, Anjali reached out to Guddi, hoping to glean insights into her own journey.

'How do you manage living alone in the JNU hostel, didi?' Anjali's voice trembled with curiosity as she posed the question to Guddi over the phone. 'I always need someone to help me move around and assist me in various activities.'

Guddi's response was nothing short of eye-opening. 'I live independently and do all my work like any other person. We even go out for meals and entertainment outside the campus,' Guddi said with a quiet confidence that resonated through the phone line.

Guddi's words pleasantly surprised Anjali and opened her eyes to a world of possibilities. Here was someone who, despite facing similar challenges, was living a life filled with independence and excitement.

For a few moments, Anjali got lost in her thoughts, forgetting that she was on the phone until Guddi's voice brought her back. 'It's great to know that you aspire to become an IAS officer. What strategy have you devised to prepare for the exam?' Guddi asked.

'Didi, I am very confused. In my school and college, my parents helped me by reading out the lessons. But, as the syllabus for CSE is huge, I am mulling hiring someone to read out the books and course material for me,' Anjali confessed, her mind swirling with thoughts.

'What are you saying? I can't believe it. On which planet are you living?' Guddi burst into laughter.

'How will someone read so much for you? Moreover, how will you cover the vast syllabus in this manner?' Guddi composed herself and asked, her tone now serious and contemplative.

'Then what should I do, didi? I have studied only in this way since Class 11. Please guide me,' Anjali pleaded.

'There are many software tools, including text-to-speech applications, that can assist you in studying and note-taking. Buy a laptop and install the necessary software to help you study independently,' Guddi advised.

Anjali's dad wasted no time and bought her a laptop the very next day. However, Anjali was at a loss when it came to operating it or choosing the right software. With no one in Sikkim to turn to for help, she felt overwhelmed and uncertain about her next steps.

After extensive research on YouTube, Anjali discovered the 'Eyeway National Helpdesk for the Blind and Visually Impaired' and located its toll-free number. They directed her to the National Association for the Blind (NAB) in R.K. Puram, New Delhi. This organization specialized in providing training programmes to empower visually impaired individuals, enabling them to lead independent and financially secure lives. Their courses included computer literacy, assistive technology and digital accessibility.

NAB appeared to be an enticing option for Anjali. However, thoughts of living alone in a far-off place soon began to worry her.

Breaking Free from the Shackles of Dependency

Anjali's parents dispelled her initial apprehensions about living alone in Delhi and motivated her to venture out.

'Anjali, this opportunity is crucial for your future. The technology training will empower you to achieve your dreams, and the institute will guide you towards living independently,' they reassured her.

Upon arriving at the NAB campus in September 2018, Anjali felt a sense of belonging. 'Here, other children are also visually impaired and will understand my challenges. No one will pity me or look at me with sympathy,' Anjali thought optimistically.

Initially, the NAB staff hesitated to admit her as the course had already begun a few days earlier. However, after persistent requests from Anjali's parents and their explanation of travelling from afar, Sikkim, they relented.

Yet, as soon as her parents bid her farewell and departed from her hostel room, a wave of emotions engulfed Anjali. Suddenly, she felt alone, grappling with the daunting prospect of surviving without them in an unfamiliar place. Tears streamed down her face as she grappled with her emotions.

'Why are you crying, sweetheart?' a gentle voice interrupted Anjali's tears and the whirlwind of her thoughts. She felt a soft hand on her head, comforting and reassuring.

'Don't cry. I am like your grandmother. I am visually impaired, too. I will be staying with you and the other girls in this room, and I will teach you how to take care of yourself,' the woman said in a soothing tone.

The old woman became Anjali's guide, teaching her how to walk independently, how to wash clothes and even how to discern if they were clean or dirty by touch alone. Her lessons infused Anjali with newfound confidence and self-reliance.

In the room, there were four other girls, along with the old woman whom they affectionately addressed as 'madam'. Anjali gradually began to feel more at ease as she made friends with the other girls. They proved to be invaluable allies, helping her catch up on missed lessons and showing her around the various facilities and areas of the NAB campus.

Anjali was astonished by the level of accessibility on the campus and inspired to witness visually impaired individuals confidently performing their tasks. Moreover, she was delighted to learn about visually challenged persons who had excelled in diverse fields, including fashion designing.

With time, Anjali mastered Microsoft Word, Microsoft Excel, Internet surfing, operating YouTube and other applications on her laptop. Since she couldn't use the mouse, she learnt various command keys of her laptop.

For the first time in her life, Anjali experienced living independently without her parents, and that too for three months. NAB not only equipped Anjali with computer skills but also instilled in her the knowledge of how to navigate through life as a blind person. She roamed around in Delhi with friends, learned new ways of doing things and got the feeling that visually impaired people are not a subject of pity and sympathy. There is no limitation on what they can do.

Anjali felt as though she had been introduced to a whole new world, one where her abilities and potential were not defined by her disability.

Riding Two Boats

Returning to Sikkim in December 2018, Anjali embarked on a unique journey, straddling two aspirations: the IAS and the Bihar Public Service Commission (BPSC). Additionally, she enrolled in an MA programme in English literature at the Indira Gandhi National Open University (IGNOU).

YouTube became her sanctuary for preparation, offering a vast array of resources at her fingertips. In addition, there was an abundance of free material, past question papers and daily quizzes available online. She devoted herself enthusiastically to her pursuit, spending countless hours in front of her laptop, save for essential activities like eating, sleeping and tending to daily chores. This period marked the beginning of her relentless dedication, her unwavering *tapasya* to achieve her ambitions.

Despite feeling somewhat underprepared, Anjali decided to take a chance on the BPSC Prelims in 2019. Although she fell short of clearing the exam by seven marks, the experience served as a catalyst for her confidence. Buoyed by this near miss, she resolved to make another attempt, this time emerging victorious and clearing the hurdle.

Thereafter, with newfound determination, Anjali embarked on her BPSC Mains journey. Answer-writing practice was crucial for success. However, she was in no position to engage a scribe for practice sessions. So, she improvised by typing her answers and seeking feedback online from a coaching institute. Reluctant to reveal her visual impairment, Anjali continued to submit typed answers, despite receiving repeated advice to submit handwritten responses in order to improve her writing skills.

Before long, Anjali began receiving praise for her answers. One day, her excitement peaked when she discovered that one of her answers had been included in the model answers published by the coaching institute on their website. This revelation served as validation of the quality of her responses, filling her with renewed enthusiasm.

Believing that cracking the BPSC mains would be easier than the UPSC, Anjali redirected her focus from UPSC Prelims preparation to BPSC mains, scheduled for November 2020. Despite the scepticism from family and friends, who pointed out the disparities between IAS and State civil service officers, Anjali remained steadfast in her decision. However, the BPSC mains turned out to be a disaster. What led to this outcome?

Grappling with Scribes

Accompanied by her father, Anjali arrived at her BPSC Mains exam centre, a government school in Patna, filled with determination and nerves. However, her resolve soon turned to dismay when she was paired with a Class 11 boy as her scribe. To her shock, the boy, who hailed from a Hindi-medium background, couldn't even read the English-medium questions for Anjali.

'Sir, how will he write the answers if he can't recite the questions?' Anjali implored the invigilator, her frustration and anxiety mounting with each passing moment.

The invigilator assured her that he would find another scribe, but forty agonizing minutes slipped by with no resolution in sight. Tears welled up in Anjali's eyes as she watched her year-long toil teeter on the brink of futility. Her dreams hung in the balance, all because of circumstances beyond her control. She had staked so much on the BPSC exam, believing it to be her ticket to success, prioritizing it over the UPSC.

Finally, another candidate stepped in as Anjali's scribe, offering a glimmer of hope. However, her command of English was only marginally better, and she also struggled with using the calculator. Anjali's anxiety mounted with each passing moment. 'Why must I suffer for circumstances beyond my control?' she silently lamented.

The invigilator, acknowledging the challenge, explained, 'We can only provide scribes from our school's students, and I've arranged for the best available.' However, his words failed to offer any comfort to Anjali.

With immense effort, Anjali soldiered on, guiding her scribe through each word, grappling with the monumental task of transferring her thoughts onto the answer sheet. The ordeal took a toll on her, leaving her drained and disheartened. Despite her unwavering determination, Anjali fell short in the exam, her dreams slipping further from her grasp.

However, when the BPSC published the marks of the Main exam, Anjali was pleasantly surprised to find that despite her scribes' challenges in accurately transcribing her answers, she fell short by just two marks. 'I was so close to cracking it despite the difficulties. I'm sure I'll succeed next time,' she resolved, feeling a surge of determination.

Anjali cleared the next Prelims of BPSC in December 2020, her third attempt, and returned to Patna for the Mains. This time, her exam centre was in a college and, on the first day, she was relieved to have a more capable scribe. However, during the sociology paper the following day, her scribe struggled to comprehend her instructions. Frustration and anger welled up inside Anjali, leading her to abandon her attempts at the paper and sit idle for almost half an hour. Then, a spark of inspiration ignited within her.

'Sir, can I write on the blackboard, and she can copy onto the answer sheet?' Anjali proposed to the invigilator. She was confident that she could write legibly in large white letters against the black background.

However, other candidates in the room objected to her idea, claiming it was unfair for Anjali to receive special accommodations. Anjali felt a surge of frustration and hurt, questioning the lack of parity between herself and other visually impaired candidates who, though not blind like her, were granted the same extra time.

Determined not to let this setback defeat her, Anjali wiped away her tears and summoned her inner strength. With renewed determination, she embarked on her paper, spelling out difficult words meticulously to her scribe. Anjali was resolute not only to complete the paper but also to excel and clear the exam.

A Painful Journey

April 2022 heralded good news for Anjali as she learned of her success in the BPSC Mains exam. Thrilled by the prospect of her first Interview, scheduled for 18 June 2022, she eagerly began her preparations. However, fate had other plans in store.

Anjali soon found herself grappling with intense bouts of stomach pain. Doctors cautioned against her proposed journey to Patna for the interview, citing grave risks to her health. Yet, the significance of this opportunity weighed heavily on Anjali's mind. With years of hard work invested in this moment, she resolved to forge ahead.

On 16 June 2022, despite excruciating pain, Anjali boarded a bus from Siliguri to Patna. With no respite from the agony, she endured a sleepless night, writhing in discomfort as the journey pressed on.

The following day, an ultrasound at a Patna hospital brought unsettling news: Anjali was diagnosed with gallbladder stones, necessitating immediate surgery due to their size. Despite the urgency of the situation, Anjali's determination to attend her Interview prevailed. Moved by her resolve and the significance of the occasion, the doctors agreed to let her go for the Interview after administering necessary medication.

Despite her illness hindering her preparation, Anjali faced the Interview with courage. She was asked about her alma maters, organic farming in Sikkim and posed questions on English literature. The Sharma family awaited the results with bated breath, their hopes soaring. The announcement of the BPSC results brought unbounded joy as Anjali was selected as a rural development officer (RDO).

And on 13 December 2022, Anjali received her long-awaited joining letter from the Bihar government, appointing her as a RDO. Her training was scheduled to commence at the Bihar Institute of Public Administration & Rural Development (BIPARD), Gaya, starting on 1 January 2023.

The selection as RDO by BPSC provided Anjali with a profound sense of relief and peace of mind. This newfound tranquillity allowed her to channel all her energy and focus into her preparations for the CSE. With the weight of uncertainty lifted from her shoulders, Anjali was able to give her all, pouring every ounce of determination and dedication into her IAS dream.

Cracking the UPSC Jigsaw Puzzle

In April 2019, on a coaching institute's website, Anjali stumbled upon an inspiring article penned by Sparsh Gupta, a blind candidate who had clinched a spot in the prestigious IAS. In his poignant narrative, Sparsh debunked the notion of physical disability, asserting that true hindrances lie within the confines of one's mind.

Sparsh's words resonated deeply with Anjali: 'It's my strong belief that there is nothing called physical disability; disability is always a mental barrier,' Sparsh said. He went on to emphasize that with firm determination and resilience, no obstacle, disability, or hurdle could deter one from realizing their aspirations. At the article's conclusion, Sparsh generously extended a helping hand to fellow aspirants with visual impairments, offering guidance and support via his email address.

Anjali's heart swelled with newfound hope and determination as she reached out to Sparsh. It was a surreal experience for Anjali to converse with an IAS officer, a dream she had nurtured for so long. Finding a mentor and guide in Sparsh became a turning point of her life.

Sparsh generously shared intricate details about the CSE journey, recounting the challenges he faced, the hurdles he overcame and the strategies he employed to conquer them. Anjali, eager to absorb every nugget of wisdom, bombarded Sparsh with questions, some of which she later chuckled at, realizing their simplicity.

In June 2019, Anjali made her first attempt to scale Mount UPSC, taking the Prelims from Gangtok with the assistance of a scribe. However, a lack of adequate preparation thwarted her success.

As the world grappled with the onset of the Covid-19 pandemic in March 2020, Anjali found a silver lining amidst the chaos. The uploading of lessons and study material by coaching academies and aspirants on the internet brought a plethora of resources within her reach. She felt a levelling of the playing field between her remote locale and bustling urban centres like Delhi. Amidst her preparations for the BPSC mains, Anjali decided to make her second attempt at scaling Mount UPSC in October 2020. A wave of joy washed over her as she discovered her roll number among the list of candidates who had qualified for the Mains.

However, in her Mains, Anjali encountered a series of setbacks. This emanated from dual mistakes—opting for Patna as her Mains exam centre and relying on a UPSC-sponsored scribe. Like BPSC's exam, in CSE as well, the scribe provided to her struggled with basic reading and writing fluency, severely impacting Anjali's performance and stopping her at the Mains hurdle.

Within a span of six months, Anjali found herself navigating through five exams back-to-back. From the UPSC Prelims in October 2020 to the BPSC Mains in November 2020, followed by the BPSC Prelims in

December 2020, the UPSC Mains in January 2021 and concluding with the MA English exam of IGNOU in February–March 2021, her resilience was truly tested.

Yet, undeterred by her setbacks, Anjali persevered. With her spirits held high, she appeared in the UPSC Prelims on her third attempt on 10 October 2021 and emerged triumphant. She opted for Delhi as her Mains exam centre. Initially, Anjali was very apprehensive about the quality of the scribe, but she was soon filled with gratitude as her scribe, a section officer of the Government of India, was very competent. However, despite her best efforts, she fell short, missing the mark by seventeen marks due to a low score in sociology, her optional subject.

Despite failures in Mains in her third attempt, Anjali remained resolute. As she geared up for the next UPSC Prelims scheduled on 5 June 2022, she reflected on the addictive nature of the UPSC's CSE journey. Once embarked upon, she realized, this path was not easily forsaken. Each setback only fuelled her determination to restart the journey, pushing her forward despite the odds.

In her fourth attempt, Anjali braved the CSE Mains in September 2022. The elation she felt on 3 December 2022, upon hearing her name among the list of candidates summoned for the Interview, was indescribable.

A Cakewalk in Dholpur House

As the date for her CSE interview approached, Anjali found herself grappling with the challenge of limited preparation time. She had joined her training as RDO at BIPARD. With her schedule packed with classes from dawn till dusk, she had little opportunity to prepare for the UPSC's Interview. However, Anjali refused to be deterred by the circumstances. Instead, she adopted an innovative approach to preparation.

Anjali decided to make the most of her time in class and engaged actively with her teachers at BIPARD, envisioning their questions as potential queries in her UPSC interview. She seized every opportunity to sharpen her responses, mentally rehearsing her answers during the lectures. On weekends, she sought out online mock Interview sessions and worked meticulously on feedback and advice she received.

While filling out her Detailed Application Form (DAF), Anjali was initially daunted by the blank spaces that seemed to mock her lack of conventional achievements. Yet, she refused to let self-doubt cloud her aspirations. She decided to list expressive writing as her hobby as during moments of emotional overwhelm, she used to pour her heart onto the pages of her diary.

On 1 February 2023, the day of her Interview, Anjali got up early. Her sister helped her in getting ready.

'Mom, how do I look?' Anjali asked her mother.

'You look beautiful and confident beta,' an overwhelmed Sanju replied, looking appreciatively at her daughter.

Arriving at the UPSC headquarters, Anjali felt a rush of apprehension wash over her. However, any lingering nerves quickly dissipated as she was greeted by a kind-hearted staff member, who guided her through the document verification process with ease and reassurance.

Entering the interview room, Anjali was struck by the warmth that permeated the air. As the panel delved into her DAF, Anjali approached each question with candour and humility. When faced with queries beyond her expertise, she didn't hesitate to admit her limitations, choosing honesty over pretence.

Despite the pressure of the moment, Anjali found herself surprisingly at ease. Drawing upon her natural gift for communication, she navigated the interview with grace and poise, her words flowing effortlessly as she shared her experiences and aspirations.

'How did it go?' Anjali's father enquired eagerly as soon as she emerged from the gates of the UPSC building, his eyes filled with anticipation. Her mother and sister stood close by, their expressions reflecting a mixture of anxiety and hope.

'As per my assessment, I did well,' Anjali replied with a gentle chuckle, enveloping her mother in a tight embrace.

Returning to Gaya, Anjali resumed her training at BIPARD the very next day. Days turned into weeks and before she knew it, her training at BIPARD drew to a close on 30 April 2023. With newfound skills and knowledge under her belt, she embarked on the next phase of her journey, a fifteen-day attachment followed by district training in Patna.

Cries of Triumph

23 May 2023 marked a pivotal moment in Anjali's journey. She had just come home for lunch after a long office meeting, but anxiety hung in the air. Buzzes and whispers about the impending declaration of the CSE-2022 results by the UPSC had her on edge. Her sister, Swati, occupied herself with the television, while their mother bustled

about in the kitchen, leaving the comforting aroma of home-cooked meals wafting through the air.

Suddenly, the familiar chime of a message notification pierced the quietude of the evening, sending a jolt of anticipation coursing through Anjali's veins. With bated breath, she reached for her phone, her heart pounding in her chest.

'Swati, has the UPSC declared the result? Could you please check quickly?' Anjali's voice trembled with excitement as she passed her phone to her sister, her eyes alight with hope.

In a flurry of activity, Swati swiftly opened the Telegram app and found a PDF file containing the result. She clicked it open, her fingers moving with practiced precision as she scrolled through the list, each passing moment fraught with anticipation.

Then, in a moment that seemed to hang suspended in time, Swati's eyes widened in disbelief as she came across Anjali's name, nestled amongst the others on the screen. 'Yippee! You've made it, Didi. Your name is at rank 450,' Swati exclaimed, her voice brimming with excitement and joy.

A wave of euphoria washed over them, mingling with tears of joy as they embraced. Anjali's mother, drawn by the commotion, hurried into the room. As Swati shared the news, a radiant smile spread across her mother's face, her eyes shimmering with unshed tears of pride and happiness.

The room erupted in celebration as the trio basked in Anjali's remarkable achievement. Sanju, overcome with pride, hurried to the kitchen to fetch sweets, eager to add to the jubilant atmosphere. Meanwhile, Anjali's phone buzzed incessantly, congratulations flooding in from friends and well-wishers.

Amidst the euphoria, Anjali's mind was filled with anxiety as the thought struck her that her rank in relation to other visually impaired candidates was critical for service allocation. With Swati's help, she meticulously combed through the list once more. They were greatly relieved to find that other visually impaired candidates known to Anjali were positioned lower down the list.

Anjali couldn't wait to share the news of her incredible success with her dad. She made a video call to her father, bracing herself for the rollercoaster of emotions that was about to unfold. As Ashok joined the call, Anjali couldn't resist the urge to playfully toy with his heartstrings, feigning disappointment as she pretended that she hadn't made it.

However, her mischievous charade was short-lived. With a gleam in her eyes and joy bubbling over, she revealed her spectacular achievement. The trio watched with delight as Ashok's expression transformed from concern to unbridled elation.

Subdued Celebration

The following day brought confirmation of Anjali's astonishing feat as the category-wise list of successful candidates was published. She was relieved to note that she had secured the second rank in her category, enough to secure her a place in the IAS according to the category-wise vacancies published by UPSC. Yet, despite the overwhelming joy that should have accompanied this revelation, a shadow of doubt crept into Anjali's mind. The scars of her past experiences and the trials she had endured whispered insidious doubts into her consciousness, planting seeds of fear in her mind.

So, Anjali made the decision to keep her incredible achievement of making it to IAS under wraps until the formal allocation of service orders arrived from the ministry of personnel and training, Government of India. She deflected enquiries about her future service, coyly suggesting that she might secure a position in the IAS, but if not, she would happily settle for the IRS. However, Ashok confidently proclaimed to his friends and relatives about her imminent ascension to the ranks of the IAS.

After an agonizing wait that stretched on for what felt like an eternity, the Government of India published the notification confirming her selection in the IAS.

After her selection, Anjali visited her native village Vyaspur with her family where a big event was organized to felicitate her. The villagers brought their kids, especially daughters, along so that they could see and talk to Anjali and get motivated. Anjali's eyes filled up as she conversed with them.

As Anjali navigated the bureaucratic intricacies of her resignation from the post of RDO to join IAS, she noticed a palpable shift in the attitudes of her colleagues. Gone were the whispers of scepticism and doubt; in their place bloomed an undeniable respect and admiration for her remarkable achievement. It was a testament to the transformative power of perseverance and the unwavering belief in one's dreams.

After pulling her down in the first two attempts, sociology, her optional subject, played a critical role in her success. Anjali had taken sociology as a minor subject in college by chance, but she fell in love with it very soon. When she was mulling writing CSE, her YouTube research revealed that it was one of the preferred optional subjects of the candidates.

But in the first two attempts, she scored an identical 208 marks in sociology and used to wish to convert it into 280 in her next attempt. God fulfilled her wish as she scored 283 in sociology in her final attempt.

Glimpse of Life on the Frontier

Anjali's journey at the Lal Bahadur Shastri National Academy of Administration (LBSNAA) in Mussoorie began in September 2023 with the Foundation Course. However, the challenges persisted. Navigating the hilly terrain was difficult, but an even more formidable challenge was grasping what was being taught in the classes, especially with the frequent use of PowerPoint presentations. To assist her, the academy started providing the presentations to her in advance, so she could go through them before class. Additionally, she was given a text-to-speech software and two attendants to help with her daily activities and moving around the campus.

With the onset of Phase-1 professional training for IAS in December 2023, Anjali embarked on an eight-week-long winter study tour, popularly known as 'Bharat darshan'. The officer trainees were divided into groups of 18 to 20 for this 20,000-km tour across the length and breadth of India.

Their mission was twofold: to immerse themselves in the country's geographical and cultural tapestry, embracing its rich heritage and diverse landscapes, and to gain invaluable insights into the functioning of various organizations, including the armed forces, public and private sectors, municipal bodies and NGOs.

While the prospect of exploring new destinations filled Anjali with excitement, there lingered a tinge of apprehension. How would she navigate the rigours of extensive travel and outdoor visits?

The exhilarating and exhausting odyssey of Anjali's group commenced with a flight from Delhi to Dimapur. From there, they embarked on an arduous eighteen-hour journey through winding hills to Mechuka in Arunachal Pradesh, their destination for the army attachment. By the time they arrived late in the evening, they were utterly exhausted.

As the first light of dawn cast its golden hues upon Mechuka, the officer trainees awoke to a sight that took their breath away. Before them lay a scene straight out of a dream. Mechuka, the 'mini-Switzerland' of India, unveiled its majestic beauty in all its glory. Captivating landscapes unfolded before their eyes, adorned with snow-capped peaks, verdant hills and emerald-blue streams meandering through the terrain like ribbons of liquid silver.

The weeklong attachment with the Indian Army offered a rare opportunity to gain invaluable insights into the operational infrastructure and indispensable role of the army in safeguarding the nation's borders. The group was taken to the forward areas of Pokhar, nestled along the Indo-China border. As they braved the bone-chilling winter temperatures, with the mercury plummeting well below freezing, the officers were confronted with the harsh realities of life on the frontier.

Amidst the adversity, Anjali couldn't help but marvel at the unwavering spirit, resilience and fortitude of the soldiers. Despite the harsh conditions, they greeted their visitors with warmth and hospitality. It instilled in her a newfound appreciation for their steadfast dedication and unyielding spirit.

As the days passed, Anjali and her companions came to realize that despite the initial fatigue and challenges, their time with the Indian Army had been the highlight of their Bharat darshan journey.

A Voyage of Self-Discovery

In Mechuka, Anjali and her colleagues also experienced the vibrant culture of the local Memba, Ramo, Bokar and Libo tribes. Their journey continued as they embarked on attachments with the Indian Air Force in Hyderabad and the Indian Navy in Kochi. From fighter planes soaring through the skies to the depths of the ocean aboard a naval ship and submarine, Anjali was awestruck by the sheer magnitude of the operations and the unwavering dedication of the servicemen and women.

From the serene waters of Kochi to the enchanting archipelago of Lakshadweep, Anjali and her companions found themselves immersed in a world of breathtaking beauty.

Though Anjali couldn't partake in the depths of scuba diving, she found solace in the stories of the coral reefs and the vibrant marine life that called them home. The return journey aboard a cruise ship was yet another unforgettable experience, as they sailed through the open seas, the horizon stretching out before them like a canvas painted with dreams.

Yet, amidst the beauty of the landscape, it was the bonds forged between the fellow officers that left the deepest impression on Anjali. From the camaraderie shared during water sports to the late-night conversations under the starlit sky, each moment was etched in her heart forever. And it was Ambika, her roommate and newfound friend, who stood by her side through it all, offering support and companionship when she needed it most.

As they journeyed through the heart of India, Anjali found herself undergoing a profound transformation. With each passing day, her confidence grew, and her perspective shifted. No longer did she see herself as weak or inferior, but as a capable and resilient individual capable of achieving anything she set her mind to.

Challenges Galore

Anjali eagerly awaited beginning her fieldwork after her training at LBSNAA. However, she was also acutely aware of the daunting challenges that lay ahead.

'I will be responsible for handling files and signing numerous papers. Finding a trusted assistant will be crucial. Are there government regulations that can help me secure one? Moreover, the increasing reliance on technology poses another hurdle. How can I effectively utilize computers, the Internet and other technologies?' Anjali pondered over these questions after a full day of intensive training.

Anjali had recognized the potential of technology to assist her. At LBSNAA, she was provided with a device called 'OrCam MyEye'. With it, Anjali would capture images of book pages, and the device would read the text aloud to her.

Yet, Anjali was also inspired by the success stories of visually impaired officers, who have excelled in their service. She understood that challenges arise to be overcome.

'Challenges come so that we can find solutions for them. I will definitely find the solution for each one of them,' Anjali assured herself with determination.

* * *

Key Takeaways from Anjali's Story

1. **Perseverance and Unwavering Belief:** Perseverance, hard work and unwavering belief in one's dreams ultimately lead to success, even in the face of great tragedies and daunting challenges. Victory may come after countless falls, so don't get disheartened by failures or demotivated by hardships. Like Arjuna, focus intently on your target and keep striving.

2. **Parental Support:** Parental support plays a crucial role in success in the CSE. Parents should also believe in their child's capabilities and patiently encourage them, even through failures. Each setback is a step closer to success.

3. **Harnessing Technological Advancements:** The world is witnessing a technological revolution and it's important to leverage these advancements. New and emerging technologies can be powerful tools to overcome obstacles and propel you towards your goals. Use them as force multipliers in your path to success.

4. **Self-Competition over Comparison:** Don't assume that candidates from reputed institutions or big cities are superior. Compete with yourself, continually stretch your limits and move steadily towards your goal. Success is about personal growth and determination, not about where you come from or your background.

5. **Overcoming Disabilities with Resilience:** Disabilities are merely mental barriers. With resilience, determination, hard work and the use of the latest technological tools, no obstacle or disability can deter you from realizing your aspirations.

Chapter 5

A Kashmiri Boy's UPSC Dream

I Want to be an Engineer

Fifteen-year-old Waseem was strolling with his friends, Mohsin and Umar, on a pleasant summer evening in June 2013, feeling the cool fragrant breeze rustling through the towering chinar trees on their faces and listening to the melodious cacophony of the birds as they were returning to their nests.

All of them were from south Kashmir's Anantnag district—Waseem from the picturesque village of Bragam and Mohsin and Umar from the nearby Nathipora village. They were Class 11 students at the Government Higher Secondary School, Dooru Shahabad.

The long evening walk was a ritual. During their strolls, they discussed endless topics. On that particular day, it was about career aspirations.

'I want to become an IAS officer. They wield so much power,' Mohsin exclaimed.

'How do you know?' Umar inquired, his curiosity piqued.

'They become deputy commissioners of districts. People go to them with their problems, like drinking water, electricity, employment or harassment by police, and they solve it all,' Mohsin explained, enthusiasm gleaming in his eyes.

'But how does one become an IAS officer?' Umar pressed further.

'There's a gruelling exam after graduation and only the top scorers get selected for IAS,' Mohsin informed.

However, Waseem remained unmoved. 'Actual change on the ground isn't brought by IAS officers, but by scientists and engineers. So, I aspire to become an engineer,' he declared firmly. Umar and Mohsin chuckled at Waseem's declaration, but Waseem stood firm in his resolve.

However, destiny had a different plan for the immensely talented Waseem.

Sparking Waseem's Passion for Science

Waseem came from a humble background. His father, Mohmad Yousuf Bhat, was a beekeeper in the agriculture production department of Jammu and Kashmir, while his mother Ruby Jaan was a homemaker. Waseem was the eldest child of Ruby and Yousuf, the other three being Arzoo, Alia and Arfat. His grandfather, Ghulam Ahmad Bhat, was a small farmer.

From the outset, Waseem was good in studies and demonstrated his intelligence when he secured third rank in the schools of Dooru Shahabad block in Class 10. Yousuf used to get disappointed if he didn't secure one of the highest marks among the students in the area.

Waseem also loved singing. In his childhood days, he used to meticulously prepare patriotic songs and eagerly wait for the arrival of army patrols to present stirring melodies. He loved the handful of toffees and occasional modest cash prize he used to receive in return.

At Iqbal Memorial Institute, Waseem found inspiration in Gulzar, a passionate science teacher, whose innovative teaching methods sparked Waseem's interest in science. Fuelled by his conviction to become an engineer, Waseem worked hard and scored a record highest marks among the students of Class 12 in the schools of Dooru Shahabad block. He also cracked JEE Mains and secured admission in BTech in the prestigious National Institute of Technology (NIT), Srinagar.

However, the elusive spot in the esteemed Indian Institute of Technology (IIT) remained out of reach as he couldn't clear JEE (Advanced), casting a shadow of disappointment over his aspirations. Regret gnawed at Waseem's heart as he pondered his decision to forego coaching in Kota, a choice that now seemed like a missed opportunity.

On his father's insistence, apart from mathematics, Waseem also studied biology in his higher secondary classes. He appeared for the NEET exam as well for admission in medical and dental colleges and scored a good rank.

The Path Unchosen

On his selection for admission in the NIT, Srinagar, Waseem's father advised him to opt for civil engineering, emphasizing the abundance of vacancies for junior engineer (civil) in the government of Jammu and Kashmir.

'As soon as you complete the course, you will get a stable government job,' he told Waseem over dinner, a night before his counselling for selection of the engineering streams.

Waseem wanted to become a computer engineer, but he couldn't tell this to his father as he had recently turned down his advice to enrol in a BDS course based on the NEET exam ranking. Moreover, he was unaware of the difference between civil engineering and computer science. So, he decided to heed his father's advice.

Waseem loved the nurturing environment of NIT, nestled by the picturesque shores of the legendary Dal Lake. It boasted modern amenities, from a central library to a campus-wide Wi-Fi network. The institution had students from all corners of India, presenting a kaleidoscope of the country's cultural diversity.

The first semester of BTech was a whirlwind of excitement. Waseem didn't realize the difference between various engineering streams as all the students studied the same subjects. However, as the third semester dawned, he found the engineering drawings and other core civil engineering courses boring.

Waseem wondered why engineering was being taught in such a boring way, filled with theory and formula cramming, without focussing on the applied aspects. 'Why do we still need to make drawings manually when there are so many modern tools like computer-aided design (CAD) available?' he wondered. A tempest of regret and uncertainty unfurled. The once-promising path now felt like a burden, a choice made in haste and without consideration for his true passion.

The C++ programming course in the third semester once again made Waseem realize his mistake. Waseem loved programming and got high scores in this paper. However, despite his best efforts, he failed to kindle his interest in civil engineering.

Reading Habit Lays a Sturdy Foundation

In the heart of adversity, a seed of resilience took root within Waseem's soul. As his interest in engineering waned, he developed a passion for reading.

With a plethora of books borrowed from NIT's library and a public library, Waseem and his friend Faizan embarked on a journey of literary exploration. Their long daily evening walks from NIT to Kashmir University became a forum for spirited discussions on a myriad of topics, including anthropology, human evolution and current affairs.

In July 2016, major disruptions erupted in Kashmir, forcing the closure of educational institutions for almost six months. The internet and telephone services were disrupted as well. Confined to his home, Waseem turned adversity into an opportunity, persisting in his quest for knowledge by regularly reading books borrowed from a local library and on the Kindle. He also read *The Hindu* newspaper daily, even though it arrived a day late in his remote village.

Classes finally resumed in the bitter cold of January 2017. As their hostel lacked heating, Waseem and Faizan sought refuge in the warmth of the centrally heated library, immersing themselves in books and periodicals for hours. Waseem also read about the Civil Services Exam (CSE) and the roles of officers of different services. The diversity of assignments for IAS officers and the positive changes many had brought to people's lives kindled his interest. Over time, he began dreaming of becoming an IAS officer.

In his fifth semester in college, Waseem shared his dream of becoming an IAS officer with his hostel roommates—Faizan, Basit and Sajjad. It elicited sceptical comments.

'It's a pipe dream. People from St Stephen's and LSR college in Delhi get selected for IAS because they have the right environment. No one from NIT Srinagar becomes an IAS officer,' they asserted.

But Waseem remained resolute, undeterred by their dismissal of his dreams.

When your determination is strong and your focus unwavering, scaling Mount UPSC is possible no matter where you start from.

Clear View of Mount UPSC from Srinagar

The visit of two popular Kashmiri IAS officers, Athar Amir and Shah Faesal, to his alma mater during the fifth and sixth semesters of his course further inspired Waseem's vision of conquering Mount UPSC.

Shah Faesal, the trailblazer who became the first Kashmiri to top the CSE in 2010, had become an inspiration and a role model for Kashmir's youth. Hailing from a remote village, Faesal's journey was marked by tragedy when his father fell victim to militant violence. Yet, fuelled by unwavering perseverance, he overcame adversities, culminating in his triumph in the prestigious CSE after completing an MBBS degree.

The allure of Faesal's TEDx Talk in NIT on 15 April 2018 drew a huge crowd. Waseem was highly disappointed as he couldn't secure an entry pass. However, one of Waseem's friends, who knew his passion for IAS and his eagerness to hear Faesal, happily parted with his pass for the inspirational address.

Athar Amir, another Kashmiri boy, had clinched the second rank in CSE-2015. He also hailed from a modest village in Anantnag district. He had secured an engineering degree from IIT Mandi before conquering Mount UPSC. He visited NIT Srinagar on 14 August 2018 and shared invaluable insights into the intricacies of the CSE, which added fuel to the fire of becoming an IAS officer that was burning in Waseem's soul.

Clarity of vision led Waseem to eschew distractions, including lucrative job placements and free coaching for the GATE exam in his final semester. Instead, he utilized this time for extensive research, gathering invaluable information about the CSE exam and devising a strategic plan to crack it.

A Life-Changing Conversation

In June 2019, Waseem completed his BTech and returned home, leaving his parents pondering his next steps, unaware of the turmoil brewing within him. Conscious of his parents' precarious financial condition and the educational needs of his three younger siblings, Waseem had decided to prepare for CSE from home. His secret desire to travel to Delhi for CSE coaching remained unspoken.

However, on the fateful evening of 19 July 2019, as the family gathered around the dinner table, Waseem's phone rang. It was his close friend Faesal. His animated voice carried across the room.

'Where are you, *bhai*?' Waseem inquired eagerly.

'I am in Delhi. I enrolled for IAS coaching yesterday. Classes will start from next week,' Faesal said, his voice carrying the excitement to Waseem's parents, who happened to overhear.

'If you want to join, please do it immediately and reach Delhi by 24 July. The classes will begin from the next day,' Faesal continued. His words ignited a spark of longing in Waseem's heart.

However, disappointment washed over Waseem the very next moment as he responded softly, 'Bhai, I can't come. I will prepare from home.' He disconnected the call and quietly resumed his dinner.

'Waseem, you should go to Delhi and join the coaching,' his dad's voice interrupted, pulling Waseem from the depths of his thoughts. Yousuf had seen deputy commissioners in his district, who were IAS officers, and was aware of the power and authority they wielded.

'Dad, the coaching fee is substantial and there will be a lot of expenses for room rent, food and other necessities. You have done enough for me and now you must take care of Alia, Arzoo and Arfat,' Waseem replied, concerned about lacing his tone.

'You don't worry about money. I will arrange it somehow. Come back as an IAS officer,' his dad reassured him, with a flicker of hope in his eyes. Ruby Jaan also supported her husband.

True to his word, Yousuf arranged the coaching fee and living expenses on 23 July 2019. The following day, with a heart filled with gratitude and hope, Waseem embarked on his journey to Delhi. His eyes gleamed with the promise of a brighter tomorrow. His friend Mohsin, an aspiring civil servant himself, accompanied Waseem to the airport.

As he bid farewell at Srinagar airport, a whirlwind of emotions swirled within Waseem. 'Sometimes, the greatest dreams take flight when least expected, propelling us towards the heights of our aspirations,' he said to Mohsin philosophically.

In the Mecca of Civil Service Aspirants

Waseem settled into a modest three-room apartment with his friends, Naveed and Faesal, in the quaint neighbourhood of Old Rajinder Nagar (ORN) in Delhi. The rent amounted to Rs 10,000 per room per month. Additionally, there were expenses for coaching classes, food, electricity, water and other necessities. As he estimated the total financial burden, Waseem couldn't shake off the concern of how his father would manage to afford such a substantial sum.

The densely packed ORN was revered as the Mecca of starry-eyed IAS aspirants. The neighbourhood teemed with a plethora of top-tier coaching institutes, bookstores, grocery outlets, libraries, roadside tea stalls and eateries, all bustling with activity round the clock. Lively discussions around CSE echoed through the streets. The omnipresent advertisements of coaching classes plastered on every pole only added to the mounting pressure, serving as a constant reminder of the fierce competition that lay ahead.

Waseem relished the freedom to move out anytime, a stark contrast to the constraints often felt in Kashmir. However, he made a conscious decision to limit his excursions outside to shield himself from the stress and influx of ideas and opinions about the course material and exam strategy.

'I will anchor myself solely to the guidance provided by my coaching centre,' he resolved.

Besides the intensity of competition, Waseem and his friends also grappled with the scorching heat and humid climate of Delhi. Food became another formidable hurdle, with none of them proficient in cooking. The available tiffin meals often proved difficult for their palates to tolerate.

Soon, Waseem got totally immersed in studies. He would attend the general studies (GS) coaching from 9 a.m. to 12 noon and anthropology coaching from 2 p.m. to 5 p.m. Thereafter, beginning with revision of whatever was taught in the coaching classes, he would self-study till 12.30 a.m. He assigned the weekends for writing tests. He also ensured that he got enough sleep to remain attentive and grasp what was taught in the coaching class.

Within two months of enrolling in the coaching centre, Waseem assessed the level of his classmates. It instilled in him a newfound confidence in his ability to crack the exam. He recognized that he wouldn't have gained this assurance had he chosen to prepare in Anantnag.

By the end of February 2020, Waseem had completed 70 per cent of the GS syllabus and syllabus of Paper-1 of anthropology. Diligently, he took careful notes during his coaching sessions, which he further enriched upon returning to their apartment.

Waseem also liked 'Lakshya', a mentorship initiative of his coaching centre, wherein 200 selected students were divided into small groups and each group was assigned to a mentor. Mentors closely guided and monitored their preparations. Over Zoom calls, their mentor Sunil would test their knowledge, discuss the exam strategies, elimination techniques to help answer tricky questions, review progress and set weekly targets. It created a competition within the group and kept their preparations on track.

One day, Neeraj Rao, who used to teach them art and culture in the coaching centre, asked the class to write answers to a few questions, collected the responses and read them.

'Who is Waseem?' he suddenly inquired, eyeing the answer sheets.

'Sir, I am Waseem.' Waseem raised his hand and got up reluctantly.

'You've written a fantastic answer. This is exactly how one should write to score well. In the CSE, it's not just about knowledge but also about how you present your answers,' he praised, approaching Waseem's desk.

Another coaching class teacher liked the way Waseem used to make prolific notes in class. 'You guys should take Waseem out for a treat and take his notes. They will help you immensely,' he told his classmates.

Such occasional pats gave Waseem immense confidence and motivation.

A Bolt from the Blue

After going on smoothly for eight months, Waseem's preparations were abruptly halted by the sudden outbreak of Covid-19. Initial attempts to continue attending coaching classes were soon overshadowed by rising concerns as reports of cases emerged from within India. The escalating numbers left them feeling increasingly apprehensive, culminating in a tense discussion within their apartment walls.

'The daily increase in cases is alarming. Should we go back home for some time?' Naveed inquired, pausing to sip his evening tea.

'There are pictures circulating in some WhatsApp groups of ambulances with staff dressed like astronauts, who forcibly took away people reported to be Covid-positive in ORN. If this is true, given how densely packed ORN is, the infection would spread rapidly, putting our lives at risk,' Faesal echoed Naveed's concerns.

'But studying at home will pose challenges. Internet connectivity is often unreliable there and access to newspapers and magazines is limited. How will we attend classes and mentoring sessions?' Waseem expressed his apprehensions about disrupting his well-oiled study routine.

'I've heard that a complete nationwide lockdown lasting several days is imminent. There may also be shortages of food and other essential items. Besides, who will take care of us if we contract Covid?' Faisal reasoned further.

'I have also heard that one of the employees of Dukes, the famous pastry shop nearby, had reported Covid-positive. So, the monster is on our heels,' Naveed supplemented.

'I agree. We should head home immediately before the situation deteriorates further. We'll make do with whatever study materials we have and, hopefully, the situation will improve, allowing us to return within a month,' Faisal proposed.

In the end, Waseem, recalling the historical spread of the bubonic plague as he had read about in one of his books, was compelled to agree.

The very next day, the trio boarded a flight to Srinagar and soon found themselves back in their respective homes. Although the price of tickets had skyrocketed, Covid-19 had served as a stark reminder of the value of life.

But how would Waseem keep his preparations on track in Anantnag?

Opportunity in Adversity

Upon arriving home, Waseem firmly outlined a set of rules to his family. Firstly, he insisted that no one approach him for physical contact or hugs for the next ten days, in order to mitigate any potential risk to them of contracting Covid-19. Secondly, he designated one room solely for his use, emphasizing that he should not be disturbed within it. Meals were to be served to him exclusively within this space.

Online classes and mentoring sessions continued but were frequently disrupted for days due to the lack of Internet. Sometimes, the Internet would be down suddenly during a mentoring session and when Waseem reconnected with his mentor after days when it got restored, he would show his annoyance as to why he had left the last session in between.

Initially, Waseem used to get very frustrated at such disruptions. But slowly, he compromised with reality, tweaked his strategy and focused on his notes and books during the disruption period. The chilly climate of Kashmir posed another formidable challenge. It necessitated the maintenance of warmth in his room, a factor that often led to inadvertent bouts of sleep.

Despite the occasional disruptions caused by Internet outages, online coaching classes proved to be a valuable asset. Furthermore, coaching institutes had archived lectures from previous years available for viewing, which proved to be very useful.

As he got extended time due to the postponement of the Prelims exam from May to October, Waseem used it to write a maximum number of mock tests. After the mock test, he would read the subject again, focusing on the topics where he didn't do well. By the end of September, he had written more than forty-five mock tests, achieving consistent high scores. This gave him immense confidence about his success in the exam.

Waseem received firm support from his family, who refrained from burdening him with any household responsibilities. His parents and grandfather constantly motivated him, reposing their faith that he will be successful—although Waseem kept reminding them about the rigour of the exam. However, Waseem's prolonged confinement within his room frequently caused concern for Ruby Jaan, prompting gentle reminders for her son to take occasional strolls.

Exam Day Scare

Waseem, Naveed and Faesal returned to Delhi in the last week of September 2020 to sit for the Prelims scheduled on 5 October 2020.

The day of the exam commenced on a daunting note. Upon attempting to book a taxi using Uber and Ola apps, Waseem was dismayed to discover the unavailability of any taxis. His examination centre was in a government school on the far-away Roshanara Road. Feeling apprehensive, he hurriedly left the apartment in search of an autorickshaw, only to find none in sight, as they had all been pre-booked by other candidates living in ORN.

With time ticking away rapidly, Waseem's anxiety intensified. He sprinted to the nearby Karol Bagh metro station in hopes of finding an autorickshaw there. Although none were available, he spotted an e-rickshaw and rushed towards it.

Initially, the e-rickshaw driver refused to transport Waseem to the examination centre, citing its considerable distance. However, he eventually relented upon Waseem's insistence and offer of double fare. Waseem heaved a sigh of immense relief as he arrived at the centre just before the commencement of the exam.

Despite the challenging nature of the GS paper, Waseem performed admirably. In the three-hour break, Waseem sat quietly in the garden of a nearby Mughal-era monument, thinking about the upcoming CSAT exam. There, he saw many aspirants discussing the questions of the GS paper instead of focusing on the CSAT paper. Some were also watching YouTube videos posted by coaching centres discussing answers of the GS paper. 'Why are the coaching centres posting videos at such a crucial time, distracting the candidates in the interregnum between the two papers?' he wondered.

Sweets Turn Sour

Upon returning to his apartment after the exam, Waseem found Naveed and Faesal disheartened by their performance, having only managed to attempt around eighty questions.

Waseem, on the other hand, had attempted ninety-six questions.

On the same day, answer keys were published on coaching centre websites. Waseem eagerly checked one of the keys and was delighted to discover that he was likely to achieve a high score of 140 in GS. Overjoyed, he promptly called his parents to inform them of his anticipated success in clearing the Prelims. They were elated and celebrated by distributing sweets in the village.

The following day, a sudden realization struck Waseem: 'I need to assess my performance in the CSAT as well,' he thought. As an engineer, he had somewhat neglected his preparations for the CSAT paper. Upon scrutinizing the answer keys, Waseem was dismayed to discover that he was not likely to get the passing marks. This meant that despite his commendable performance in the GS paper, he would fail to clear the Prelims.

Seated alone in his room, Waseem's anxiety intensified, and he found himself unable to contain his tears. After some contemplation, he reached out to his mother and confided in her about his concerns. As any loving mother would, she offered reassurance, expressing her unwavering confidence in her son's abilities. Nonetheless, Waseem remained tense and decided to seek counsel from his mentor at the coaching institute.

'Be patient and cross-reference the answer keys from English-medium coaching centres after a couple of days. Errors are common in keys uploaded immediately after the exam, as well as in answers provided by Hindi-medium coaching centres for the comprehension part,' said his mentor. This advice calmed Waseem's nerves.

When Waseem checked the CSAT answer key from another coaching centre, he was filled with relief. It indicated that he was likely to score between ninety and ninety-five marks, well above the qualifying score.

Overcoming First Attempt Challenges

After a brief respite spent exploring the vibrant streets of Delhi with his friends, Waseem plunged headfirst into his preparations for the Mains exam. He began with anthropology, his optional subject. It didn't take long for him to realize that his study approach thus far had been primarily geared towards the Prelims, leaving him with a lot of ground to cover for the Mains.

The new mentor from the coaching institute prescribed him a rigorous regimen of answer-writing practice, delving into past years' questions and meticulously comparing his responses with model answers. However, the suggested strategy demanded a significant investment of time—a luxury Waseem found himself sorely lacking. A vast expanse of syllabus was still awaiting his attention. Undeterred, he resolved to focus on studying from his meticulously curated notes.

Waseem crafted a rigorous twelve to fourteen-hour daily study routine, methodically accounting for each minute. This approach also helped him by leaving no room for the encroachment of his mind by negative thoughts or self-doubt. He divided the day into two distinct blocks—one dedicated to GS and the other to anthropology.

Waseem harboured a lingering doubt that whispered through the corridors of his mind like a faint echo.

Its source was the pervasive belief that filling more answer sheets would increase the likelihood of scoring higher marks. However, Waseem found himself at odds with this notion because his small handwriting allowed him to complete each paper within the main sheet itself, without needing a single additional sheet.

Another idiosyncrasy set him apart from his peers, drawing disapproving glances from his mentor. While others adhered to the conventional wisdom of tackling exam questions from beginning to end or starting from the best answer, Waseem defied tradition, opting instead to work in reverse order, starting from the last question and working his way back.

One more formidable challenge lay in Urdu, his Indian language for the CSE. Having studied Urdu only up to Class 10, Waseem faced an uphill battle, grappling with the intricacies of the language. It was here that his sister, Arzoo, became his saviour, offering her assistance with grammar and patiently guiding him through the labyrinth of linguistic nuances. In her innocent curiosity, she pondered aloud the multitude of subjects an aspiring IAS officer must master.

For the ethics paper, Waseem's approach was to write simple and lucid answers punctuated with quotes and examples. For this he, meticulously curated a forty-page document in a tabular format, containing important definitions and examples, besides quotes relevant to each term. The compendium proved to be very handy as immediately on reading the question, he recalled the relevant quotes and examples.

The anthropology exam turned out to be very tough, with a veritable maze of unfamiliar terms and concepts. Yet, Waseem's reservoir of knowledge, nurtured through readings beyond the confines of the UPSC syllabus during his college days, proved to be very useful.

Another valuable tool in his arsenal for success in the exam was representation of his thoughts and concepts through diagrams. Waseem had drawn hundreds of relevant diagrams in a separate notebook, which proved to be precious in all the papers.

However, amidst the steady rhythm of his preparations, there lingered moments of doubt. In his first attempt, the paucity of time didn't let him write the Mains test series in exam-like conditions. It left Waseem grappling with a nagging sense of inadequacy, a fear that his preparations were superficial.

But in the quietude of the night before his optional paper, a message from his teacher pierced through the veil of doubt. With words of encouragement and praise, he affirmed his answer-writing capabilities in the only test paper he could attempt and urged him to embrace the prescribed time limit.

An Oasis in the Midst of an Unauthorized Colony

Amidst the fervour of Mains exam preparation, Waseem and his friends stumbled upon an advertisement of the Hamdard Study Circle (HSC). The institution provided residential coaching to CSE aspirants from minority communities and other backward classes. Drawn by the promise of single-occupancy AC rooms and a modest monthly fee of Rs 6500, they sat for its entrance exam. Soon, their names glimmered on the list of selected candidates, unveiled in December 2020.

However, Waseem found himself ensnared in a dilemma. While the allure of HSC's affordability tempted him, the comforting familiarity of ORN held him in its grasp, especially with the looming spectre of the Mains exam. After much soul-searching, he opted to remain anchored in ORN till his Mains exam, fearing that any disruption to his routine might tip the delicate balance of his preparations.

But the convenience of ORN came at a steep price. With no time to spare for cooking amidst the frenzy of exam preparations, he was compelled to survive for days together on processed items like potato wafers and chocolates.

After the Mains exams had concluded, Waseem journeyed to Sangam Vihar, the humble abode of HSC, dubbed as Asia's largest unauthorized colony. As his autorickshaw navigated the labyrinthine streets, he encountered a scene that defied expectation. Narrow thoroughfares were strewn with refuse, while trenches scarred the earth on either side. The air buzzed with the clamour of vehicles and the chatter of pedestrians, each vying for their slice of space amidst the pandemonium. Amidst this hubbub, Waseem couldn't help but ponder the circumstances of his friends, Naveed and Faesal.

But as Waseem stepped through the imposing gates of the centre, a wave of relief washed over him. He was transported to a realm far removed from the tumult outside. Before him stood a majestic structure, its lush green grounds extending a welcoming invitation. Naveed greeted him with a warm smile, guiding him to his assigned room.

HSC fostered an excellent environment for preparation, offering abundant opportunities for peer learning through answer-writing sessions, periodic tests and classes. The sense of camaraderie flourished as the aspirants came together to celebrate festivals and birthdays, strengthening the bonds of friendship. There was a craze for gyms, often eliciting playful comments from seniors, like, 'I am not sure whether you will go out of HSC as a civil servant, but I am very confident that you will go out as a wrestler.'

A Race to Gym from the Chai Tapri

After enduring the gruelling journey of one-and-a-half years, the burden of preparations on Waseem's shoulders had eased post the Mains exam. Yet, the haunting spectre of uncertainty, the fear of not clearing the Mains echoed in his mind unabated.

But undeterred by the looming apprehension, Waseem commenced preparation for the Interview. He devoured the contents of three newspapers daily. He also rallied fellow aspirants into a discussion and mock Interview group. Constructive feedback and encouragement by peers solidified his confidence. He watched videos of good public speakers, too, dissecting the nuances of their delivery with keen discernment.

On 22 March 2021, whispers of an impending announcement of the Mains result permeated the air. An atmosphere of palpable tension descended upon HSC and the collective pulse of the community quickened. Yet, amidst the rising tide of apprehension, a glimmer of levity emerged as playful memes, saying, '*Yehi raat antim, yahi raat baki* [This is the last night, the only night that remains]', began to circulate within social media groups.

On the following day, from the crack of dawn, Waseem found himself tethered to his phone, fingers poised to refresh numerous WhatsApp and Telegram groups. The UPSC website, besieged by a deluge of eager aspirants, continuously displayed only an enigmatic 'error' message.

As the day wore on, frustration blended with anxiety cast a pall over Waseem's spirits. To divert the tumultuous sea of emotions raging within him, he walked to the chai *tapri* at the gate of HSC. Amidst the cacophony of thoughts clamouring for attention, a beep pierced through the haze of uncertainty, signalling the arrival of a message. Waseem clicked the PDF file containing the results of the Mains exam posted by someone on the Telegram group. A surge of trepidation coursed through his veins. Steadying his breath, Waseem steeled himself for the moment of truth, fingers trembling as he punched his roll number in the search option, heart hammering in his chest.

Then, like a beacon of hope in the darkness, his roll number materialized on the screen. Joy erupted within him and a tidal wave of relief washed over his senses. He raced towards the HSC gym to share the news with Naveed and Faesal. Naveed lifted Waseem onto his shoulders as their friends cheered. The jubilant crowd then made their way to the tea stall to celebrate.

Gearing Up for the Final Summit

Interview preparations began in full swing. Waseem appeared in a series of mock Interviews and used the feedback to hone his responses and refine his approach. Yet, just as momentum reached its peak, a resurgent wave of the Covid-19 pandemic compelled UPSC to postpone the Interview. HSC was closed, forcing Waseem and his friends to go back to Kashmir.

Undeterred, Waseem again transformed his humble abode into a bastion of preparation. He immersed into the depths of online newspapers and magazines to stay abreast of current affairs. He also prepared himself for every conceivable question that might arise from his Detailed Application Form (DAF), especially important issues concerning his home state, like tourism, security and the economy of Jammu and Kashmir. He pored over the transcripts of past Interviews and trained his mind to navigate the tricky questions.

As the sands of time trickled away, Waseem faced a dilemma: whether to focus on preparing for the impending Interview or to shift his energies towards the next Prelims. Eventually, he resolved to dedicate all his time and energy to preparing for the Interview. When the UPSC announced the Interview schedule, Waseem hurried back to his humble abode in Delhi, the HSC.

On the eve of his Interview on 15 September 2021, as rain lashed against the windows with relentless fury, Waseem decided to seek refuge in Jammu and Kashmir house in Lutyens Delhi as the road outside HSC was flooding with water. As his autorickshaw navigated the floodwaters that had engulfed the streets, a poignant question lingered in his mind—'Why can't we find solutions to such civic problems?'

Birthday Bonanza

On the eve of 21 September 2021, tension was mounting among the aspiring civil servants at HSC. Whispers of an impending announcement of the CSE-2020 final results echoed through its corridors. Sleep eluded Waseem and his fellow aspirants, who had faced the Interview panel.

As the dawn of 22 September approached, they woke up with hope mingled with apprehension. Yet, to their dismay, the anticipated declaration of results failed to materialize. Social media murmurs hinted that the declaration of results had been postponed to 24 September, prolonging their torment.

On the fateful day of 24 September, Waseem sat hunched over his laptop, his fingers incessantly refreshing the UPSC website. The minutes stretched into hours; each passing moment infused with mounting tension.

Then, as the clock struck 6.30 p.m., the long-awaited moment arrived. With bated breath and trembling fingers, Waseem scrolled through the list of ranks, his heart pounding with trepidation. Rank after rank flashed before his eyes, each one intensifying the knot of anxiety tightening in his chest.

As he traversed through the ranks, the numbers blurred into a haze of uncertainty and despair threatened to engulf him. He saw 150, 175, 200 . . . but still, his name remained elusive. The weight of anticipation bore down on him, threatening to crush his spirits.

Just when despair seemed poised to triumph, a glimmer of hope pierced through the darkness. With a surge of adrenaline, Waseem's eyes widened with excitement as he stumbled upon his name etched at rank 225. Joy erupted within him, dispelling the shadows of doubt that had threatened to consume him.

In that moment of triumph, every ounce of doubt and fear melted away, replaced by a profound sense of accomplishment. Tears of joy streamed down his cheeks.

In a heartbeat, Waseem's phone lit up, with Mohsin's name flashing on the screen.

'*Mubarak bhai, tumhara selection ho gaya hai* [Congratulations brother, you have been selected]', Mohsin's voice erupted with excitement, having glimpsed the results before Waseem.

'I'll rush over to your place and share the news with your family,' Mohsin declared eagerly before ending the call.

Waseem wasted no time and dialled home. His father and sisters, Arzoo and Alia, were busy adding new curtains to the windows. With trembling hands, Waseem relayed the news to his father, who jumped with joy upon hearing Waseem's words. Arzoo and Alia erupted into a frenzy of screams and dances. Rushing to join them, Waseem's mother, who had been in the adjacent room, seized the phone. Upon hearing her son's voice, her emotions overflowed, tears streaming down her cheeks in unbridled pride and happiness.

Despite Waseem's attempts to explain that his rank was 225 and he would need to attempt the exam again, his words were drowned out by the exuberant celebrations of his family. They were simply overjoyed by the news.

Before long, the beautiful village of Bragam was engulfed in merriment as Waseem's extended family, his childhood friends and relatives from his mother's village congregated to celebrate his achievement. In HSC, too, the night resonated with the sounds of jubilation, marking the triumph of Waseem and two other inmates, who had cleared the exam.

In the early hours of the morning, Waseem boarded a flight bound for Srinagar, his heart fluttering with anticipation. At the airport, he heeded his father's request and changed into a crisp suit and tie.

As Waseem stepped out of the Srinagar airport terminal, he was cheered and garlanded by a jubilant crowd of friends and relatives, who had come to receive him. As he made his way to his village, Bragam Dooru, Waseem was met with a sight that filled him with awe and gratitude—a vast throng of approximately 5000 people had gathered outside his home.

Word of Waseem's achievement had spread like wildfire through the tranquil hamlet and neighbouring villages. Tents had been erected and the air was filled with the aroma of cooking food. The rhythmic beat of drums infused the atmosphere with festivity. The presence of numerous media personnel underscored the significance of the moment, highlighting the immense reverence for the IAS and other civil services in Kashmir.

Amidst the throng, people jostled eagerly to capture selfies and record videos with Waseem, each vying for a moment in the spotlight. For Waseem, it was a revelation—a testament to the profound impact his achievement had on his community and beyond.

Adding to the joyous occasion was the serendipitous alignment of dates—25 September marked not only Waseem's triumph but also his birthday. As the festivities continued into the night, the crowd gradually dispersed, leaving behind an intimate gathering of family members and close friends. With laughter, music and heartfelt camaraderie, Waseem revelled in the warmth of his loved ones, cherishing every moment of his special day.

A Steep Fall

Three days whirled by in celebrations and meeting people. But amidst the fleeting flow of friends, relatives and media personnel, Waseem stood firm in his resolve—he would write the exam again and become an IAS officer. His maiden attempt had yielded a respectable 225 rank, igniting a flame of confidence within him.

Yet, the next Prelims loomed just fifteen days away. Having focused on Interview preparations after his Mains exam, Waseem hadn't dedicated much time to Prelims practice. Still, he exuded confidence, believing that clearing the Prelims would now be a breeze.

On the evening of 28 September, as the family gathered for supper, Waseem shared his wish to appear in the next Prelims. His parents were taken by surprise.

'But you told us you had cleared the exam. Why the need to write it again?' his mother asked innocently.

'Maa, I passed the exam, but my rank is 225. With this rank, I'll get into the Indian Revenue Service (IRS), not the IAS,' Waseem explained patiently.

'But why does it matter? What's the difference?' she queried, still perplexed.

'Maa, IRS officers handle income tax cases only, while IAS officers become deputy commissioners and district magistrates. They wield more authority and can do a lot to help people,' Waseem simplified.

'I understand what Waseem is saying. I also want him to become an IAS officer,' his father interjected.

Ruby Jaan, Waseem's mother, couldn't shake her worry. Her son would have to endure another year of gruelling study sessions, living away from home, with unpalatable food that could impact his health and strain his eyes. But for her son's dreams, she reluctantly agreed.

Despite the constant influx of relatives and friends, Waseem persisted in his studies, seizing whatever precious moments he could find amidst the chaos. He had chosen Srinagar as his exam centre.

At the exam centre, Waseem's familiar face, known from the coverage in the local media after his selection, attracted attention. To shield himself from distractions, he donned a mask and immersed himself in his exam.

However, Waseem's overconfidence led to a lapse in concentration. He approached the exam casually, hastily selecting options without giving them due consideration. When the answer keys were released, Waseem was filled with regret and frustration, realizing the gravity of his errors.

Despite his disappointment, he clung to a glimmer of hope that he might still clear the Prelims. Yet, that hope was dashed when the results were announced—he had failed to clear the Prelims by a mere two marks.

The news shocked his family even more than it did Waseem himself. They couldn't fathom how he could fail when he had successfully navigated all three stages in his previous attempt. The unpredictability and challenges of the exam left them bewildered.

Reflecting on his failure, Waseem recognized the harsh truth—he had been too overconfident and careless. It was a hard lesson learned. He realized that success in this rigorous exam couldn't be taken for granted and that outdated preparations were insufficient to crack it.

After enduring a period of despondency, Waseem found renewal within himself, viewing his failure as an opportunity to lay a solid base. With the next Prelims just six months away, he resolved to embark on rigorous preparations immediately for both the Prelims and the Mains and secure a top rank in the CSE-2022.

Waseem was soon in HSC, preparing his strategy to conquer Mount UPSC. By then, the marks sheet of CSE-2020 had been published. Waseem carefully analysed his weaknesses and potential areas of improvement. He found that he had performed well in essays and Interview, but there were shortcomings in GS. There was some scope for improvement in the optional subject, too.

Shubham Kumar, the topper of CSE-2020, became an inspiration for Waseem. He watched Shubham's videos, where he emphasized studying from model answers to previous years' questions. Motivated by this, Waseem visited Karol Bagh and purchased a set of model answers from a renowned coaching centre. He also enrolled in a test series to further refine his answer-writing skills.

Thereafter, Waseem curated a comprehensive timetable from November 2021 to March 2022 for the Mains and from April 2022 to June 2022 for the Prelims preparation. He wrote many mock tests both for GS Mains and anthropology and saw his scores and confidence rising. He also wrote twenty mock tests for Prelims, simulating exam-like conditions.

Waseem's perseverance paid off as he cleared the Prelims, marking the beginning of his intensive Mains preparation. It revolved around studying model answers, doing test series and multiple revisions. Waseem would start his day by writing answers to previous years' questions for an hour and doing self-evaluation.

He allocated time for each question—seven-and-a-half minutes for ten markers and ten minutes for fifteen markers, ensuring he stayed within the allotted time limits. Even on the day of Mains papers, he would wake up early and write answers of three or four questions, so as to get the flow of writing. As expected, Waseem cleared the Mains exam.

The Interview Odyssey

In his first Interview back in 2021, Waseem had brimmed with confidence, armed with six months of arduous preparation to face the daunting board. Little did he know that a tumultuous rollercoaster awaited him and that the very first question would shatter his overconfidence.

'The coaching centres for this exam are mushrooming. Aren't they against equity and equal opportunity for candidates?' The chairperson's inquiry pierced through the air as the interview commenced. Expecting questions on

Kashmir or topics related to his DAF, Waseem was caught off guard.

Waseem took a moment to compose himself before responding. 'Ma'am, in today's world, knowledge has become more accessible. There's an abundance of free resources available online for candidates, who cannot afford coaching. Additionally, many governments offer free coaching to underprivileged students. For instance, in Kashmir, we have the 'Parwaaz' scheme. While coaching provides guidance, success can also be achieved through self-study, utilizing online resources effectively,' he answered, hoping to steer the conversation towards Kashmir and invite questions on the topic.

Yet, the relentless barrage of questions surrounding coaching for the next ten minutes left him feeling drained and disheartened. A sigh of relief escaped him when the conversation shifted to the security situation in Kashmir and other parts of India, including incidents of stone pelting on security forces. Prepared and armed with data, Waseem tackled the topic with confidence.

Then, out of the blue, came a question that caught him off guard. 'What do you think makes a good teacher?' a member of the board inquired.

'A good teacher is not merely someone who imparts knowledge, but the one who empowers students to become self-motivated learners,' Waseem replied without hesitation

Exiting the Interview room, Waseem carried with him a mix of emotions—doubt mingled with determination, uncertainty intertwined with hope. However, when the marks were revealed, he was left astounded by the unexpectedly high score of 184.

Fast forward to his second Interview in 2023, Waseem strode in the corridors of Dholpur House with the confidence of a warrior. Armed with the invaluable experience gained from his previous encounter and buoyed by the commendable marks he scored; he faced his new panel with a quiet determination.

The Interview started on expected lines, with questions about tourism in Jammu and Kashmir. Other members asked about related topics like security in the region. Surprisingly, there were no questions about civil engineering or anthropology.

Emerging from the Interview room, Waseem exuded an air of confidence, convinced that he had delivered his best performance yet. However, when the scores were finally unveiled, Waseem found that his score of 182 was less than his previous Interview score by two marks.

Transported from Nagpur to Mussoorie

On 19 December 2022, following his Mains exam, Waseem commenced his training at the National Academy of Direct Taxes, Nagpur. But soon after arrival, illness struck like a sudden tempest. He was swiftly admitted to the hospital and subsequently transferred to the intensive care unit (ICU).

The ICU walls reverberated with the incessant cacophony of beeping monitors. As he lay in the ICU for ten days, battling illness amidst the spectre of death, he confronted the fragility of life. The once all-consuming pursuit of success in the CSE dwindled in significance against the stark reality of his own mortality.

Days flew by and before long, it was May 2023. The impending announcement of the CSE results cast a heavy shadow of uncertainty over Waseem and his peers. Among the twenty-five IRS officers from his batch, who had received Interview calls, the fierce competition meant that only a handful were likely to ascend to the coveted ranks of the IAS.

On 23 May 2023, tension hung thick in the air with the impending announcement of the CSE results. Waseem's resolve remained unyielding. However, with each passing moment, the impending revelation loomed larger, threatening to engulf him in a storm of uncertainty.

'Why are you so anxious, Waseem? I'm sure you'll make it this time,' his friend Pavitra, sitting next to him in class, attempted to soothe his anxiety.

'I've put in a lot of effort this time. This is going to be my last attempt because after this, we'll receive regular postings in the IRS and I won't have the time to take the exam again,' he said, trying to shake off the tension that still gripped him tightly.

Pavitra's reassurances couldn't bring solace to Waseem and his anxiety persisted. After lunch, he decided to skip class and retreat to his hostel room, hoping to find respite in slumber. However, the lull was short-lived. An unexpected call from Faesal shattered the calm. The call disconnected before Waseem could answer it, sending shockwaves of speculation rippling through his mind.

'Why did Faesal call at this time? Something must have happened. Has the result been published? He wouldn't have called if I hadn't been selected,' Waseem pondered anxiously. Without delay, he opened Telegram and located the much-awaited PDF file. With trembling hands, he clicked open the file and glanced at its first page.

And there it was, like a beacon of hope amidst the tumultuous sea of uncertainty—his name, boldly emblazoned at rank seven. A wildfire of jubilation erupted within him, propelling him into a frenzy of excitement. Bursting forth from his room, his exultant cries drew the attention of a group of friends returning to the hostel after lunch. The weight of years of perseverance lifted, replaced by the sweet embrace of accomplishment. The jubilant celebrations began instantly and continued through the night, joined by four other IRS colleagues of Waseem, who had also been selected for the IAS.

Waseem applied for leave and made his way back home, where he was greeted by a throng of eager faces and the comforting embrace of his mother, Ruby Jaan. The media swarmed around him, capturing the essence of his victory. However, the villagers were puzzled by the renewed fervour. 'What has happened now? The boy had been selected in IAS two years back. What's the reason for the fresh celebrations?' they wondered aloud.

Ruby Jaan, Waseem's mother, felt a wave of relief wash over her. Her son's relentless dedication had finally borne fruit. He would no longer have to toil tirelessly, as his hard work had paid off.

* * *

Key Takeaways from Waseem's Story

1. **Total Commitment:** Success in the CSE cannot be taken for granted, nor can it be achieved with casual, half-hearted or outdated preparations. Overconfidence and carelessness are recipes for failure. Many candidates fail in the Prelims stage even after successfully navigating one or more stages of the exam in earlier attempts.

2. **Master the Art of Presentation of Answers:** In the Mains exam, it's not only your knowledge that matters but also how you present your answers. Candidates must learn from model answers, toppers' answer copies and other sources. Practicing answer-writing is crucial for success.

3. **Pursue the Field of Study that Excites You:** In school and college, selecting fields of study based on your interests is paramount. Don't let your opinion be swayed by parents, friends or relatives.

4. **Cultivate a Reading Habit:** Developing a reading habit is essential. It expands your knowledge base, which is beneficial at all stages of the CSE. It also enriches your overall perspective.

5. **Seek Focused Guidance:** Obtaining guidance from too many sources will only confuse and stress you. Avoid the influx of numerous ideas and opinions about course material and exam strategy. Depend on select, reliable sources for guidance.

6. **Quality over Quantity in the Mains Exam:** It doesn't matter how many sheets you fill in the Mains paper or in which sequence you attempt the questions. What matters is the clarity, depth and precision of your answers.

Chapter 6

The Numero Uno

Top Students Pursue Medicine and Engineering

The dusky twilight on this March 2014 evening had gradually yielded to the artificial glow of streetlights and neon signs. The honking of cars, rhythmic ringing of bicycle bells and animated chatter of vendors and residents were slowly fading away. In their modest apartment in East of Kailash, South Delhi, the Sharma family gathered around their dining table. Rachna Sharma and Sunil Dutt Sharma sat with their children, Shruti and Aditya, while Amma, Rachna's loving mother, completed the circle.

As dinner concluded and amma retired to her room, the peaceful evening gave way to a lively debate. Shruti, a bright-eyed Class 10 student at Sardar Patel Vidyalaya, had brought home a circular from school about selecting subjects for Class 11. Such animated exchanges were a familiar sight in Indian households as children prepared to transition to higher classes or get ready to join college.

'The choice seems quite clear, beta. Ours is a family of engineers and doctors. You should choose science subjects and prepare for IIT-JEE,' Shruti's father remarked, casting a glance at the circular.

'Papa, I have earnestly explored the engineering option. However, it fails to ignite my passion,' Shruti confessed, with a hint of reluctance in her voice.

Rachna interjected with a gentle yet persuasive tone, 'All right, then you should aspire to become a doctor like your grandparents.'

Shruti's grandfather, Devendra Kumar Vats, and grandmother, Satya Bala Sharma, were well-known doctors in their native village. Several of her cousins and relatives also pursued careers in the medical profession.

Shruti listened attentively but dared to voice the stirrings of her own heart. 'Maa, I have been thinking a lot about this and I truly believe that humanities would be a better fit for me.'

Her parents exchanged a sceptical glance, grappling with the unexpected deviation from the well-trodden path they had envisioned for their daughter.

'What career path do you see for yourself in that? Bright students like you opt for the science stream. It provides stability. First secure a job, then you can choose to do whatever you want,' Sunil said, his tone tinged with concern.

But Shruti stood her ground. 'Papa, nowadays there are a lot of career options for humanities students as well,' she explained, her voice steady with determination.

Her father's brows furrowed in contemplation. 'Not many. You will be left with very limited choices, like working in an NGO or pursuing journalism,' he countered.

Rachna, echoing her husband's sentiments, shared a common refrain of Indian parents. 'Just remember, whatever you choose, don't take the easy route. Work hard for a few years and your life will settle,' she advised.

Undeterred, Shruti played her trump card to win her parents' approval. 'Papa, there's also the option of civil services. Many humanities students become IAS and IPS officers. I want to pursue that path,' she declared firmly.

Her parents looked at each other, a silent conversation passing between them as they weighed the merits of Shruti's proposal and her unwavering determination.

'Yes, that's a good option. But you must take mathematics and economics, too, to widen your choices,' Rachna said, her voice tinged with the echoes of her own unfulfilled aspirations to qualify for the civil services examination (CSE).

'All right, papa, mummy,' Shruti nodded reluctantly, accepting the compromise.

Her younger brother, Aditya, a silent observer to the familial drama unfolding before him, felt a spark of hope flicker within his heart. 'If mummy and papa have allowed Shruti to pursue the subjects of her choice, perhaps they will also allow me to pursue cricket, my passion,' he mused, a smile tugging at the corners of his lips.

Shruti's choice soon invited comments from neighbours and relatives. 'Oh, we thought she was a good student!' they exclaimed, unable to hide their surprise.

A Nurturing Environment

Roots of Shruti's family lay in the tranquil village of Athai, nestled amidst the verdant landscapes of Bijnor district of Uttar Pradesh. Her grandparents had established their

Ayurveda practice in the nearby village of Basta. Shruti's father was an architect and also managed their family school in Basta.

Following Shruti's birth, despite her grandparents' reservations, her parents decided to move to the bustling metropolis of Delhi in search of better education and career opportunities for their children. However, conscious of the vitality of remaining connected with one's roots, for every vacation, Shruti's father would lead them back to Basta. There, Shruti revelled in the simple joys of rural life, playing with her cousins and relishing local candies like 'Laila ki ungli' and 'imli ke gole'.

From her earliest years, Rachna instilled in Shruti a love for learning. Even as a toddler, Rachna would lovingly prepare her school bag, filling it with a diary, pen and tiffin. Every morning, Shruti embarked on her daily 'school' adventures to her makeshift classroom, nestled in a corner of her room. There she would sketch and scribble for hours, savouring her tiffin in between. She dreamt of being an astronaut in her initial years.

We learn a lot of things subconsciously or sublingually in our school. That's why it's very important to have a good school environment. Her parents' quest to provide the best education to Shruti led to her admission in the Cambridge School, New Friends Colony. The school was known for imparting knowledge through innovative approaches and fun activities. The presence of a library in every class nurtured her voracious appetite for reading. However, it also invited occasional reprimands from her parents for indulging in novels.

Later, starting from Class 6, Shruti was enrolled in the prestigious Sardar Patel Vidyalaya in Lodhi Estate, New Delhi. She soon fell deeply in love with her school, which fostered an environment where every student was empowered to reach their full potential. She liked the school's unique award system, based on 'merit cards' rather than traditional ranks. The school fixed qualifying standards in each competitive area, including sports, and awarded merit cards to all those students who crossed the standards. It taught Shruti to compete with herself.

Her days at school were filled with excitement and discovery as she eagerly participated in a myriad activities and events in the 'musical afternoons', 'activity weeks' and 'food festival'. Shruti loved her school so much that when she was not heeding to her mother, Rachna's threat of not sending her to school made Shruti quickly fall in line.

Shruti eagerly awaited the annual activity week in the school, a time when the students put away their books and bags for cultural enrichment and sporting prowess. The days used to be filled with cultural activities, elocution, recitation, storytelling, motivational talks and sports. She would enthusiastically prepare poetry and prose, both in English and Hindi, for months; she loved reciting them during the activity week, earning numerous merit cards.

Another big annual attraction was the school's food festival, which attracted Shruti to her school for years even after she had passed out. It used to be a culinary extravaganza that brought together students and parents in celebration of traditional and healthy cuisine from across the country and beyond.

During her school days, Shruti found a profound sense of fulfilment and joy in social work. Besides teaching children of economically weaker sections (EWS) in and around her school, she lent her time and energy to Muskan, an NGO devoted to supporting differently abled and mentally challenged children and adults. Tales of officers effecting transformative change appearing in the daily newspapers resonated deeply with Shruti and fuelled her passion.

Besides nurturing academic excellence, the school also fostered the seeds of leadership and camaraderie through the student executive, a body elected by secret ballot. Besides being the cultural affairs secretary, in Class 12, Shruti threw her hat into the ring for the coveted position of general secretary. Shruti was a high achiever in academics, too, scoring 98 per cent in her Class 10 and 95 per cent in the Class 12 examinations.

At the Crossroads Again

The euphoria of achieving a staggering 95 per cent in her Class 12 exams was but a fleeting moment of celebration for Shruti. The family was in a huddle soon to take a very important decision about Shruti's life—which subjects to choose for her bachelor's degree programme.

'Mom, dad, I really want to pursue history (honours),' Shruti voiced her heartfelt desire as she flipped through the pages of Delhi University's undergraduate admissions brochure.

Sunil exchanged a worried glance with Rachna, his brow furrowed in concern. 'But Shruti, economics (honours) offers better job prospects. Think about your future, beta,' he implored.

Rachna nodded in agreement. 'Yes, Shruti. Economics is a solid choice. It opens a lot of opportunities for you,' she affirmed, her eyes reflecting her maternal concern.

Shruti hesitated, her heart torn between her passion and practicality. 'I understand, but I fear there will be too much math involved in economics. History feels like the right fit for me,' she confessed.

With a heavy sigh, Sunil leaned forward, his gaze fixed on Shruti. 'Beta, I fail to understand your reluctance. You've excelled with a high 97 per cent marks in maths and an impressive 98 per cent in economics. We want what's best for you,' he reasoned.

In her desperation to sway her parents' decision, Shruti wielded her most potent weapon. She argued that history was indispensable for success in the CSE. Moved by her impassioned plea, Sunil and Rachna relented, seeing within her words a resolute determination to become an IAS officer.

However, unbeknownst to her parents, Shruti was yet to solidify her career path, and her proclamation was merely a means to pursue her passion for history.

Another battle ensued over the choice of college. Shruti was drawn to the historic allure, iconic institutions, picturesque surroundings, extracurricular activities and vibrant campus life of Delhi University's North Campus. She yearned to join the prestigious Saint Stephen's College despite the arduous two-hour daily commute. Rachna and Sunil, on the other hand, favoured the practicality and convenience of Lady Shri Ram College, an equally esteemed institution located close to their home. Yet, through persistent persuasion, Shruti once again managed to sway her parents' decision.

Middle-class families, especially those who are the first generation to migrate to urban areas, often uphold conservative values. Shruti's parents were no exception, enforcing restrictions on her outings to once a week and staunchly prohibiting sleepovers at friends' houses. In college as well, she had to forgo activities that went on late into the night.

You Are Not Career-Oriented

Parents often etch milestones in the life journey of their children—age to complete studies, age to pick up a job, age to get married and so on. Shruti's parents did so as well. Rachna, in particular, who had experienced financial dependence all her life, wanted Shruti to be financially independent as soon as possible.

As she entered the final year of her bachelor's degree, Rachna and Sunil asked Shruti about her career plans and urged her to start preparing for the CSE. They admonished her for delaying things unnecessarily, not being decisive and career-oriented and reminded her of the promise she had made.

Shruti's parents advised her to join a coaching institute to prepare for the CSE. Shruti, on the other hand, wanted to seriously pursue her bachelor's studies without distraction. However, she agreed on the condition that she may be allowed to stay in a paying guest accommodation near the coaching institute.

'For the first time in life, I will be free to participate in the evening activities in college and go out with friends without any restriction, Moreover, I will get to know the pattern of CSE,' she thought. Little did she know that living alone would be full of challenges and make her realize the importance of home and family.

Soon, Shruti and her mother were on the hunt for a room in Karol Bagh. They were shocked to see the small size of the rooms and a complete lack of ventilation. After days of search, they zeroed in on a room in a flat which had some access to natural light. Shruti would attend college in the morning and go to the coaching class in the evening.

The charm of living alone disappeared swiftly as Shruti got the taste of the Karol Bagh world. Politics and fights between flatmates, theft of food items kept in the common refrigerator, harassment by the flat-owner, horrible food of the tiffin service and the burden of cleaning the room and washing her clothes left her harried. Another challenge was inculcating self-discipline as there was no one to wake her up on time, adhere to the study timetable and eat properly.

She also noticed that many of the aspirants living in Karol Bagh were just enjoying themselves, wasting their time and their parents' money and were not serious in their studies. They lived in Karol Bagh just to convince their parents that they were preparing seriously for the CSE.

Shruti soon realized that coaching didn't offer significant overall value and self-study was a better option. The sprawling halls of the coaching institute accommodated over a thousand students, making for a crowded and impersonal learning environment. During the lengthy two-and-a-half-hour sessions, valuable time was squandered by teachers in frivolous banter and casual conversations.

The coaching classes resembled a scripted spectacle, particularly evident when Shruti accidentally found herself in a class she had already attended. She couldn't help but notice the mechanical repetition that characterized the session—even the jokes were recycled, delivered with uncanny precision at the same moments as before.

But there were some pleasant changes, too. Shruti enjoyed the freedom to go out without seeking permission. She could attend more college fests and events. She also witnessed a change in the behaviour of her parents, who started treating her as grown-up, someone more mature, who could move out independently and manage on her own. Moreover, coaching provided her with an understanding of the exam pattern.

However, the trek to conquer UPSC is seldom simple and straightforward.

A Tryst with Academics

As Shruti approached the final year of her BA (honours), her ambitions were clear: a year dedicated to conquering the heights of Mount UPSC. But fate often leads us down unexpected paths, as she soon discovered.

As the end of her undergraduate journey loomed closer, Shruti learned that nearly everyone in her class was fervently preparing for the entrance exam for admission to the prestigious MA programme at Jawaharlal Nehru University (JNU). Succumbing to peer pressure and the allure of a highly regarded programme, Shruti took a leap of faith and filled out the form for the exam.

The exam results delivered a surprise. Shruti emerged as the top scorer. Despite the months of rigorous preparation, many of her classmates were unable to clear the entrance test. Shruti's remarkable achievement filled her parents with pride. It became a prominent topic of discussion during their post-dinner conversation.

'Shruti's exceptional performance demonstrates her immense potential,' remarked Sunil. 'I firmly believe that she should redirect her focus towards UPSC instead of joining the JNU.'

'Papa, I'm passionate about studying history,' Shruti voiced earnestly. 'Moreover, pursuing an MA will provide a solid foundation for my CSE preparation, especially with history as my optional subject.' Her enthusiasm for history ran deep.

'If Shruti is truly dedicated to pursuing an MA in history, then let her follow her passion. She can continue her IAS preparation alongside,' Rachna chimed in, offering her support to Shruti.

Shruti felt immense gratitude towards her parents, realizing that despite their logical persuasion, they never imposed their choices on her. The ultimate decision was always hers. Rachna frequently supported Shruti in these decisions, occasionally siding with her against Sunil.

JNU revealed itself to Shruti as a vibrant hub of intellectual discourse and political engagement. She found herself swiftly embraced by a diverse community and newfound friends. The 24x7 dhabas offered not just food but a space for camaraderie and lively conversations. Equally captivating were the university's libraries, especially the history department's Centre for Historical Studies (CHS) library, whose serene surroundings and resident peacocks stole Shruti's heart.

Shruti discovered a genuine love for her course. She found the curriculum and course design to be of exceptional quality. The professors were highly esteemed within academic circles. Students were allowed to attend any lecture. The institution promoted academic writing and thinking through a rigorous system of paper writing. Papers were meticulously scrutinized and intensely discussed, fostering a culture of academic excellence.

However, Shruti soon realized that a career in academia, though intellectually stimulating, would not be fulfilling for her. She observed that academic life revolved around writing papers and engaging in lengthy, intense discussions on minor nuances, with few opportunities to make a direct impact on people's lives. Consequently, she became disillusioned with academia and decided to leave the MA programme prematurely to focus her energies on preparing for the CSE.

Shruti's decision surprised her professors, who implored her to reconsider. However, despite their efforts to dissuade her, Shruti remained resolute.

A Chance Discovery in Basta

One evening, while Shruti was engrossed in her preparations, she received a phone call from her father, who was visiting Basta at the time.

'Shruti, did you know about the Residential Coaching Academy (RCA) in Jamia Millia Islamia?' Sunil's voice carried a blend of surprise and excitement. 'They offer free coaching to civil services aspirants, along with library, hostel and mess facilities at a nominal cost.'

'Dad, how did you find out about this?' Shruti's surprise mirrored her father's unexpected revelation.

'I stumbled upon an advertisement in the newspaper about their upcoming entrance examination,' Sunil explained, his tone filled with enthusiasm. 'I believe you should consider taking the entrance test. It's conveniently located close to our home,' he explained.

Nestled within the confines of Jamia Millia Islamia, the Residential Coaching Academy (RCA), Centre for Coaching & Career Planning, operated under the joint funding of the University Grants Commission (UGC) and the ministry of minority affairs. It offered free coaching programmes to compete for the CSE and other job opportunities for aspirants from minority communities, scheduled tribes, scheduled castes and women.

Shruti effortlessly sailed through the three-stage entrance examination of RCA held in 2019. However, she decided to initially utilize only the library facility and attend selected classes while residing at home.

RCA provided a conducive and competitive environment for preparation. Here, she observed a higher proportion of dedicated aspirants compared to Karol Bagh. Many among them had triumphed through one or more stages of the CSE.

It took Shruti a while to become integrated into a small, tight-knit group of fellow aspirants at RCA. They could often be found engaged in lively discussions on significant topics, whether in the tranquil ambience of the RCA lawn or over steaming cups of 'chacha ki chai'. Chacha recognized her from a distance as Shruti used to bring her own red coffee mug and drink two strong coffees.

They also engaged in rigorous answer-writing sessions. An excellent culture of peer learning developed as they exchanged their answer sheets and provided feedback to each other. Soon, Shruti shifted to RCA hostel, where she found wonderful friends in Shumra, Mini and Kranti.

Witnessing the dedication and diligence of her peers served as a constant source of motivation for Shruti. Whenever fatigue threatened to dampen her spirits or her efforts faltered, the sight of her determined companions tirelessly toiling away reinvigorated her resolve.

However, the outbreak of Covid-19 soon brought about an unexpected twist. RCA abruptly closed its doors, instructing students to vacate the hostels and discontinued the mess facility. Electricity and drinking water supplies were cut off. While Shruti was fortunate to reside nearby and wasn't significantly impacted, the situation dealt a severe blow to many students hailing from distant locales.

Among them was Kranti, a determined aspirant from Assam grappling with the harsh realities of her humble background. Having lost her father at a young age, returning to Assam spelled the end of her UPSC journey. In this hour of crisis, Shruti happily extended an invitation for Kranti to stay at her home. Kranti would later crack the Assam CSE and become an Assam civil services officer.

Mini, another aspirant, faced a similar predicament and found refuge in Shruti's home during the subsequent wave of Covid-19. Following in Kranti's footsteps, Mini persevered and triumphed, cementing a place in the IPS through CSE-2021.

During the Covid-19 pandemic, Shruti and her friends utilized mobile apps for group discussions and collaborative studying. They divided the task of notetaking, with one person leading each topic and preparing comprehensive notes on Google Docs, while others contributed to enrich them. The extended time provided by the pandemic proved invaluable in refining and solidifying these notes.

As the fresh dates for the Prelims-2020 were announced, Shruti felt confident in her preparations. However, fate had other plans. Little did she anticipate that a minor oversight would lead to a major blunder, threatening to derail her carefully laid plans.

Taking on the Linguistic Challenge

After the Prelims-2020, Shruti's heart brimmed with confidence. Wasting no time, she delved into preparations for the next challenge, the Mains. By the time the results of the Prelims were announced, and she emerged victorious, Shruti had covered a significant portion of the syllabus. However, her jubilation soon turned to disbelief and dismay.

As she sat down to fill out the Detailed Application Form-1 (DAF-1) on the UPSC portal, Shruti was in for a rude awakening. Certain crucial information, such as her optional subject, Indian language paper and the examination medium, had been prefilled in DAF-1 based on the details submitted by her in the Prelims Application Form. While filling it out, Shruti made a monumental mistake by selecting Hindi-medium for her GS and essay papers.

As Shruti gazed at the pre-filled, non-editable information in her DAF-1, a sinking feeling settled in the pit of her stomach. Her eyes remained locked on the words before her, her mind struggling to comprehend the gravity of the situation.

Desperately, she searched for a solution, frantically scouring every corner of the Internet for a way to rectify her mistake. She also reached out to her friends, hoping for guidance or a shred of reassurance, but their responses only echoed her own sense of helplessness.

In a moment of vulnerability, Shruti turned to her mother, tears streaming down her cheeks as she confessed her mistake. Her mother, too, was stunned by the revelation, grappling with the reality of their predicament.

For the following days, Shruti and her mother travelled to the UPSC headquarters. They penned numerous applications and met many officers with fervent pleas to amend Shruti's medium of examination. They also met an aspirant at RCA who had faced a similar ordeal a year prior. Everyone uttered the same words: 'Nothing can be done now.'

Shruti was faced with an agonizing ultimatum: proceed with the exam in the Hindi medium or forfeit this attempt. Despite her father's suggestion to opt out and focus on the following year's preparations, Shruti decided to face the challenge and write the Mains exam in the Hindi medium.

Shruti would study her notes in English, painstakingly translate them into Hindi using Google Translator, and then study the translated versions. Her friends, Stanzin Wangyal, who would later crack the CSE to bag a position in the IRS, and Vishakha offered invaluable support during this challenging time.

However, as Shruti delved into her preparations, the task proved to be daunting, with a vast array of technical terms to grasp and a lack of writing practice in Hindi. She couldn't finish any of her papers within the allotted time. Each exit from the examination hall was marked by tears of frustration and disappointment.

Still, Shruti harboured a glimmer of hope amidst the shadows of her linguistic limitations. But her optimism was swiftly crushed when the results were announced. However, a silver lining appeared when the UPSC released the marks for the Mains examination. Shruti had fallen short by just one mark. With her spirits buoyed by this realization, Shruti envisioned her triumph in her next attempt and immediately devoted herself wholeheartedly to preparations.

She meticulously studied the syllabus and selected one or two reliable sources for each subject. She also analysed previous years' questions. Thereafter, she continually augmented her notes with additional information, data, examples and quotes from newspapers and other reading materials to enrich her answers. She made sure that all the information on a topic was neatly organized in one place, rather than scattered throughout her notes.

Upon completing the syllabus, Shruti turned to test series and answer-writing practice. After each round of answer-writing, she did self-evaluation to see how she could make them better, both by better structuring and adding more points. Studying the answer sheets of previous years' toppers, she extracted valuable insights to improve her answers.

Shruti's mantra was minimal sources, multiple revisions and consistent answer-writing practice. She also recognized the importance of prioritization, time management and leveraging one's strengths.

'I Am Not Going to Write This Exam Again'

On the evening of 10 October 2021, after her Prelims exam, Shruti sat amidst her scattered notes, her face streaked with tears. Her mother and a close friend sat by her side, offering words of comfort. The answer keys uploaded by three prominent coaching institutes painted a bleak picture of her chances to progress to the next stage of the exam.

Shruti's confidence plummeted. So, instead of starting her Mains preparations, she decided to join MA (Sociology) at the Delhi School of Economics. Yet, fate had a surprising twist in store for Shruti. When the results of the Prelims exam were finally unveiled, contrary to the grim predictions of the coaching institutes, she had cleared the Prelims comfortably.

Buoyed by this unexpected triumph, Shruti threw herself back into her preparations with renewed vigour. Although she had already laid a solid foundation after the last Mains exam, the ensuing months were a gruelling odyssey as the syllabus seemed never-ending.

In Mains, Shruti did well in the compulsory languages, essay and GS papers. She was eagerly looking forward to the five days gap between her GS and optional papers. However, fate dealt Shruti another cruel blow. On the evening of her last GS paper, Shruti started feeling weak and feverish. Her condition deteriorated the next day, with symptoms strongly suggestive of Covid-19, although she refrained from getting tested.

Shruti noticed that many candidates were coughing and sneezing in the examination hall during the GS and essay papers. There were even rumours circulating about the possible postponement of the remaining papers due to the ongoing wave of Covid-19. Those who got themselves tested and disclosed their illness found themselves barred from sitting in the exam.

The five-day break was crucial for Shruti to revise her optional subject. However, she was so sick that she couldn't even get out of bed for three days. The prospect of attempting the optional papers seemed dauntingly distant, sending chills down her spine.

Fortunately, on the eve of the exam, Shruti's condition improved slightly. The next morning, she swallowed a fistful of medicine and mustered every ounce of strength to make her way to the examination centre and somehow completed the exam. As she emerged from the crucible of examination, she felt a profound sense of relief.

Returning home, she declared, 'I am not going to write this exam again. It's so taxing, both physically and mentally.'

The next day she joined sociology classes at the Delhi School of Economics.

A Cascade of Tears

Despite facing multiple challenges during her preparation phase, Shruti was confident she would clear the Mains exam. Her belief was validated on 17 March 2022, when the UPSC published the results, opening the door to Dholpur House for the Personality Test, or Interview.

With her Interview scheduled for the initial week, a tide of stress surged within her.

Shruti embarked on a hurried preparation spree, meticulously listing the maze of questions that might stem from her DAF. To stay abreast of current affairs, she turned to clarifying wisdom of podcasts like '3 Things' by the *Indian Express* and 'Cut the Clutter' by ThePrint. Additionally, she appeared in a handful of mock Interviews, where her performance garnered overwhelmingly positive feedback, bolstering her confidence.

On the morning of the interview, dressed in a beautiful saree, Shruti radiated a blend of expectations and nervous energy. Accompanied by her parents and a couple of close friends from Jamia, she arrived at the illustrious UPSC headquarters. Little did she know, fate had a swift agenda in store for her.

As the first candidate in her cohort of six, she scarcely had time to acclimate herself to the hallowed halls of Dholpur House. Within mere moments of her arrival, she found herself seated outside the imposing interview room.

Upon stepping into the room, Shruti was struck by its setting. In stark contrast to the spacious chambers and expansive tables she had encountered during her mock Interviews, this room was modest in size, with board members seated in close proximity to one another. Besides the chairman, four other figures adorned the room.

The very first question, probing the framework of the juvenile justice system in the country, rattled Shruti's composure. Though she endeavoured to respond, the chairman's gentle urging for greater specificity left her momentarily flustered.

As the Interview unfolded, Shruti found herself adrift in a sea of dissatisfaction. Few and far between were the moments where her analytical prowess and penchant for shaping opinions could shine. The landscape was dominated by factual inquiries, often leaving her to apologize to the board for her inability to provide answers.

The barrage of questions delved into the realm of facts and history, testing Shruti's depth of knowledge. From inquiries about the cyclical nature of history to specific events such as the Champaran Satyagraha, the Maurya dynasty, World War dynamics and the assassination of Lord Mayo, each query demanded a nuanced understanding. Furthermore, the panel probed her insight into governance matters, including sustainable development goals (SDGs).

The confidence that had blossomed within Shruti, nurtured by the echoes of encouragement from her mock Interviews, swiftly dissipated like morning mist. With each passing moment, the weight of her disillusionment grew heavier, casting a pall over her aspirations to leave a lasting impression and secure high marks.

As Shruti emerged from the imposing gates of Dholpur House, she saw her parents who awaited her, exuding confidence in their daughter's performance. However, as Shruti drew near to them, a cascade of tears streamed down her cheeks, stirring a deep well of concern within them. With her mother enveloping her in a warm hug, she poured out her heart, recounting the tumultuous experience of the interview. Rachna consoled her not to worry and that something good was in store.

In an effort to uplift her spirits, Shruti's parents took her to the nearby Carnatic Cafe for brunch. An unspoken agreement hung in the air: 'Refrain from broaching the subject of the Interview.' Yet, the echoes of the Interview lingered in the corners of Shruti's mind. The hope of achieving a high rank to secure a place in the IAS seemed to have slipped from her grasp.

'Can I Believe My Eyes?'

On 30 May 2022, Shruti was overwhelmed with anxiety. Rumours abounded regarding the imminent release of the CSE-2021 results by the UPSC. Clutching her phone like a lifeline, she obsessively refreshed the Telegram app every thirty seconds.

As the clock struck 12 noon, a collective gasp rippled through the group chat as a PDF was shared. Trembling with apprehension and clutching onto a silent prayer in her heart, Shruti mustered the courage to click open the document, mentally preparing to scan the list from the bottom. However, as her eyes darted across the first page, they were met with a sight that sent shockwaves through her being. There, adorned in black and white, was her name, boldly etched at the coveted rank one. It felt surreal, as if she had stumbled upon a shimmering oasis in the parched desert of her dreams.

In moments of unimaginable triumph, doubt crept in like a shadow, casting a veil of uncertainty over Shruti's elation. Was it a hoax? With bated breath, she closed her eyes, her heart pounding in her chest as she awaited confirmation. With trembling hands, she checked her roll number and name once more, desperately seeking reassurance. Though she anticipated her name to be somewhere in the final list, securing All India Rank-1 surpassed even her wildest dreams.

Apart from her mother, only her amma was present at home. Shruti's father had departed for Basta the previous evening and Aditya was away playing cricket.

Shruti scrutinized her name multiple times, double-checking her roll number. There was no indication in the group chat of the PDF being a counterfeit. Finally, she mustered the courage to share the monumental news with her mother, who responded with a mix of jubilation and incredulity. 'Is it true, Shruti?' Rachna asked repeatedly, her voice quivering with emotion. Together, they pored over the document once more.

As the reality began to sink in, Rachna shared the news with amma, enveloping her in a tight embrace. Tears of joy streamed down their cheeks as they held onto each other for a long time. Yet, amidst the euphoria, the magnitude of the achievement still seemed unreal, requiring time to fully grasp its significance.

Shruti dialled her father's number, her heart throbbing with excitement as she delivered the life-altering news. As Sunil absorbed the revelation, waves of pride and joy washed over him, rendering him speechless. He immediately embarked on the journey from Basta to Delhi, eager to celebrate his daughter's triumph.

Still clad in casual home attire, with oil splattered in her hair, Shruti sat in disbelief as she witnessed her name splashed across television screens. Soon, a deluge of phone calls inundated Shruti's world. The most gratifying aspect of it all was witnessing the radiant smiles on her mother and amma's face.

Suddenly, a knock at the door shattered the tranquility of the moment. Rachna hurried to answer it, only to be greeted by Najma Akhtar, vice chancellor of Jamia, bearing a bouquet of flowers. Behind her, a throng of media personnel clamoured for attention, their cameras flashing like stars in the night sky. Amidst the chaos, Najma Akhtar extended her congratulations, enveloping Shruti in a warm embrace.

The onslaught of media interviews began in earnest, the number of reporters swelling with each passing minute. Their house soon resembled a bustling newsroom, with journalists spilling onto the stairs and even onto the roof of the building. In a bid to manage the crowd, Shruti had to come downstairs, while Rachna frantically reached out to relatives and friends for assistance.

The media persisted long into the night, their presence stretching past midnight despite repeated pleas for departure. As dawn broke, they returned with renewed vigour, their requests for interviews unabated. The next day, too, turned into a relentless cycle of inquiries, with relatives flocking in droves and the phone ringing incessantly.

Shruti soon realized that her success had propelled her into the spotlight. The day after the results were announced, she accompanied her mother to the nearby Haldiram's sweet shop to pick up some sweets for their visitors. However, as soon as she entered, she found herself surrounded by people who recognized her. Many of them requested autographs and photos with her. Likewise, a few days later, during a brief trip to Shimla, she encountered a similar situation on the bustling Mall Road.

For Shruti, a private and reserved individual by nature, the mounting pressure became unbearable. However, there was much more pressure in store for the would-be bureaucrat.

Bracing for a Social Media Storm

Just two days had passed since Shruti's sudden surge into the spotlight and already the weight of fame and expectation bore down heavily upon her. As she rose from bed, a silent prayer escaped her lips, hoping for a reprieve from the constant stream of visitors, phone calls and interview requests. Meanwhile, Rachna was bustling in the kitchen, preparing steaming aloo parathas for breakfast, while Shruti's father sat engrossed in the morning newspaper. The serenity of the room was abruptly shattered by the sudden ring of Sunil's phone.

'Why is Shruti posting anti-government stuff on social media?' the caller, a friend of Sunil, inquired with concern.

'What social media posts?' Sunil responded, his expression clouded with confusion.

'Don't you know that her posts on Instagram and Twitter are going viral?' the caller explained, taken aback by Sunil's lack of awareness.

'Which post? I don't think Shruti has posted anything,' Sunil replied, his confusion deepening.

'Oh! You don't know about such a big controversy? Let me share links to some posts. You need to immediately counter them,' the caller insisted, leaving Sunil pondering over the unexpected turn of events.

For the next few minutes, confusion hung thickly over Shruti and her parents. While Shruti did have Instagram and Twitter accounts, they were strictly private and hadn't been accessed for days. The unsettling thought that her accounts might have been compromised by hackers loomed ominously in their minds. Hastily, Shruti logged in to her accounts, her heart racing with anxiety.

However, their suspicions were only compounded as they discovered that no recent posts had been made; her accounts lay dormant for months. Bewilderment gripped Shruti as she pondered why her father's friend sounded so deeply concerned about her social media activity.

Within minutes, Sunil's friend sent links to some Instagram and Twitter posts. As they clicked them open, a profound shock swept over them. They were confronted with fake accounts pretending to be Shruti Sharma, adorned with her photographs. To their astonishment, these counterfeit accounts boasted lakhs of followers.

As they sifted through the deceitful posts, it felt as though the ground had been yanked from beneath their feet. Malevolent actors had capitalized on Shruti's newfound national prominence and had used fake accounts to disseminate numerous controversial posts. Among them were critiques of the government's Agniveer scheme for recruitment in the defence forces.

The responses poured in by the thousands, with some rallying behind her purported views while others vehemently condemned her for the posts. Shruti's name had become a trending hashtag on social media platforms.

Shruti took swift action, filing a complaint with the police against the perpetrators. Additionally, she took to her own Twitter and Instagram handles to debunk the falsehoods and raise awareness about the existence of these fraudulent accounts. Simultaneously, she reached out to her fellow high-ranking candidates from the CSE, enlisting their support in disseminating warnings about her counterfeit accounts through their social media channels.

Shruti also found herself in the midst of social media buzz due to a couple of minor controversies. Firstly, during an interview on a YouTube channel, she discussed the Aryan invasion theory, elaborating on its various aspects. Unfortunately, someone cherry-picked one aspect of her response and blew it out of proportion, sparking controversy.

Additionally, a tweet surfaced after Shruti's success, suggesting that JNU students were not only active in protests but also topping UPSC exams. This remark quickly snowballed into a controversy, with some individuals tweeting against JNU, while others rallied in its defence.

Shruti had initially planned a solo trip abroad immediately after her UPSC success and she had even convinced her parents, gaining their approval. However, the whirlwind of media controversies and the constant stream of visitors disrupted her plans. Then, a dark cloud descended upon the Sharma family as Rachna, Shruti's mother, was diagnosed with cancer.

While most people relish the joy of success after conquering Mount UPSC, for Shruti, the period post-result was unexpectedly hectic and emotionally draining.

In the Majestic North Block

Rachna and Sunil were overjoyed when Shruti received a letter informing her that she would be felicitated on 7

June 2022 by Dr Jitendra Singh, Union minister of state for personnel, public grievances and pensions.

On the morning of that day, Shruti got ready for the big occasion, clad in a blue and white cotton saree. Sunil was already prepared, eager to escort her. However, Shruti couldn't shake off her sadness, knowing her mother's illness prevented her from accompanying them.

Very soon, the father–daughter duo found themselves in the majestic North Block of the central secretariat. All the twenty rank holders of CSE-2021 invited to the event were super excited. Even more thrilled were their proud and beaming parents, who accompanied them. Shruti relished interacting with her batchmates for the first time, having previously seen some of them on television or in newspapers.

They were ushered into a conference room to their allotted seats on one side of an oval table. The minister and senior officers of the department sat on the opposite side. Each topper was felicitated by the minister with a memento and parents joined their wards during the felicitation, beaming with pride as they posed for pictures.

A thunderous round of applause erupted from the achievers as the minister hailed their batch as the architects of the 'Century India', poised to chart a new course for the country as independent India approached its centenary. He also expressed immense pride in the historic achievement that, for the first time, the top three rank holders in the CSE were all women.

Upon returning home, Shruti briefed Rachna about every minute of the felicitation function. She observed immense pride gleaming in her mother's eyes, momentarily overshadowing all her pain and illness.

In a Mesmerizing Oasis

Joining the Lal Bahadur Shastri National Academy of Administration (LBSNAA) in Mussoorie was a breath of fresh air for Shruti. Accompanied by her father, she felt a pang of longing for her mother, who couldn't join them on this journey.

Days at the academy were a flurry of activities, from classes to outdoor adventures, including invigorating treks and a memorable village visit in Puducherry. Apart from Mini, who had been Shruti's friend since their Jamia days, Shruti formed close bonds with Ankita, Naman and her roommate.

Before they knew it, the two-month-long Bharat darshan study tour was on the horizon. However, Shruti found herself torn. Her heart weighed heavy with sadness as she longed to stay by the side of her mother, who had been admitted to AIIMS, New Delhi, for treatment. Despite her own struggles, Rachna selflessly urged Shruti to embark on the Bharat darshan.

After concluding their attachments with the three armed forces, the group set foot on the enchanting islands of Lakshadweep. They found themselves spellbound by the unspoiled natural splendour and ethereal allure of Lakshadweep.

Without hesitation, Shruti donned snorkelling gear and plunged into the azure depths of the sea. An enchanting underwater tableau unfolded before her eyes—coral reefs, adorned in hues as vibrant as a painter's palette, schools of fish darting among the intricate coral gardens, graceful sea turtles gliding serenely through the oceanic expanse. As night descended, the beach came alive with a soft, ethereal glow as bioluminescent algae cast a spellbinding light upon the sand.

The group stayed in the beautiful Bangaram island. It was so small that Shruti and her friends could encircle the entire island on foot. Yet, amidst the tranquil rhythms of island life, there was one evening in Lakshadweep that etched itself into their memories with an indelible ink.

On the serene shores of Bangaram, Shruti and her friend Divya found themselves drawn to the kayaking boats. They each claimed a vessel and set out into the vast blue. After some time, they lay back in their boats, letting the rhythmic lullaby of the ocean calm them into a peaceful nap amidst the open sea.

As Shruti and Divya dozed peacefully in their kayaks, unbeknownst to them, their fellow batchmates glided by. When they woke up, refreshed and invigorated, an idea struck Shruti like a bolt of inspiration.

'Let's circle around the island in our boats,' Shruti suggested to Divya, who readily agreed, unaware of the challenges that awaited them.

As they paddled away from the shore, the sun sank lower in the sky and with each passing minute, darkness descended. Despite their determination, the daunting task ahead became apparent forcing them to abandon their pursuit and return to the guest house.

In the guest house, their batchmates grew uneasy upon finding no trace of Shruti and Divya, especially as darkness slowly descended over the island. Recalling seeing the duo napping in their kayaks some distance from the shore, concern rippled through the group.

Fearing the worst, one of them decided to place a call to the administration.

As Shruti and Divya paddled closer to the guest house in their kayaks, they noticed a commotion on the shore. Spotting them, their friends ran towards them, exclaiming with a mix of anger and relief, 'Where have you two been? You've scared us!'

Shruti and Divya glanced around, their hearts sinking as they saw the local administration assembled with a sizeable rescue team, poised to venture into the ocean in search of them. Overwhelmed by embarrassment and guilt, the duo realized the gravity of their actions and the unnecessary panic they had caused among their friends and the community.

A Big Invite

Shruti's heart danced with excitement as she read an email on her phone screen. It was an invitation from the President of India, beckoning her to the prestigious Republic Day 'At Home' function. A surge of pride swelled within her. The honour was bestowed upon the male and female toppers of the CSE and a couple of other prestigious exams.

Filled with exhilaration, Shruti wasted no time in booking her ticket and making her way to Delhi on 25 January 2023. The following afternoon, adorned in an elegant silk saree, she arrived at the grand Rashtrapati Bhavan lawn for the highly anticipated event.

As she stepped onto the meticulously manicured lawn, a radiant smile graced Shruti's lips. Surrounded by a sea of dignitaries, she was awestruck by the sight of the President, the

Prime Minister and esteemed guests, including the President of Egypt, who was the chief guest at the Republic Day parade. Cabinet ministers, the national security advisor, ambassadors and other notable figures lent an air of grandeur to the occasion. Alongside fellow toppers, Shruti eagerly scanned the crowd, each sighting eliciting a surge of excitement.

Their enthusiasm reached new heights when they had the opportunity to engage with the finance minister, Nirmala Sitharaman. She sought their input for the impending budget, prompting lively discussions among the group as they eagerly shared their suggestions.

After exchanging pleasantries with the dignitaries, they moved on to enjoy some tea. Here, they found themselves in the company of numerous senior officers, engaging in lively conversations.

Before bidding farewell, Shruti and her friends succumbed to the temptation of capturing numerous photographs against the backdrop of the majestic Rashtrapati Bhavan and within its expansive corridors.

A Tearful Goodbye

Upon Shruti's request, she was assigned to Meerut district for her district training, a place close to Delhi, so she could stay near her ailing mother. Each passing day saw Rachna's health decline despite the tireless efforts of doctors at AIIMS. After a relentless year-long battle with cancer, Rachna peacefully departed this world, leaving Shruti to hold her in a final, loving embrace.

Shruti was utterly devastated. Rachna had been her everything, her guiding light and unwavering source of support. She had made numerous sacrifices for the education and career advancement of her children. Rachna's heart had swelled with pride and happiness upon Shruti's success in the CSE. She had longed to witness Shruti's journey as an IAS officer unfold.

From Rachna, Shruti had learned invaluable lessons in resilience and boundless positivity. Rachna's innate kindness and her passion for uplifting others had left an indelible mark on Shruti's soul. Though Rachna was physically gone, her spirit would forever dwell within Shruti, guiding her path and igniting an unyielding determination to bring meaningful change to the lives of those she would serve as an IAS officer.

A Formidable Test

'Who's that young girl stepping out of the sub-divisional magistrate's (SDM) car?' inquired an elderly farmer, gesturing with his calloused hand towards the government vehicle that had just pulled up.

'Perhaps the SDM's daughter,' speculated his colleague, his kurta pajama worn and a thick moustache adorning his face.

'But what brings her here? Where's the SDM to find a solution to our pressing problem?' pondered the first farmer, his curiosity piqued.

Amidst the commotion, local administration and police personnel hurried towards the girl as she stepped out of the car and made her way towards the group of protesting farmers.

The young woman was none other than Shruti Sharma. She was assigned the role of SDM just a week prior.

This responsibility came abruptly when the regular SDM, Aojasvi Raj, took a month-long leave.

After a late night spent addressing complaints of illegal mining in the area, Shruti had found little reprieve as her phone continued to ring incessantly, disrupting her sleep. The local tehsildar informed her that hundreds of farmers had staged a dharna. Their demand: access to the national highway directly in front of their village.

Shruti's nerves kicked in. New to the district and inexperienced in her current assignment, she hadn't yet encountered such crowds. Feeling the weight of responsibility, she promptly dialled Aojasvi, the regular SDM and her senior in service, seeking guidance.

'Access to and exit from the national highway is under the jurisdiction of the National Highways Authority of India (NHAI),' he informed her. 'We don't have the authority to intervene in this matter.'

'But sir, what should I tell them? How can I persuade them to end their protest?' Shruti's voice trembled with worry.

'Stay calm and composed. Listen to their grievances attentively and assure them that we will do everything in our power to address their concerns,' Aojasvi advised, his tone reassuring.

Shruti made her way through the throng of farmers and took a seat among them. The crowd, predominantly composed of male farmers with a scattering of females, buzzed with energy. Behind them stood a line of tractors and trolleys that had transported the farmers to the protest site. The police struggled to maintain order, urging the crowd to settle down and refrain from sloganeering.

The tehsildar introduced Shruti and indicated that she would hear their grievances and escalate them to higher authorities for resolution. A wave of commotion swept through the crowd when, in a moment of vulnerability, Shruti admitted that the issue lay within the jurisdiction of NHAI and that the district administration's options were limited.

However, she swiftly regained control of the situation, assuring them that she had fully comprehended the gravity of their genuine demand. She pledged to immediately escalate the matter to the highest level of state government and NHAI officers for prompt resolution.

'But when can we expect this to be done?' one of the farmer leaders pressed.

'We will expedite the process, but it requires coordination with senior officials in Lucknow and Delhi. Please allow us at least two months,' she responded calmly.

After a long conversation and negotiations on the timelines, Shruti breathed a sigh of relief as the farmers agreed to end their dharna. The incident offered Shruti invaluable insights, giving her a glimpse into the formidable challenges that IAS officers face daily in the discharge of their duties.

* * *

Key Takeaways from Shruti's Story

1. **Harness the Power of Peer Discussion and Collaborative Learning:** Forming a small group of like-minded IAS aspirants can be incredibly beneficial. Collaborate in making notes, engage in honest peer reviews and provide constructive feedback. Discuss complex issues and constantly motivate each other. It acts as a force multiplier, helping cover the vast syllabus efficiently and effectively.

2. **Exercise Extreme Caution while Filling Application Forms:** Fill out the exam application forms with utmost care. The information submitted is not editable and mistakes can cost candidates dearly. Ensure every detail is accurate, especially the information concerning your category, medium of exam, home state and service preference to avoid unnecessary complications.

3. **Avoid Premature Self-Evaluation of Prelims Performance:** Refrain from rushing to evaluate your performance using answer keys posted by coaching institutes. Do not get disheartened if predicted marks are lower than expected; cut-offs vary each year. Remember that assessment based on answer keys can be inaccurate. Continue preparing diligently for the Mains.

4. **Understand the Subjectivity of Interview Assessments:** Recognize that the Personality

Test or Interview assessments are subjective. The board appreciates an honest 'no' over attempting to answer questions you are unsure about. Do not be discouraged if you fail to answer some questions or if the Interview doesn't go as expected.

5. **Be Cautious with Media and Social Media After Success:** Post-success, be very careful in media interviews as facts can be twisted and statements cherry-picked. Monitor social media posts concerning you and be aware of any fake accounts created in your name.

Chapter 7

IAS Triumph over American Dream

Hurricane Creates a Mental Storm

It was raining cats and dogs in Houston, USA, on 28 August 2017, as Hurricane Harvey unleashed its fury. The Houston metropolitan area, part of the state of Texas, was battered by winds blowing at 200 km/hour and unprecedented rainfall reaching up to 50 cm. The catastrophic flooding brought the city to its knees, causing extensive damage to homes, businesses, infrastructure and the environment. Life was brought to a standstill for nearly twenty days. Thousands were displaced and many fatalities were reported.

Amidst this chaos, a twenty-four-year-old Indian man sat by his two-bedroom apartment's window. Although his eyes were fixed on the devastation outside, his mind was immersed deeply in thought. Confined to his home like many others for the past four days, he survived on the provisions he had managed to procure before the stores ran out of stock. This nature-induced incarceration had provided him ample time and opportunity to ponder over his life and future. The storm building up in his mind over the past few months had intensified in tandem with the hurricane.

The young man was Lavish, a graduate of the Indian Institute of Technology (IIT) Bombay. His fully furnished apartment, provided by his employer, Shell, had been his sanctuary since he joined the company's Texas office two years ago. Shell, a globally renowned Fortune 500 oil and gas giant, had offered him a handsome salary package, including a luxury sedan.

Lavish fondly recalled the day he had landed in Houston. The transfer adviser from his company had given him a warm welcome, provided a tour of the city and extended invaluable help in settling down. She assisted him in opening a bank account, obtaining a social security number, securing a driver's licence and moving into his apartment. Within fifteen days of his arrival, Lavish was pleasantly surprised when she handed him the keys to a brand-new luxury sedan.

The office environment was warm and welcoming. Lavish was part of a culturally diverse team led by Brad Rodgers, a native Texan. His teammates hailed from Kazakhstan, Nigeria, Spain and Malaysia. Invitations to their homes during Christmas and New Year added a personal touch to their harmonious professional relationships. Lavish had developed a close bond with Manish Srivastava, an IIT Guwahati alumnus, who became his friend, philosopher and guide and with Danny, his Malaysian colleague.

However, despite his professional success and peaceful life, Lavish was not happy. What was bothering this young man?

Realizing the American Dream

Hailing from a humble background, as a student at IIT Bombay, Lavish's primary focus was on earning money to repay his education loan and help his family purchase a new house. So, in the fourth year of his BTech, when the placement season began, he set his sights on the companies offering the highest salary package, rather than preferring any particular sector or nature of work. Competition was fierce, but he had spent the past two years relentlessly improving his academic performance and excelling in research.

Shell, a Fortune 500 company known for its liberal packages and top-notch employee facilities, was scheduled to come on day one of placements. Lavish prayed fervently for an opportunity with this global giant. He had prepared meticulously, seeking guidance from seniors already working at Shell.

The initial hurdle, an aptitude test, proved to be a breeze. Next came a psychometric test designed to evaluate decision making abilities, conflict resolution and consistency in thought processes. Despite many candidates dropping out, Lavish successfully navigated this obstacle.

The ultimate challenge was the e-tray test, an online assessment that simulated a real-world work environment to evaluate the skills and abilities of candidates for a specific role. In this phase, candidates were provided with a computer loaded with company policies, rules and regulations, connected to the company's server. They assumed the role of a project manager, facing real-life situations in a simulated live company environment.

Candidates had to assess situations, communicate with virtual teams and make various business decisions. The selection criteria revolved around the speed and accuracy of decisions, coupled with the candidate's ability to justify them. This demanding phase was followed by two rounds of interviews.

The evening brought a moment of euphoria for Lavish when he learned of his selection by Shell with a lucrative compensation.

In August 2015, Lavish joined Shell's upscale office in Bengaluru. The infrastructure and working environment were excellent. Employees were respected and given a lot of flexibility. The workforce was diverse, with employees from many countries. He also got the opportunity to visit numerous countries, savouring the perks of business class travel and luxurious stays in five- or seven-star hotels, with full flexibility to spend money for business requirements.

His dedication, technical acumen and skills quickly caught the attention of his superiors. Merely ten months after joining, he received a summon from his boss, Muthu Subramanyam.

'Do you have an interest in specializing in one of Shell's technologies?' Muthu enquired as soon as Lavish entered his chamber. The general manager, Sandy Lundie, was seated beside him.

'Shell has patented technology for emission reduction. We have numerous projects in this domain, but there's a lack of expertise in the Asia–Pacific. Given your strong research background and simulation expertise, we're considering sending you to Houston, USA, to learn and subsequently establish a team in India,' Sandy explained.

Delighted by the opportunity, Lavish readily agreed to shift to USA. On the evening of 30 October 2016, a chauffeur-driven Mercedes awaited Lavish outside his apartment in Bengaluru to transport him to the airport. A sense of achievement washed over him as he enjoyed the warm hospitality in the business class of an Emirates flight to Houston.

Mount UPSC Overshadows America's Allure

After living in Houston for a year, an internal storm started brewing in Lavish's mind. Despite achieving the highly sought-after 'American dream', Lavish began feeling homesick and was engulfed by a profound sense of emptiness.

During the past year, he had enthusiastically travelled across the USA, meeting and staying with many seniors from IIT Bombay. He was disheartened to find that, although they were working in renowned companies, they could afford only modest apartments and had to perform household chores themselves. What was more disheartening was that their job profiles and pay packages were not very different from his. The scope for professional growth and enhancement in income appeared marginal at best and the work was highly repetitive. Life was monotonous, too.

Moreover, there was no job security. As Lavish was preparing to leave for the USA, Shell underwent a massive layoff due to crashing oil prices. Many of his friends lost their jobs and those who remained were shuffled into roles they disliked. Another round of layoffs occurred after Lavish left the country.

The abundance of free time on weekends in the USA intensified the churning in Lavish's mind. He started feeling a void in his life. He had paid off his education loan and bought necessities for his parents and brother. The monthly salary started to look like merely a number in his bank account, making no significant real change in his life. Gradually, he began gravitating towards a career in the coveted IAS.

During his childhood, Lavish had no awareness of civil services and no one in his family held a government job. However, he couldn't escape the occasional taunt from friends: 'Are you a collector?' This phrase, often used when someone asserted authority or delivered a preachy discourse, left a lasting impression on his young mind. It ingrained the belief in him that a collector, an IAS officer, wielded significant authority.

Subsequently, at IIT Bombay, Lavish struck up a friendship with his classmates Rinku Meena and Hanuman Prasad Meena, both hailing from Rajasthan. From the outset, the duo harboured a clear goal—to become IAS officers. They regaled Lavish with stories of the respect, power and perks that IAS officers enjoyed. Lavish also started noticing that people in powerful positions, such as the RBI governor, MD of Air India, collector of Udaipur and many names on the inauguration boards of various buildings at IIT Bombay were IAS officers. Entry into the IAS appeared to be a sure shot way to achieve professional and social success. Therefore, he was not surprised when Rinku declined campus placements and headed straight to Delhi after completing his BTech to prepare for the CSE.

Lavish recalled Rinku and Hanuman's tales about respect and power of IAS officers when he had a series of distressing encounters while living in Bengaluru: harassment by police, government offices, local vendors and even the security guard of his apartment building.

'I have studied at a top-notch institute, published research papers internationally and earn a decent income. Yet, I face harassment from guards and police constables. Even if I accumulate vast wealth, will it guarantee me respect in society and shield me from such harassment?' Lavish pondered helplessly.

Further, during his travels abroad, Lavish observed diplomatic counters at airport immigration, where the process was even faster than business class. Interactions with diplomats left him awestruck, realizing they represented the nation on the global stage.

In the last two years, while Lavish was in the USA, many of his seniors were selected for the IAS and IPS. Some of his close friends and classmates were preparing for the exam, too. Inspired by their achievements, Lavish started gathering information about the CSE and stumbled upon the Baswan Committee's report. It recommended reducing age limits and the number of attempts for civil service aspirants. This ignited a sense of urgency in Lavish as he pondered, 'I am already twenty-four years old. If I want to appear for the CSE, now is the right time; otherwise, I might regret it for a lifetime.'

While Lavish was still mulling over his career options, his close friend from IIT, Shreyans Kumat, with whom he frequently discussed CSE preparations, quit his job to prepare for the CSE full-time. Additionally, Piyush Prasad, one of Lavish's seniors at Shell in Bengaluru, also encouraged him to pursue his IAS dream. Lavish's allure for Mount UPSC intensified further.

As the relentless rain pounded the windows and Hurricane Harvey ravaged Houston, Lavish's mental storm also reached its peak, sweeping away the American illusion. He decided not to apply for an extension of his contract in the USA and return to India.

Goodbye, Shell

On 1 May 2018, Lavish was deeply engrossed in his work at Shell's Bengaluru office. He had submitted his resignation the previous day, marking the beginning of his one-month notice period. Around 6 p.m., he received a call from his boss, Brad.

'I was surprised to see your resignation email. Why are you quitting, Lavish? Have you received a better job offer?' Disappointment and disbelief were evident in his voice.

Lavish's revelation left Brad stunned.

'Did I hear you correctly? You want to leave a high-paying job at Shell to sit at home and study for two years for a job with almost zero probability of success?' Brad questioned, unable to see the logic.

'Yes, Brad. That's precisely why I need to quit—to dedicate myself fully to studying and emerge successful,' Lavish explained, providing insights into the realm of civil services. He shared details about the job profile of IAS officers, the perks, respect and authority associated with it and the immense job satisfaction they experience.

Brad listened attentively but remained unconvinced. Initially, he suggested that Lavish consider a lighter assignment within Shell and simultaneously prepare for the exam. Undeterred, Lavish insisted on giving his all for a shot at success. Recognizing Lavish's determination, Brad proposed a sabbatical leave, allowing him to return to the company after two years if his pursuit of the UPSC dream didn't unfold as planned.

Emma, another general manager, based in the Netherlands, echoed similar sentiments, encouraging Lavish to explore social sector roles within Shell. Believing that Lavish wasn't thinking rationally, she counselled him on rational decision-making and even presented him with a book, titled *Thinking Fast and Slow*, urging him to think slow, think rationally rather than emotionally.

However, Lavish's immediate general manager, Sandy, expressed reluctance regarding the idea of a sabbatical leave. 'Shell can't be a fallback option,' Sandy, deeply attached to the company, conveyed with a hint of disappointment. Lavish, too, felt that returning to the same company if he failed to scale Mount UPSC would be a step down and pressed for the acceptance of his resignation.

Convincing his family was another formidable task. His decision was met with resistance from his family initially, who believed he could juggle work and studies. With their financial situation more stable than before, they had plans for a new house in a good locality and Lavish's marriage. However, he assured them that securing another job would not be a challenge if the UPSC endeavour didn't pan out.

The stage was set for Lavish to embark on the arduous journey to scale Mount UPSC.

Triumph in Battleground Kota

By quitting a highly coveted and well-paying job at Shell, Lavish had made an extraordinarily bold decision. Many IAS aspirants struggle to make such monumental choices, often attempting to balance two boats and consequently losing out on their dreams.

But sleep eluded Lavish that night. The words of Brad, Emma and Sandy haunted him. The uncertainty of success in the CSE also engulfed him. He felt a pang of guilt for postponing his parents' dream of buying a new house. With teary eyes, he recalled how his mother had worked tirelessly, stitching clothes for hours after her job at the bank to earn the money needed for his coaching after Class 10.

However, this was not the first time Lavish faced intense competition and endured a rigorous study schedule for an extended period. He had surmounted similar challenges twice before: a decade ago, when he moved to Kota for two years of IIT-JEE coaching after Class 10 and later, during the three years of his BTech studies at IIT Bombay.

Lavish vividly remembered 19 April 2009, when, just twenty days after finishing his Class 10 exams, he travelled from Udaipur to Kota with his mother. He felt a wave of gratitude for his *nanaji* (maternal grandfather), who had paid the exorbitant coaching fee of Rs 1.3 lakh, as Lavish's family was grappling with severe financial hardships.

For the next two years, a tiny PG room, devoid of basic amenities like an air conditioner, cooler, heater or geyser, was home for the fifteen-year-old Lavish. It was highly unsuitable for Kota's extreme climate—scorching at forty-eight degrees Celsius in summer and bone-chilling at one degree Celsius in winter. To save money, he survived on half-tiffin service twice a day.

With the gleaming dream of IIT success, when Lavish entered his coaching institute on the first day, he was left in disbelief. An expansive sea of bicycles stretched from the institute's gate, covering an area equivalent to four football fields. Behind this sea of cycles loomed a colossal seven-storeyed building. The campus buzzed with about 10,000 students, revealing the magnitude of the academic endeavour he had embarked upon.

When Lavish interacted with some of his classmates, he was further shocked to discover that nearly everyone had been the top student in their respective schools. Many gave the impression that they had already mastered the entire syllabus. 'If there are so many exceptionally bright students in just one institute, do I stand any chance of securing one of the limited seats in an IIT?' he had wondered, a sinking feeling settling in his heart.

However, he soon mustered courage, strengthened his resolve and plunged into his preparations with steadfast determination, dedicating an astonishing fourteen to sixteen hours daily to studying. Despite being an ardent cricket fan, he refrained from watching a single match of the Cricket World Cup that year, prioritizing his studies.

The pivotal day of the IIT-JEE exam arrived on 11 April 2012. Lavish felt a surge of nervousness as this single day held the power to shape his destiny. However, he performed well, as revealed by the answer keys published the following day.

On the night of 24 May 2012, joy filled the air when he learned that he had achieved a remarkable rank of 254 in the IIT-JEE. Fascinated by the intricate workings of machines, Lavish chose mechanical engineering over much-coveted computer science and electrical engineering. IIT Bombay, with his *chachaji* and *mausiji* residing there, was his obvious choice. His cousins had painted vivid pictures of the city— its towering buildings, bustling local trains, serene beaches and the aura of Bollywood actors.

On 20 July 2012, Lavish, accompanied by his parents and brother, boarded a train from Udaipur to Mumbai, ready to embark on a new chapter in his life.

Illusion Shattered

The campus of IIT Bombay was awe-inspiring, surrounded by natural beauty—mountains and the Sanjay Gandhi National Park on one side and lakes on the other. The campus boasted amenities Lavish had never seen before: a swimming pool, gymnasium, badminton and tennis courts, a mess serving delectable food and vast green spaces.

Overwhelmed, Lavish felt a profound sense of relief and liberation. 'The era of hard work and struggle is over, and I will now live my life. Big multinationals will soon be vying for me with lucrative job offers,' he whispered to himself, a lingering echo from the conversations that used to resonate in Kota. This complacency led to wastage of a lot of time in movies, games and social media. Lost in his own world, he missed many classes, too.

However, the placement season of his seniors a year later shattered his illusion. Much to his surprise, many seniors who had paraded around, projecting an air of 'coolness', struggled to secure employment. Anxious and perturbed, Lavish sought advice from successful seniors on how to navigate the final year's job hunt. Sleep eluded him as he absorbed the harsh truth about what corporates sought in potential employees—a high cumulative performance index (CPI) above nine in academics and a distinct 'spike' in the curriculum vitae (CV).

Pondering over the elusive concept of a spike in the CV, Lavish wondered how to attain it. His seniors explained that a spike could stem from exceptional achievements in extracurricular activities, research endeavours or holding leadership positions.

Lavish decided to wake up from slumber and study hard. He also decided to look for a research opportunity, which soon came when Professor S.V. Prabhu, an authority in fluid mechanics, sought assistants for a research project on vortex shedding.

Lavish threw himself wholeheartedly into the research project with Prof. Prabhu, dedicating hours after class, on weekends, holidays and semester breaks. He learned the skill sets of creating an experimental setup, conducting research, documenting findings and presenting the results. In the process, he also acquired skills in software development, designing and image processing.

His relentless efforts bore fruit when IIT Bombay recognized him with an award for exceptional undergraduate research. Furthermore, his research paper earned a coveted slot for presentation at an international conference on fluid mechanics in Paris.

Leveraging the strength of his research experience, Lavish secured a reputed international paid internship in Paderborn, Germany, after completing his third year. Simultaneously, Lavish remained committed to his studies achieving remarkable CPI scores of 9.67, 9.93, 9.7 and a perfect 10 in the last four semesters, earning the institute's prestigious academic excellence award.

His meticulous planning and years of hard work culminated in securing a much-coveted, high-paying job at Shell on 1 December 2014.

Returning to 1 May 2018, Lavish found himself standing at the threshold of yet another formidable challenge in his life: scaling Mount UPSC. However, the recollection of his past struggles and triumphs in Kota and Mumbai served to strengthen his resolve, imbuing him with the confidence necessary to confront this arduous challenge and emerge triumphant.

Is the Struggle Really Worth It?

On 5 June 2018, Lavish entered the bustling world of IAS aspirants in Delhi. A stranger to the city, he sought refuge in a community hostel in Karol Bagh. It offered modest, shared rooms at a monthly rent of Rs 10,000, inclusive of two simple meals. Lavish, determined, brushed aside the discomfort, choosing to concentrate solely on his goal.

Selecting the optional subject for the Mains proved to be challenging. Despite warnings from friends, including Shreyansh, Lavish was drawn to the familiar terms in the syllabus of mechanical engineering and was motivated by a few high scores in the subject. 'Why can't I be one of the high scorers?' Lavish reasoned, reflecting on his strong performance in mechanical engineering during his BTech. The next day, Lavish headed straight to Daryaganj market to purchase the recommended second-hand books. He also enrolled himself in a coaching institute for GS.

The transition from the corporate work culture to an environment demanding intense focus presented a formidable challenge. Lavish had grown accustomed to frequent meetings and discussions, where prolonged attention wasn't a prerequisite. His routine had revolved around checking emails every fifteen minutes and taking breaks every hour.

When Lavish delved into the syllabus for the GS, the vastness of the curriculum overwhelmed him. 'Prelims is less than a year away. Will I even be able to cover the syllabus? Even if I clear the Prelims, there'll hardly be any time to prepare for the optional subject, essays and GS for the Mains exam. Will I be able to do well in humanities, a field I haven't explored since high school?' he wondered, grappling with the labyrinth of uncertainties ahead.

As Lavish delved into mechanical engineering, he encountered another stark reality. Nearly 40 per cent of the CSE syllabus was not covered during his BTech. A significant portion from the rest had faded from his memory. Compounding the issue, while IIT professors favoured books by foreign authors, for the CSE, books by Indian authors were recommended.

Amidst this emotional upheaval, Lavish faced another setback. Scoring a mere thirty marks in his first GS mock test and consequent scathing feedback from the examiner cast a gloom over him. For a moment, he doubted his ability, plunging into a depressive phase, feeling that he was not capable of cracking the CSE.

What intensified his gloom was the news of the Indian Prime Minister's visit to Houston. Lavish saw the videos and photos of the 'Howdy Modi' event and reminisced about his comfortable life in Houston.

'If I had not decided to write CSE, I would have been in Houston, participating in this programme. I was living a good life, traveling across the globe, earning good money. Here I am slogging for eighteen hours a day in an old, shabby, shared hostel room. I have lost money and comfort and even lagged in my career. Is this struggle worth it? Even if I get a high rank, what if I land in some bad cadre?' A slew of questions wrecked his mind.

Every IAS aspirant encounters depressive phases during their preparation journey. The earlier you overcome it, the sooner you are likely to taste success.

Fortunately, Lavish didn't allow this phase to continue long and uplifted his mood quickly. 'I have never been unsuccessful in a competitive exam. I must do this not only for myself but for my family. Moreover, when my classmates and other IIT alumni can do it, why can't I crack the exam?' he told himself.

A few days later, the news that Shreyans Kumat, his best friend in Kota and IIT Bombay, had cleared the Mains injected Lavish with renewed strength. It reignited the same fire within him that burned during his IIT-JEE days in Kota and later in his second and third year in IIT Bombay.

Crafting a Winning Formula

Lavish meticulously scrutinized previous years' examination questions. It indicated a misalignment between the curriculum taught in coaching classes and questions asked by UPSC. Consequently, he opted to prioritize self-study while selectively attending coaching sessions on polity and economy. Additionally, he searched for insightful lectures on geography and economics available online.

Lavish gradually boosted his attention span. He also effected a drastic change in his routine and started studying in the calm of the nights. As December rolled in, Lavish conducted a meticulous assessment of his progress, time remaining for the Prelims and the duration required to prepare for different topics. Armed with this analysis, he crafted a schedule with daily-weekly-monthly targets, incorporating time for tests and revisions. Committed to meeting his daily targets, Lavish sacrificed sleep, resting at times for only three to four hours a day.

In January 2019, Lavish became part of a group of three other like-minded aspirants in the hostel: Manish Dhariwal, Mukul and Dixit Jain. Besides helping each other, they also evolved a healthy competition among themselves. A prominent coaching institute's daily five-question challenge became a staple exercise for them. They also engaged in joint discussions to understand the nuances of each problem and discover smart strategies for tackling questions effectively.

To simulate exam conditions, the trio attempted approximately forty full-length question papers of a test series in their hostel on predefined dates and timings. This collaborative effort not only fostered discipline but also provided mutual motivation during moments of low morale. Lavish also discussed exam strategy with his 'chai friend' Gourav Sharma, a senior from IIT Bombay. Lavish immensely benefited from his crisply drafted notes, memorizing techniques, question paper analysis and visualization of the exam content.

From February 2019, he committed himself entirely to Prelims preparation. After each test, he meticulously analysed his performance, dissecting every mistake to discern whether it was due to inadequate preparation, lack of knowledge or a hasty reading of the questions.

While filling up the CSE application form, Lavish had also casually opted for the Indian Forest Service (IFS), whose Prelims exam was common with CSE.

The Prelims exam was held on 3 June 2019. Analysis of the answer key post the exam hinted at Lavish scoring above 140 marks. When the results were declared, as expected, he cleared the exam, both for the CSE as well as the IFS, bringing waves of joy.

However, the Mains, scheduled to commence on 19 September 2019, loomed a mere 100 days away, worrying Lavish. At that time, the news of Shreyans clinching an impressive fourth rank in the CSE-2018 in his inaugural attempt vastly boosted Lavish's sagging spirits.

Amidst the labyrinth of Mains preparations, Lavish grappled with a dilemma familiar to many aspirants—whether to complete the syllabus before diving into answer-writing practice and mock tests or to concurrently study and write tests. Lavish opted for the latter which provided him the much-needed writing practice as well as valuable insights into his weaknesses. He also regularly wrote full-length test papers, self-evaluated his answers and noted areas for improvement. Past years' topper copies were another potent learning tool.

Just a few days before the Mains exam, Lavish and his friends enrolled in mock examinations at an 'exam simulator'. These simulators, established by prominent coaching centres, create a specialized examination environment that mirrors UPSC examination halls. They publish a mock examination schedule with the same sequence, duration and breaks as the actual civil services Mains examination. These mock examinations, held a few days before the Mains, provide candidates with crucial practice and help them acclimate to the exam conditions.

After completing the CSE mains on 27 September 2019, Lavish found himself utterly drained of energy. So, he promptly escaped to Udaipur. Following a hiatus of twenty-five days, he returned to Delhi and resumed preparations for IFS Mains, scheduled from 1 December 2019.

Smartly Navigating DAF

The eagerly awaited good news arrived on the midnight of 15 January 2020. Lavish and Mukul had cleared the CSE Mains. The IFS Mains results were announced the very next day, and the duo had triumphed in this as well.

A surge of new energy coursed through Lavish's veins at the realization that he was just one step away from his goal. However, the next moment, anxiety gripped him as he contemplated the stark reality that success in the Interview meant nothing if his name didn't feature in the final list. He tried to temper his family's exuberance, explaining to them that the CSE is akin to a snakes and ladders game. Even if a snake bites you at the last stage, you may regress to zero and have to embark on the journey anew.

The IFS Interview was scheduled for 11 February 2020, while the CSE Interview was slated for 25 March 2020. Since many Interview questions are based on the details provided by candidates in the Detailed Application Form (DAF), Lavish had filled out the form meticulously. He avoided unnecessary details but made sure to include information about his scholarships, awards and research papers. Recognizing that his work experience set him apart from other candidates, he underscored it to invite questions during the interview. Before submitting the DAF, he sought feedback from his seniors who had cracked the exam in the past.

Choosing preferences for services proved to be a daunting task. Initially drawn to the prestige and opportunities to live in foreign countries, Lavish was tempted to fill the Indian Foreign Service as his first choice. However, a perception of monotony in work and the desire for a broader range of challenges led him to favour the IAS. As he wasn't inclined towards uniformed services, he ranked the Indian Police Service a few notches lower.

Another challenge in completing the DAF was indicating preferences for cadres. Naturally, Rajasthan and Madhya Pradesh were his first and second choices, with Madhya Pradesh holding sentimental value as it was close to Udaipur. However, deciding on the third choice proved challenging, leaving Lavish torn between Uttar Pradesh and Karnataka. Seeking guidance from his friend Shreyansh, he received valuable advice.

'Lavish, you will spend your life in the cadre, so you should think holistically and long-term. Consider the needs of your parents, wife and children. Karnataka has big cities with good connectivity, including Bengaluru, with good health and education facilities and ample employment opportunities. Language might pose a challenge initially, but it's not difficult to overcome,' Shreyans advised, and Lavish nodded in agreement.

Looking at transcripts of Interview questions posted by candidates on the internet, Lavish noted that questions about the meaning of a candidate's name were favourites among Interview boards. Oddly enough, he found himself ignorant about the meaning of his own name. Throughout school and college, Lavish endured classmates teasingly attributing the meaning of his name to *'Kaam Dev'*, the Hindu God of erotic love, desire and pleasure—a label he disliked. So, Lavish decided to craft his own interpretation. Combining 'love' from English with 'ish', meaning God in Hindi, he defined Lavish as the person whom God loves.

Delving into other aspects of his DAF, Lavish explored the origin of his last name, Ordia. Moreover, hailing from Udaipur, he researched the city, its tourist attractions and the tourism industry. Additionally, he delved into Delwara, his mother's village, drawing connections to Dilwara Jain temples in Mount Abu due to the similarity in names.

To grasp the Interview landscape, Lavish downloaded Interview transcripts spanning the last six years from various platforms. Using keywords like 'tourism', 'Udaipur', 'Rajasthan', 'mechanical engineering' and 'oil and gas', he sifted through the transcripts for questions related to these topics. He also analysed ongoing interview transcripts to stay updated on current discussions happening in the Interview rooms.

Lavish also appeared in a series of mock Interviews. While some feedback was constructive, a few interviewers delivered harsh criticism, even mocking him, which took a toll on his confidence.

An Invitation to the World of Forests

The crisp morning of 11 February 2020 found Lavish at the majestic UPSC office in Dholpur House, eager and ready for the IFS interview. Little did he know that the first question would catch him off guard.

'Why have you been sitting at home for the past five years?' the chairman of the board inquired, throwing Lavish into momentary confusion.

Undeterred, he began detailing his work experience at Shell, only to discover that the board had been provided with his DAF-1, which outlined his hobbies. DAF-2, containing crucial details about his professional journey, was not placed in their folders. This unforeseen glitch steered his Interview away from the anticipated path.

Despite Lavish's efforts to convey his experience, the board remained fixated on the limited information presented in DAF-1. They posed unpredictable questions, such as asking him to interpret a quote from a wall calendar and discerning nuances between war and battle, conflict and dispute. Leaving the Interview room with a sense of disappointment, Lavish couldn't shake off the feeling that his performance had fallen short of his expectations.

It was around 5 p.m. on 4 March 2020, when Lavish was gearing up for a mock Interview for the CSE at a prominent coaching institute. Suddenly, a burst of excitement erupted as one of his friends, a junior from IIT Kanpur sharing the same hostel, rushed in.

'Congratulations, Lavish! You've cracked the IFS exam!' The friend enveloped Lavish in a hug, delivering the news with contagious enthusiasm.

'Wow! That's indeed great news. But what's my rank?' inquired Lavish, elated and curious.

To his sheer delight, Lavish discovered that he had secured the second rank in the IFS exam. An outpouring of congratulatory messages flooded in, leaving him pleasantly surprised as he hadn't invested as much effort into preparing for the IFS Mains as he had for the CSE. Furthermore, his Interview experience had not been as encouraging. As the exam patterns of IFS and CSE are similar, his expectations of a good result in CSE soared.

Suddenly, Lavish received a cascade of phone calls from the coaching institute he planned to attend for the mock Interview, urging him not to skip it. Resisting the temptation to celebrate, he decided to proceed with the mock Interview.

As Lavish arrived for his mock Interview, he was met with a reception fit for royalty. The institute's staff extended a warm welcome, and the mock Interview board members, rather than subjecting him to the usual grilling, engaged in a congratulatory competition.

Upon exiting the Interview room, the institute staff insisted that Lavish meet the institute's owner, who awaited him in his Kalu Sarai office for a special Interview. Initially resistant, Lavish eventually relented. Transported from Karol Bagh to Kalu Sarai, Lavish joined a gathering of successful IFS candidates, all summoned by the institute's staff.

In an expansive studio filled with numerous cameras, the institute's owner interviewed Lavish, exploring his background, preparation strategy and his advice for future aspirants. The clear intent behind the interview was the marketing of the institute. Despite assurances that he would be provided transport to his hostel after the session, this commitment was completely overlooked.

The next day, Lavish was surprised to see an advertisement published by the coaching institute in the newspapers featuring his picture. The claim unabashedly asserted that Lavish had been a student at the coaching institute, although he had just attended a mock Interview there. It dawned on him why the images of high achievers often grace the advertisements of all prominent coaching institutes.

However, with new vigour, Lavish shifted his focus to the impending CSE interview scheduled for 25 March 2020.

Navigating the Probing Missiles

To prepare for the CSE interview, Lavish formed a close-knit group consisting of Mukul, Prakhar and Prateek—his comrades from the hostel, all of whom had received Interview calls from UPSC for the first time. They engaged in lively discussions on current affairs, simulating formal Interviews by probing each other with questions from DAF and questions sourced from contemporary issues and past Interview transcripts.

Just as the crescendo of their preparations reached its peak, the symphony was abruptly halted by the onslaught of the Covid-19 contagion. Sensing the impending lockdown, Lavish hastily gathered his essential books, boarding a train bound for Udaipur mere hours before the Prime Minister's nationwide lockdown announcement.

The next three months were filled with uncertainty, hopelessness and restlessness. Lavish had been unemployed for nearly two years. He often found himself contemplating the opportunity cost of the time he was investing in preparing for the CSE.

The long hiatus came to an end when UPSC proclaimed fresh Interview dates three months later. From the picturesque city of Udaipur, also called Venice of the East, Lavish reignited his preparations, engaging in online mock interviews and lively discussion sessions with friends on WhatsApp.

Yet, in this quest for focus, Lavish encountered frequent disruptions from his family members, oblivious to the intensity of his preparations. His grandmother would often intrude into his study sanctuary, bearing tea or snacks even in the midst of a mock Interview.

Recognizing the unique circumstances of the pandemic, where face shields and masks were mandatory in the Interview, Lavish practiced donning a suit, face shield and mask to acclimate himself to the challenges of the real Interview scenario. His glasses would quickly fog up and beads of sweat adorned his face by the Interview's conclusion.

A few days before the crucial date, Lavish made his way to Delhi. On the pivotal morning of 28 July 2020, he summoned an Uber from his hostel to Dholpur House. Despite the exhaustive preparations, a palpable nervousness accompanied him as he waited in the hall for his turn. Seeking assurance that his voice wouldn't falter before the board, Lavish made a visit to the washroom and practiced his responses in front of a mirror.

As the moment arrived, Lavish was ushered into the Interview chamber. The interrogation began with questions focused on the tourism sector, an apt choice given Lavish's roots in Udaipur, a prominent tourist destination.

'Should we shut down the tourism industry amidst the Covid-19 pandemic, or do you have a strategy to keep it running without adverse health impacts?' The chairperson's probing question hung in the air, setting the tone. The inquiry then pivoted to the demand for the reopening of masjids for namaz. 'Should we agree, or do you believe it's an ill-advised demand,' one of the members inquired.

The trajectory of questions shifted seamlessly to Lavish's professional past at Shell. One board member delved into his mechanical engineering background and the energy sector, presenting challenges that left Lavish momentarily stumped. The chairperson, unfazed, delivered another tricky question, probing, 'If you don't secure a position in IAS but find success in another service like the Indian Audit and Accounts Service, would you regret leaving Shell?'

From Corporate Cubicle to Collector's Chair

On the crisp morning of 4 August 2020, Lavish rose at his customary hour, around 10 a.m. Soon, his grandmother presented him with a cup of steaming ginger tea. Lost in contemplation, Lavish relished the fragrant tea intertwining with his musings. However, an unexpected phone call from Prakhar, his preparation friend in the Delhi hostel, disrupted the tranquillity.

'Congratulations, Lavish! You've cracked the CSE,' the friend exclaimed, his voice vibrating with excitement.

'Thanks, buddy, but what's my rank?' Lavish's elation, while genuine, was laced with a palpable curiosity about his standing in the prestigious exam.

'You've done phenomenally well. You are in the top twenty,' the friend declared, leaving Lavish grappling with disbelief.

Swiftly unlocking his phone, Lavish found himself bombarded with a deluge of congratulatory messages. Seeking confirmation, he navigated to the PDF file of the results on the Telegram app and diligently scrolled to locate his name. It proudly occupied the eighteenth position. Still teetering on the edge of disbelief, Lavish decided to verify the result on the UPSC website.

The confirmation swept Lavish away on a tide of excitement. To release the surging emotions within, he ascended to the roof of his house. With clenched fists raised to the sky, Lavish shouted into the expanse, a euphoric release echoing through the quiet air. It was more than a celebration; it was a cathartic moment of liberation, a personal 'moksha' from the relentless grip of the CSE cycle.

Descending from the rooftop, Lavish hurried to his grandparents' room, eager to share the news that had set his heart ablaze. As he conveyed the life-altering revelation, tears of sheer happiness welled up in his grandparents' eyes. In haste, they dialled Lavish's parents, Hema and Mukesh, eager to extend the joyous news. Soon, the homestead became a bustling hive of activity, inundated with the presence of extended family members and jubilant relatives.

Amidst the incessant telephone calls and the sweet aroma wafting from boxes cracked open in celebration, Lavish found himself caught in a surreal experience. The festivities were in full swing, yet he remained in a state of numb disbelief, as if witnessing a story unfold before his eyes.

After a few days, Lavish joyously visited Delwara, his nanaji's village, where an air of festivity defied the ongoing Covid-19 pandemic. Despite the challenges, the villagers poured out to welcome him with tilak and garlands, leading Lavish on a procession to visit every house in the village. The villagers affectionately dubbed Lavish's grandfather as *Collector sahab ke nana* [the collector's grandfather]'.

On 10 October 2020, Lavish embarked on the momentous journey to the Lal Bahadur Shastri National Academy of Administration (LBSNAA), tucked away in the beautiful Himalayas.

The Covid-19 Onslaught

After seven months of rigorous training in Mussoorie, overflowing with enthusiasm, Lavish eagerly reported for further training to the state Administrative Training Institute (ATI) of Karnataka in Mysore. Little did he know that the path ahead would be fraught with unexpected challenges.

The country was reeling under the deadly second wave of Covid-19. So, Lavish and his fellow IAS trainees of the Karnataka cadre were tested for the contagion. In a twist of fate, Lavish's test results turned positive. The revelation baffled him as he displayed no symptoms whatsoever. Despite his pleas to undergo quarantine within the confines of ATI, Lavish was admitted to a ward in the district hospital.

Stranded in an unfamiliar place, Lavish, still grappling with the nuances of the Kannada language, felt a sense of trepidation. The following morning, a catering attendant threw a meagre meal of ragi balls and a small polythene packet containing sambar on his bed. Devoid of any utensils at his disposal, Lavish faced a conundrum on how to consume the food. Left with no option, Lavish pricked a small hole in the polythene containing the sambar, risking a spill and somehow managed to swallow the ragi balls with it. His eyes turned moist at his helplessness.

Wary of the forced idleness, Lavish strolled out of the ward while engaged in a conversation with a friend over the phone. The echoes of a doctor's stern reprimand soon chased him back to his bed, where he lay, sheepishly accepting the scolding.

Four seemingly interminable days passed in the hospital ward populated by the ailing, many dependent on oxygen support. The toilets emanated a disconcerting odour, and the atmosphere reeked of helplessness. Desperation mounted as he pleaded with the doctor for release.

The doctor, moved by Lavish's tearful entreaties, succumbed to compassion after verifying through a scan that Lavish was indeed in perfect health. Returning to the ATI, Lavish was met with another cruel twist of fate—his dadaji had tested positive for Covid-19 and was hospitalized. His condition was reported to be serious. Desperate to be by his grandfather's side, Lavish faced a heart-wrenching denial of leave by the ATI. Fate, in its relentless stride, dealt Lavish a personal blow with news of his dadaji's death on 30 May 2021.

Learning the Ropes the Hard Way

After completing his training at ATI, Lavish embarked on his journey to Mandya district for his further training. However, a tough phase awaited him there, too. The first formidable task was arranging decent accommodation as the PWD guest house was under renovation. Culinary challenges proved to be the next daunting test as Lavish was not used to the local food. Surviving on a diet of fruits and curd-rice, he lost 8 kg in two months.

Navigating through meetings conducted entirely in Kannada, Lavish found himself bored and frustrated. The language barrier compounded with the absence of proper food, suitable accommodation and companionship fuelled his internal turmoil. His frustrations, penned in the compulsory monthly demi-official letters to his counsellor at LBSNAA, conveyed a poignant struggle. In one candid expression, he wrote, 'Kannada sounds to me as if someone is shaking a pot filled with pebbles.'

As the months unfolded in Mandya, Lavish fortunately encountered a silver lining in the form of Manoj and other Marwari acquaintances, who swiftly transitioned into valued friends. This newfound companionship not only alleviated his solitude but also brought respite in terms of food.

After feeling lost for a month, Lavish decided to take control of his training. He arranged attachments with various government offices, delving into the intricacies of their operations. Beyond his professional pursuits, he delved into the rich tapestry of Mandya's history and culture, discovering gems like the KRS Dam, Asia's first hydro-power plant constructed in 1902.

Witnessing the entire silk production process, from silkworm rearing to weaving, further enriched Lavish's understanding of the district. Slowly but surely, life in Mandya metamorphosed into a more pleasant experience.

Midway through his district training, Lavish, along with his fellow IAS officers, was summoned for a two-month-long Bharat darshan. A subsequent Karnataka darshan deepened his connection with the state, revealing its inherent beauty. Engaging with other Karnataka cadre batchmates, Lavish came to the realization that his initial tribulations in Mandya were an exception rather than the rule.

Assistant Secretary's Revolutionary Ventures

Returning from their district assignments, Lavish's batch found themselves back at LBSNAA for an eight-week Phase-II training. It was a fleeting interlude preceding the much-anticipated three-month stint in various ministries of the Government of India as assistant secretaries. The mere thought of navigating the corridors of power, situated in the grandeur of the central secretariat, stirred a palpable excitement within Lavish.

However, his initial elation waned when Lavish was assigned to the ministry of consumer affairs in Krishi Bhavan. His expectations of a glamorous assistant secretaryship in the majestic North Block or South Block were quashed. Moreover, a prevailing notion that consumer affairs entailed minimal activity further dimmed his spirits.

But soon Lavish found himself proven wrong. The department was plunged into novel and dynamic realms, including cryptocurrencies, surrogate advertisements and online commerce. Its zealous secretary spared no effort in ensuring Lavish's involvement in departmental activities, often extending work hours until 8 p.m.

Lavish enjoyed working with senior officers of the department. He proposed an omni-channel for registering complaints from consumers from different sources, including consumer helpline, chatbot, website, emails and social media tags. Adding another layer to this digital ecosystem, Lavish worked on *'Jagriti'*, a consumer-oriented chatbot. Empowered by natural language processing, Jagriti would address consumer queries, comprehensively transforming the call centre into a perpetual 24x7 service sans human intervention.

Yet, Lavish felt that his pièce de resistance was the assisted judgment writing system, which held the promise of revolutionizing the landscape. Confronting the staggering backlog of over five lakh pending consumer cases, the system aimed to create a comprehensive database, meticulously indexing and categorizing cases sector-wise, product-wise and section-wise. Harnessing the power of machine learning and drawing insights from past judgments, this system envisioned generating editable draft judgments. Lavish, testing the proof of concept, handed the mantle of implementation to the secretary, consumer affairs.

A Fresh Start in Bidar

Following the culmination of his training, Lavish assumed the role of sub-divisional magistrate (SDM) in Bidar, situated at the trijunction of Karnataka, Maharashtra and Telangana. Given his prior experiences in Mandya, Lavish approached his new assignment with tempered expectations.

To his surprise, Bidar welcomed him with open arms. The staff and locals displayed remarkable warmth and hospitality. Language ceased to be a barrier, with Hindi and Urdu serving as a common means of communication for most. Lavish found solace in the delectable and varied cuisine. The pleasant weather, clean air and water and positive vibes further added to the charm of Bidar. The proximity to Hyderabad, just two-and-a-half hours away by road, and a direct flight from there to Udaipur, provided a convenient connection to his home.

Lavish felt not only welcomed but genuinely happy. In the shadows of Bidar's ancient alleys, the seeds of a new chapter started sprouting.

* * *

Key Takeaways from Lavish's Story

1. **Embrace Sacrifice and Bold Decisions**: Scaling the heights of Mount UPSC requires more than just a dream; it demands sacrifices and bold decisions. Balancing multiple priorities dilutes your focus. Success will only grace your efforts when you commit with unwavering determination and wholehearted preparation.

2. **Select Your Optional Subject with Strategic Precision**: The choice of your optional subject can make or break your preparation. Deliberate carefully over all options and avoid hasty decisions. Make a strategic choice that aligns with your strengths and interests, giving you a competitive edge.

3. **Conquer the Mental Challenges**: Every IAS aspirant faces moments of doubt and depression. The quicker you overcome these mental hurdles, the sooner you will reap success. Draw inspiration from your strengths and successes, the achievements of your peers and those with similar backgrounds. High spirits and good mental health are vital for triumph in the CSE.

4. **Leverage Mock Tests and Simulations**: Mock tests, answer-writing practice and exam simulations are crucial for excelling in the CSE. Aim to complete around thirty mock tests for Prelims, engage in ample answer-writing practice for Mains and, if possible, join an exam simulator.

5. **Use DAF to Your Advantage**: Filling out your DAF meticulously is of utmost importance. The board will often base questions on the information you provide. Highlight your strong points and unique attributes. Avoid including details you cannot discuss confidently during the Interview.

6. **Harness the Power of Group Discussions and Mock Interviews**: Group discussions and mock Interviews with friends are invaluable tools for Interview preparation. Simulate the UPSC Interview environment to get a feel of the actual day.

Chapter 8

Becoming an IAS Officer: The Success Mantras

In the first seven chapters, we have delved into the inspiring life stories of seven young heroes, who have successfully scaled Mount UPSC in recent years. Lakhs of civil service aspirants reading this book will undoubtedly be eager to imbibe the winning strategies and learn success mantras from these role models. In this chapter, we will explore the effective strategies employed by our heroes and other IAS toppers to crack the prestigious CSE. These have been grouped into the following sections:

1. Winning Strategies
2. Key Success Mantras
3. Cracking the Prelims
4. Scoring Victory in the Mains
5. Impressing the Interview Board

Let's discuss each of these elements in detail.

Winning Strategies

Let's start by mapping out the best strategies to scale the heights of Mount UPSC:

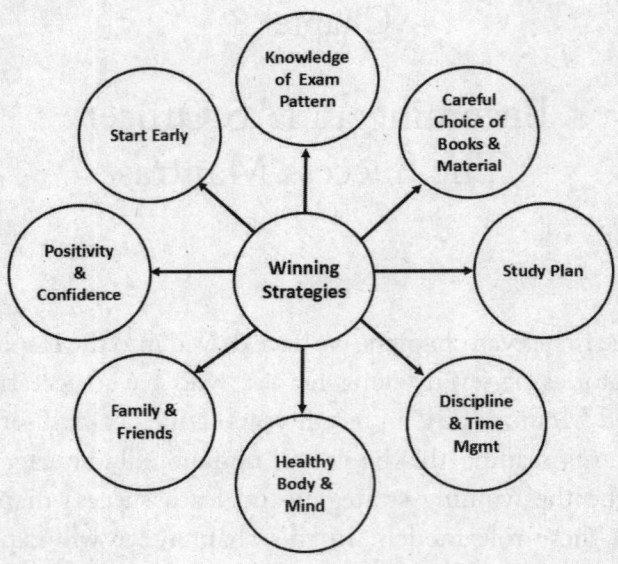

Start Early, Understand the Rules of the Game

Embarking on the journey to become an IAS officer requires strategic planning and a thorough understanding of the process. Starting your preparation during or immediately after graduation provides a distinct advantage. Your connection with academics gives you an edge over older competitors, allowing you to build a solid foundation and allocate ample time for revisions and mock tests. Additionally, if you are still enrolled in a college or university, you have access to valuable resources such as libraries, hostels and academic support. With age on your side, there is also less pressure to settle down quickly. However, starting early might mean sacrificing some aspects of the full college experience.

Consider the stories of our seven heroes. Satyam began his preparation as soon as he entered the final year of his graduation. Anjali and Waseem started right after graduating, while Shruti dived in after a brief foray into postgraduate studies. Shruti felt that balancing college studies and UPSC preparation was challenging and believed it was better to finish graduation before starting the journey to conquer Mount UPSC.

Picking Pearls from the Ocean

Navigating the sea of recommended reading material for the exam can be intimidating for aspirants. The seven heroes of this book emphasized simplicity in preparation and advocated for quality over quantity and underscored the importance of selective reading.

Remember, the UPSC seeks not specialists, but well-rounded individuals with a broad understanding across diverse fields. Overloading yourself with excessive resources can create confusion, instil fear and erode confidence. A decluttered preparation table enhances focus, boosts morale, streamlines your preparations and sharpens your intellectual acumen.

NCERT books have been the bedrock of civil service preparations for generations. They clarify basic concepts and theories, build a solid foundation and provide a comprehensive grasp of various subjects. In 1993, when

I embarked on the arduous trek to scale Mount UPSC, I was advised to start with Class 9 to Class 12 NCERT books. Even today, these books are cherished for their reliability, coherence, accuracy and accessible language. Depending on your subject knowledge, you may start with Class 9 and Class 10 or with Class 11 and Class 12 NCERT books.

Once you've established your base with NCERT books, carefully select standard books and reference material to deepen your understanding. Resist the urge to hoard books; instead, choose one or two authoritative sources per subject. Seek guidance from mentors or successful candidates to curate your reading list. Moreover, focus only on the topics in the syllabus and prioritize thorough understanding and multiple revisions over the sheer number of books.

Supplement your learning with reliable online resources. Websites of government organizations and reputable research institutes offer a wealth of current information and data. Magazines like *Yojana* and *Kurukshetra* provide valuable insights into crucial areas such as governance, agriculture and economics.

Understand concepts deeply and cultivate critical thinking and analytical skills rather than rote learning. The UPSC values your ability to reason and solve problems more than your capacity to memorize facts. Engage in discussions with fellow aspirants to sharpen your understanding and gain new perspectives.

By maintaining a focused, organized approach grounded in reliable resources, you can navigate the vast sea of information with confidence. Remember, it's not about collecting every pearl, but about stringing together the most precious ones to create a masterpiece of knowledge.

Charting Out an Effective Study Plan

Antoine de Saint-Exupéry, the famous French poet and author, once said, 'A goal without a plan is just a wish.' For an IAS aspirant, a meticulously crafted plan is the key to transforming dreams into reality. An effective plan ensures comprehensive coverage of the syllabus, allows time for mock tests, revisions, answer-writing practice and, ultimately, prepares you for success.

Given the vast syllabus of the CSE, breaking it down into manageable parts is crucial. Setting monthly, weekly and daily targets helps cover the entire syllabus methodically, with sufficient time allocated to each topic. Prioritize challenging over weaker subjects and ensure ample time for revision, mock tests and answer-writing practice. However, while your targets should push you, they must also be realistic to prevent burnout and loss of enthusiasm.

Avoid common pitfalls, such as investing excessive time on low-yield subjects like world history or post-Independence history, which typically have fewer questions. Bharat, one of our seven heroes, regretted devoting twenty-five days on these subjects. A careful analysis of high-yield topics by analysis of previous years' questions can help you enhance the yield for the time and effort invested.

Shruti advised setting content-based rather than time-based targets and prioritizing high-yielding syllabus areas. Satyam analysed the total pages he needed to study, and the number of revisions required, setting daily targets accordingly. He visualized his progress over three and six months, systematically working towards these milestones.

Recognize that a one-size-fits-all approach doesn't work. Everyone has a unique learning style and preferred study timings. Blindly following someone else's strategy or online hacks can lead you astray. Tailor your strategy to suit your style, learning abilities, schedule, preferences, strengths and weaknesses for maximum efficiency.

Periodic analysis of your progress is crucial. Be honest with yourself about your advancement and don't hesitate to adjust your strategy when needed. Flexibility is strength, not weakness. An integrated approach for Prelims and Mains preparation is immensely beneficial. Viewing both stages as parts of a single examination with a shared syllabus ensures a more cohesive and efficient study strategy. The knowledge gained during Prelims is highly relevant for the GS papers of the Mains exam. One essential strategy is to complete a thorough round of Mains preparation before the Prelims. This allows ample time for revision after the Prelims and honing answer-writing skills critical for the Mains.

Leveraging technology can act as a force multiplier in your preparation. Use interactive platforms and apps for group discussions to amplify your learning and for collaborative note-making. Podcasts and YouTube channels can help you to stay updated on current affairs.

Discipline and Time Management: Twin Pillars of Success

For IAS aspirants, maintaining an organized and disciplined routine is of utmost importance. Consistently meeting weekly and monthly targets is critical, as every missed deadline adds pressure and increases the workload. For this, you need to step out of your comfort zone, regularly push your boundaries and consistently challenge yourself.

Judicious time management is another vital success factor. There's no perfect number of hours to study; it's the quality of study that matters, not the quantity. However, it's necessary to study with full concentration. Additionally, your schedule should allow flexibility to switch between topics based on mood and preference to help keep your mind fresh and engaged.

Creating a daily study schedule and logging the time spent on various activities helps manage time effectively and reduce wastage. For instance, Satyam analysed his daily time expenditure on paper before retiring for the night. This practice of self-reflection helped him identify and eliminate time wastage, honing his discipline.

Remember, the path to scale Mount UPSC is a marathon, not a sprint. Preparations can become exhausting and difficult over time. So, incorporate regular breaks and moments of recreation into your schedule.

A Healthy Mind Resides in a Healthy Body

The journey to Mount UPSC is long, arduous and both physically and mentally taxing. In this gruelling expedition, besides your intellect, your health is an asset.

Aspirants often dedicate more than twelve hours a day to their studies for months on end. Many endure subpar living conditions, subsisting on unappetizing food provided by hostels and tiffin services.

The combination of a sedentary lifestyle, intense academic demands, relentless competition, tight deadlines and an ever-expanding syllabus can extract a heavy toll on both body and mind. Add to this the setbacks encountered in mock tests, the stress of answer-writing practice and the looming fear of failure. In this challenging environment, the importance of health becomes paramount.

Regular physical activity, even brief walks or simple stretches, can reoxygenate your brain, enhancing cognitive function and memory retention. Mindfulness practices like meditation, yoga and deep breathing exercises sharpen concentration and reduce stress levels. Additionally, ensuring sound sleep is fundamental, allowing vital organs to rest and rejuvenate, thus maintaining peak efficiency.

Cultivating Positivity and Confidence

The path to becoming an IAS officer is strewn with challenges. Aspirants face formidable mental trials and emotional setbacks. Take Minnu, who faced the abyss of depression after failing to clear the Prelims in her fourth and fifth attempts, despite reaching the Interview stage in her third shot. Satyam broke down just days before the Mains, fearing he was not fully prepared. Shruti was in tears after her Prelims in her second attempt and again after her Interview. Waseem experienced a negative phase when he failed to clear the Prelims in his second attempt, despite securing the 225 rank in his first attempt.

External pressures often compound internal struggles. Mockery from teachers, derision from relatives and societal scepticism can erode confidence. Yet, it's precisely in these moments that the seeds of future triumph are sown. Satyam endured barbs from teachers like, 'Look, collector sahab has come to the class today,' and 'You don't even know the basic concepts; how can you dream of becoming an IAS officer?' Minnu was mocked by colleagues after her unsuccessful attempts. Bharat faced derision from a cousin, who told his mother, 'Why is he sitting at home? Ask him to take tuition for my children and earn some money.'

Surround yourself with positive affirmations and motivational resources like books, videos and success stories to keep your spirits high. Minnu, for instance, found inspiration in a film about a dedicated and hardworking district collector whenever she felt low. Bharat's mother suggested that he light a lamp and pray briefly each day to maintain focus and positivity.

Embrace the three Cs: consistency, confidence and calmness. Consistency in your efforts, confidence in your abilities and calmness in the face of challenges. Stay calm when things don't go your way and keep putting in your best effort. Sometimes, it takes time to find a study rhythm. Build your knowledge brick by brick, be consistent with your study routine and don't lose momentum, even if you face setbacks or obstacles. Trust your preparation and stay committed to your goals.

Each day of dedicated study and each obstacle overcome is a brick in the edifice of your success.

The Vital Role of Family and Peers

The journey to the heights of Mount UPSC is a demanding one, requiring relentless dedication and perseverance. Amid this gruelling process, the support of family, close friends and peers can make the journey smoother and the victory even sweeter.

Emotional and financial support from family and close friends can alleviate the pressures of preparation, allowing aspirants to focus entirely on their studies. The encouragement and understanding of loved ones provide a strong emotional foundation, helping candidates to stay positive and persistent through the ups and downs of the journey.

We have repeatedly seen in the stories of our seven heroes that family members make significant sacrifices to ensure the aspirant can study without distractions. This emotional backing is crucial, especially during moments of self-doubt and fatigue. Knowing that your family believes in you can be a powerful motivator to keep pushing you forward.

A supportive peer group is critical, too. It can foster a sense of camaraderie, making the preparation phase less lonely and more engaging. Peer discussions can enhance understanding of complex issues, clear doubts, reinforce knowledge and solidify concepts in your mind. Interactions with fellow aspirants can introduce new viewpoints and insights that you may not have considered.

Shruti joined a small group of aspirants at Jamia, who practiced answer-writing together and evaluated each other's responses. This collaborative approach allowed them to learn from one another and improve their skills collectively. They also used Google Docs to compile and share notes. 'Having a good group helps a lot; we added to each other's knowledge,' Shruti explained.

Similarly, Lavish formed a small peer group for discussions. They would set specific dates and times for mock tests, simulating exam-like conditions to enhance their preparation. 'Sometimes, when you feel low and start thinking about giving up, such a peer group keeps you motivated. You learn from each other and keep pushing each other,' Lavish added.

Coaching versus Self-Study

The question of whether to join a coaching institute is a critical one that plagues many IAS aspirants. Satyam initially joined a coaching institute but soon realized that much of his time was wasted. He decided to stay ahead of the coaching curriculum and attended only those classes that covered topics he found challenging during self-study. Satyam observed that many coaching teachers spent considerable time on stories, jokes and anecdotes, which he found unproductive.

Similarly, Lavish, after attending a few classes and analysing past years' questions, noticed a disconnect between the questions asked by UPSC and the coaching curriculum. He reduced his attendance in coaching classes and relied more on relevant online lectures.

Anjali triumphed purely through self-study. Shruti also found coaching classes unhelpful due to their large size and irrelevant discussions. 'There is a general impression that if you have to write the CSE, you need to join a coaching institute. But this is not true. You can get guidance from other sources, too,' she said.

On the other hand, Waseem benefited significantly from coaching classes and the mentorship programme offered by his coaching institute. Bharat and Minnu attended coaching classes specifically for their optional subjects.

Discussions with successful candidates and extensive research reveal that joining a coaching centre is not essential for success in the CSE. It's possible to conquer Mount UPSC without enrolling in coaching classes. Candidates may seek guidance from blogs of successful candidates, online videos and discussions with those who have cleared various stages of the exam. Moreover, those who wish to join coaching but can't afford it can benefit from government-sponsored coaching classes. Some state governments also provide scholarships to bright students to cover their coaching expenses at private academies.

However, candidates should be cautious and not blindly follow toppers or individuals who post videos and materials online. Self-proclaimed UPSC 'experts', often found at tea stalls in coaching hubs, on YouTube, in libraries and other places, can mislead candidates with so-called perfect strategies. It is crucial to prepare a personalized strategy based on one's own analysis, interests, strengths and weaknesses.

The D-Day Tips

No matter how diligently you've prepared, your ultimate success hinges on your performance on exam day. It's natural for pressure to mount and many aspirants find themselves sleepless the night before, overwhelmed by anxiety that can undermine months of diligent study. Managing this pressure and reducing anxiety is crucial. Remind yourself that you're not alone in this struggle—every aspirant faces pre-exam jitters. Keep reassuring yourself that you have put in the hard work and deserve to succeed. Aim for a good night's sleep before the exam to ensure you're well-rested and alert.

In the days leading up to the exam, it's essential to adjust your routine. Some aspirants, like Satyam and Lavish, study through the wee hours, sleeping in the morning. However, if you follow a nocturnal schedule, you must realign your body clock a few days before the exam to ensure you're fully awake and alert during the test.

A day before the exam, make sure you have your admit card and identity proof ready to avoid any last-minute panic. Satyam experienced a stressful situation on the morning of his first Mains paper when he couldn't locate his admit card and Aadhaar card. This led to significant time loss and made his blood pressure soar, which impacted his concentration. In the panic, he forgot the quotes, examples and data he had memorized for the paper that day.

If you live in a bustling hub of civil services aspirants, it's wise to arrange transportation to the examination centre well in advance. Other candidates may pre-book all available autos and taxis, making it challenging to secure transport at the last minute. Waseem faced this challenge and nearly missed his Prelims due to the non-availability of transport.

On the day of the exam, stay hydrated, take deep breaths, meditate and pray if it helps. Stay relaxed and maintain full concentration while writing. Keeping a calm and focused mind is key to performing well under pressure.

Remember, your hard work has prepared you for this moment. Stay confident, trust in your preparation and approach the exam with a positive mindset. Your dedication and perseverance will pay off.

Key Success Mantras

After discussing crucial preparation strategies, let's now delve into some key success mantras, as depicted in the figure below:

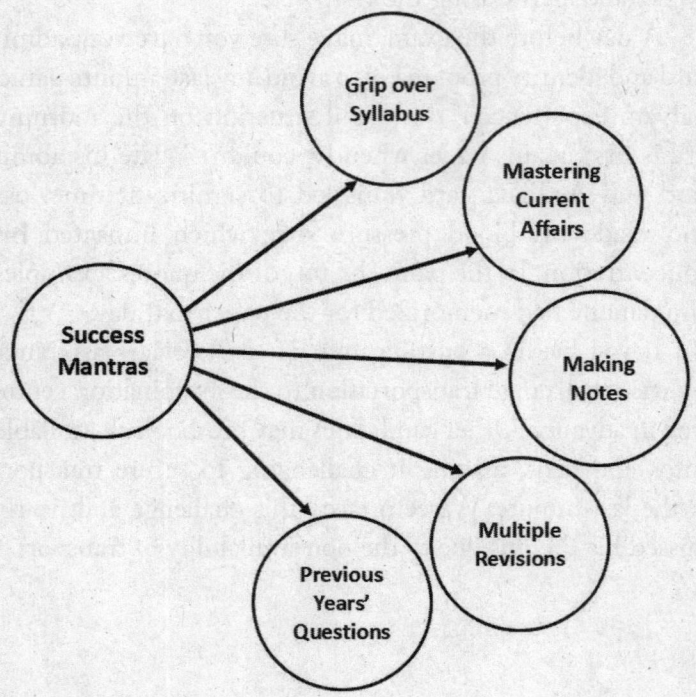

A Firm Grip over the Syllabus

Mastering the CSE demands a comprehensive grasp of its extensive syllabus. For the Prelims, UPSC provides a broad list of topics, while for the Mains, a detailed syllabus covering a wide range of subjects is outlined. Your first critical step is to meticulously read and revisit the syllabus, noting each topic and sub-topic. This thorough familiarity forms the bedrock for effective and targeted study.

Given that all exam questions are syllabus-based, strategic reading is key to acing the exam. Aimless reading across myriad sources is suicidal. IAS toppers don't just study the syllabus; they live it. This constant reminder serves as both motivation and guide

At first glance of the syllabus, its sheer scope may seem overwhelming. But don't let its size overpower you. Like ascending Mount Everest, success is achieved step by step. Each revision makes the challenge more manageable. Consider the syllabus a treasure trove of knowledge, to be unravelled layer by layer, revealing fresh perspectives and nuanced insights.

Reading, analysing, absorbing and thoroughly memorizing the syllabus for each paper will help you draw a clear roadmap for preparation and ensure efficient use of your time. It guides you on what's crucial to study and what can be omitted. A strong grasp of the syllabus enables you to filter relevant information from irrelevant material and connect it to the pertinent parts of the syllabus in whatever you read—be it newspapers, magazines, articles or books. This understanding is invaluable for effective notetaking and revisions.

Display the syllabus visibly at your study space, let it be the first thing you see each morning. This constant visual cue keeps you focused, aiding in topic recall and linking them to current events. Identify challenging topics early and devise a strategy to tackle them.

Mastering Current Affairs

Current affairs form a vital and dynamic segment of the syllabus. It demands substantial attention and time due to its pervasive presence across all papers of the CSE. Integrating insights gleaned from current affairs into your answers and essays amplifies their depth and contextual relevance, fosters a holistic viewpoint, demonstrates a profound grasp of real-world implications and improves your vocabulary and expression. Thus, every IAS topper underscores the importance of staying abreast with the latest national and international developments.

Various coaching institutes publish periodic compilations on current affairs. However, despite the availability of these compilations, all the seven heroes in this book recommended reading at least one newspaper daily while preparing for the Prelims and the Mains exams, and two newspapers for the Interview. They emphasized that there is no substitute for reading newspapers.

It's also advisable to read one current affairs monthly magazine. Some aspirants supplement their current affairs knowledge with news analysis podcasts or by browsing reputable online platforms for daily updates. However, candidates shouldn't spend more than one hour reading daily newspapers while preparing for the Prelims and Mains exams. The focus should be on issues, not just news.

Understand why an issue is in the news, gather background knowledge, its current status, understand different sides of the issue, related opportunities and challenges and suggestions or opinions regarding the way forward. Additionally, note down relevant statistics.

Scripting Success through Notes

Effective note-making stands as a cornerstone of success for many IAS aspirants. Notes serve not just as repositories of information but as powerful tools to organize thoughts, bolster understanding and ensure efficient retention and revision. Research has shown that writing by hand significantly improves memory retention due to the increased cognitive processing involved compared to typing.

Make concise and purposeful notes, consolidating key points, concepts, facts, formulas and examples gleaned from various sources. IAS toppers advise structuring notes around keywords from the UPSC syllabus, consolidating information from various sources. This approach ensures that all relevant information is consolidated in one place, rather than being scattered across multiple sources.

Utilize bullet points, diagrams, maps, flow charts and mind maps to simplify complex topics, aid memorization and enhance the quality of your answers. Key points, important facts, formulas and relevant examples should also find a place in your notes. Many aspirants prefer files or folders over notebooks as they make it easier to add information on a topic as preparation progresses.

Among our seven heroes, Minnu prepared comprehensive notes for each paper. Satyam read a topic from two or more sources simultaneously and made rich, detailed notes. He preferred using loose sheets instead of a register. Waseem meticulously prepared notes during coaching classes, leaving space on the side to enrich them later at home.

However, Shruti advised against making notes from every book. According to her, certain books like Lakshmikanth and Spectrum are succinct and akin to notes themselves, making additional note-taking redundant. Instead, she read directly from these sources. She maintained paper-wise notebooks with the syllabus on the first page. Whenever she found relevant articles, data or information, she pasted them under the corresponding syllabus heading. This helped her compile information and data on each topic.

Waseem had made a compilation of definitions, examples of freedom fighters, philosophers and administrators and quotes in a tabular manner. This made it easy to recall quotes and examples instantly during the exam.

The Power of Revision

Given the vast and diverse syllabus, covering a multitude of subjects, it's natural for the aspirants to forget what they have studied over time. Consistent and thorough revision not only solidifies your understanding but also builds the confidence needed to succeed. Revision aids in retention, deepens comprehension, reinforces concepts and helps identify weak areas. Without diligent revision, knowledge gained risks fading into obscurity, undermining months of dedicated preparation. Multiple rounds of revision are, therefore, critical success mantras for aspirants.

For IAS toppers, revisions occupied a central place in their preparation strategy. Shruti underscored its significance, stressing, 'In the crucible of the exam, only deeply ingrained points come to your aid. That's why multiple revisions are indispensable.' The number of revision rounds depends on an individual's retention capacity and the time available.

Many aspirants adopt the practice of revising daily, reviewing what they studied at the end of each day. It reinforces learning and ensures vital concepts remain fresh. Revisiting NCERT books to reinforce basic concepts after an advanced session on a topic is a sound strategy. Prioritizing the revision of subjects or topics where you feel less confident is valuable, too.

It's a common practice among aspirants to write important terms, definitions, examples and formulae on sheets of paper and paste them in their study space for frequent review and memorization. Some aspirants make a separate set of micro notes, which are compact summaries focusing on critical points and data across various topics, for quick multiple revisions and enhanced retention.

Incorporating the latest developments while revising provides an edge in the competitive exam landscape. It can enhance your answers, making your preparation more robust and comprehensive.

Scanning UPSC's Mind with Previous Years' Questions

A repository of previous years' questions is a treasure trove for IAS aspirants. Meticulous analysis of these questions can reveal critical insights into the exam's pattern, format and recurring themes. It also helps candidates understand the difficulty level, recognize the most useful study materials and align their preparation with the examiners' expectations. Additionally, it aids in discerning recent trends and pinpointing high-weightage topics that need to be prioritized. The possibility of encountering repeated questions from previous years adds another layer of importance to this practice.

Previous years' questions are readily available, both in print and online, often categorized by topic for convenience. Aspiring IAS candidates are advised to obtain question papers from the last twenty-five years. A smart strategy is to solve these questions immediately after completing a topic. This approach not only reinforces learning but also significantly boosts confidence by providing a realistic gauge of one's preparedness.

Many aspirants also benefit from practicing questions posted daily on the websites of prominent coaching institutes.

Cracking the Prelims

Mock Tests: The Key to Cracking Prelims

Success in the UPSC Prelims hinges on one pivotal practice: taking mock tests. As a critical component of preparation, mock tests are indispensable for every aspirant. So, candidates must allocate ample time in their schedule for a substantial number of mock tests. Many aspirants enrol in mock test series offered by coaching institutes, regularly taking these tests, evaluating their performance, revising weak areas and adjusting their study plans accordingly. Participating in a test series also allows aspirants to gauge their preparation against their peers.

When self-assessing mock test answers, it's essential to meticulously analyse incorrect responses, challenging topics and tricky questions that were missed due to insufficient details. For instance, Lavish took numerous mock tests and meticulously analysed his mistakes. He identified whether the errors were due to gaps in knowledge, misreading questions or other reasons. Similarly, Waseem initially tackled topic-wise mock tests after completing each subject, analysed his mistakes and revisited the material to strengthen his understanding. Some candidates also maintain a 'mistakes book', meticulously noting down errors made in test series to ensure they do not repeat them.

Mock tests serve several crucial purposes. They familiarize candidates with the exam format, develop exam temperament, improve speed and accuracy, enhance time management and highlight knowledge gaps and areas for improvement. Many IAS toppers, including Waseem, took forty to forty-five full-length tests before the Prelims. Taking these tests in a simulated, time-bound environment further refines time management skills and helps candidates cope with exam stress.

Bharat also underscored the importance of mock tests: 'By taking mock tests, you get an idea of the status of your preparation.' However, candidates should avoid taking mock tests too early in their preparation, as low scores can impact confidence and motivation. According to Satyam, 'First study vigorously and do revision, then appear in mock tests. Focus on the topics where you scored low and improve them.'

Neglect CSAT at Your Peril

In the quest to conquer the UPSC Prelims, many aspirants overlook a crucial component: the GS Paper-2, known as the CSAT. This paper's qualifying nature often leads candidates to neglect its preparation, mistakenly believing it to be a minor hurdle. However, this oversight can be disastrous. Despite needing only sixty-six out of 200 marks to pass, underestimating CSAT has derailed many aspirants' dreams. Even some candidates who had cleared all three stages of the exam failed in the CSAT in subsequent attempts aimed at improving their rank. Minnu, for instance, failed to clear the Prelims twice despite performing well in GS Paper-1 because she did not score the qualifying marks in CSAT.

Besides neglecting CSAT during their preparations, diluting focus on the day of the Prelims can also contribute to failure in CSAT. On that day, in the three-hour break between the GS Paper-1 and CSAT, many candidates spend time analysing their performance in GS-1. It can dampen their spirits and subsequently their CSAT performance.

Minnu experienced this firsthand; her focus on assessing her GS-1 answers and browsing the Internet during the break ruined her mood and contributed to her poor performance in CSAT twice. Waseem also observed that many candidates wasted valuable time post GS-1 exam analysing their performance instead of focusing on CSAT. Some coaching institutes exacerbate this by posting videos discussing GS-1 answers during the break.

The difficulty level of CSAT has been increasing, making it crucial for aspirants to give this paper due attention. Satyam warns, 'With a lot of analytical skills and mathematics, CSAT is now becoming like the Common Admission Test (CAT) conducted by the IIMs.' His advice is straightforward: 'Three months before the Prelims, solve last year's CSAT paper under exam-like conditions. If you score less than 100 marks, you need to devote some time to preparing for CSAT.'

Preparation for CSAT should involve solving previous years' papers to build comfort with the format. If difficulties persist, seeking assistance to learn tricks and shortcuts is advisable. Waseem suggested that candidates should pre-identify the types of questions they can solve efficiently and focus on those sections, rather than wasting time on difficult questions. Minnu, after analysing her strengths and weaknesses, concentrated on comprehension, reasoning and simple mathematics, where she excelled.

Thus, adequate preparation for CSAT, coupled with a strategic focus on one's strengths, is essential to avoid letting this paper shatter your IAS dreams.

Scoring Victory in Mains

Choosing the Right Optional Subject

Choosing the right optional subject is a crucial step in your quest to become an IAS officer. It requires careful thought and strategic planning. With 500 marks riding on it, the optional subject can significantly influence an aspirant's overall score and their chances of becoming an IAS officer. Conversely, an ill-considered choice can lead to undue stress and may force candidates to switch subjects after one or more attempts.

Consider Bharat, who initially chose geography based on superficial Google research. He later regretted this decision and changed his optional subject in his final attempt. Lavish faced a similar predicament after selecting mechanical engineering without thoroughly examining its syllabus and how it aligned with his undergraduate studies.

On the other hand, Minnu chose geography out of a genuine love for the subject, despite not having studied it since Class 10. Anjali opted for political science and international relations, a subject she enjoyed and had studied as a minor in college. For Shruti, history was a natural choice, being both her favourite subject and her major in college. Waseem selected anthropology after carefully assessing his strengths and interest in the subject.

The choice of an optional subject requires careful consideration of several factors. Aspirants should thoroughly analyse the pros and cons of each potential subject, delve into the syllabus, review previous years' question papers and evaluate the availability of study materials. Key factors to consider include interest in the subject, academic background, syllabus overlap with GS papers and strength and comfort.

Your optional subject should be one that you enjoy studying, especially when you need a break from the GS papers. Passion for the subject can sustain motivation and make the study process more enjoyable. Prior knowledge or academic experience in the subject can save time and help in scoring better. Significant overlap of syllabus of optional subject with the GS papers can be advantageous. Assessing your strengths and comfort with the subject matter is crucial for building confidence and performing well in the exam.

IAS toppers advise completing the optional subject's syllabus at least once before the Prelims. This strategy is crucial because the window between the Prelims and Mains is brief, and this period should be utilized for revision and in-depth study rather than initial learning.

Honing Your Writing Skills

In the Mains, success hinges not just on what you know, but also on how effectively you can express that knowledge within a limited time frame. Completing each paper on time is a formidable challenge that requires not only speed but also the ability to articulate thoughts coherently. Strong writing skills are, therefore, crucial for success in the Mains exam.

'Answer-writing is the only way to prepare once you have the basic content,' says Shruti. 'No matter how much knowledge you have, if you can't write structured answers, it's of no use.'

Developing writing skills is not an overnight process but one that demands consistent practice over time. Regular answer-writing sessions helps aspirants hone their analytical thinking, articulate thoughts clearly, present arguments logically and integrate knowledge across subjects. It ensures you address the core aspects of each question and design your answers effectively within the stipulated time.

Practicing answer-writing and self-evaluation of answers also promotes better content retention, improves grasp of the subject, enhances time management skills and helps adhere to word limits, all while boosting confidence. Shruti's revision strategy revolved around answer-writing. 'After writing answers, I would sit with my notes to self-evaluate and see what else I could add or how I could structure my answers better.' She also studied answer sheets of previous years' toppers, noting good practices from their answers.

Aspirants are well advised to start answer-writing practice early in their preparation. Begin by writing answers to questions in NCERT books. As your preparation progresses, practice with previous years' questions. Some candidates make it a habit to write answers to ten questions daily. They should also learn from model answers provided by coaching centres and focus on enhancing their analytical and critical thinking abilities.

If you can afford it, join a Mains test series of a reputable coaching institute and work on the feedback provided. Practicing full-length papers within the same time constraints as the actual exam can significantly improve your performance. After completing a test, compare your answers with the model answers, identify gaps and update your notes accordingly.

Some IAS toppers suggest writing the four GS papers on two consecutive days before the actual exam to be fully battle-ready. Lavish and his friends participated in a simulator at a coaching centre one week before the Mains exam. These simulators replicate the exam environment and schedule, providing invaluable practice under conditions that mimic the real thing.

Power of Structure and Presentation

Beyond the speed of writing, the content, structure and presentation of your answers can elevate your name to the top of the final list of successful candidates. Understanding the demands of each part of a question is crucial. While your answers do not need to meet the editorial standards of newspapers, they must be simple, well-structured, coherent, lucid and concise, showcasing conceptual clarity. Writing in bullet points with crisp sentences is preferable. It's better to present fewer points clearly and effectively than to include more points with less clarity.

A well-structured answer starts with a clear introduction that provides context. This could be a brief background of the topic, a relevant quote or a definition of a key term. The introduction sets the stage for the rest of your answer and should capture the essence of the question.

In the body, directly address the specific question and provide a comprehensive response that covers all aspects of the question. This can be achieved by dividing the question into parts with innovative sub-headings that include keywords from the question. Develop a multidimensional perspective by analysing issues from various angles, such as social, political, economic and environmental. Incorporate case studies and examples in your answers. Some candidates, like Waseem, preferred writing case studies in boxes alongside their answers. Finally, conclude with an optimistic, forward-looking statement.

Proper presentation of answers is critical as it makes the examiner's task easier. Attractive, readable and understandable answers stand out among the pool of responses. Ensure your answers are visually appealing, with clear headings, bullet points and adequate spacing. Incorporate relevant terminologies and underline them. For instance, in a case study on leadership, use terms such as 'motivation' and 'empathy' and highlight them for easy identification. Underlining important points can also be beneficial.

Studding the static portion of your answer with current affairs helps in presenting a broader picture. Quotations from reports, indices and data can substantiate your answers and demonstrate a well-rounded understanding of the topic. Use graphs, diagrams, flowcharts, maps and tables liberally. These tools not only save time but also present data clearly and concisely. Tables can help organize data effectively, making it easier for the examiner to locate information. Maps are useful for answering map-based questions and aid in the retention of data and facts. Avoid repetition of what you have presented in diagrams and flowcharts; use the text to provide supplementary information.

Overcoming the Ethics Challenge

GS Paper-4, or the ethics paper, is a unique part of the Mains exam. It covers a broad range of topics including human values, ethics in public administration, accountability and probity in governance. Success in this paper requires a nuanced understanding of ethical concepts, the ability to apply these concepts to real-life situations and skills to present answers with clarity and depth.

Case studies form a significant part of the ethics paper. Candidates are presented with scenarios wherein they apply ethical principles to solve problems, demonstrating their practical understanding of the subject. To excel, candidates should practice analysing case studies, identify the ethical dilemmas involved, consider various stakeholders' perspectives and propose balanced and justifiable solutions.

Personal introspection can provide unique insights and add depth to the answers.

Staying updated with current affairs, especially issues related to governance, public administration and social justice, is crucial. Incorporating examples from real life, current events and historical instances can enrich your answers, making them more engaging and impactful for the examiner.

Practical strategies can significantly enhance your preparation for the ethics paper. Maintaining a compilation of definitions for all relevant keywords and key phrases, alongside real-life examples and references to bona fide personalities, can be immensely helpful. For instance, Minnu started identifying ethical angles in daily news and considering how she would address these issues as a civil servant. She also drew examples and stories from cultural epics like the Ramayana and Mahabharata, as well as religious texts like the Bible and the life of Buddha.

Satyam and Bharat collected examples from their personal lives and identified role models for various values. Shruti, on the other hand, maintained a separate notebook where she jotted down noteworthy quotes from books, magazines or newspapers, organizing them under relevant headings for easy reference during her preparations.

Crafting Compelling Essays

Reflecting on my first attempt at the CSE in 1993, I distinctly remember the introduction of the essay paper. This paper is not merely a test of creative writing skills. It evaluates a candidate's ability to think critically, express ideas clearly and present balanced perspectives on various issues.

Crafting compelling essays requires a strategic approach, balancing depth of content with clarity of expression.

Candidates are required to write two essays. To score high marks, these essays must be a fine blend of structured thinking, coherent presentation and a deep understanding of the chosen topics. Regular practice on a range of subjects, from philosophical musings to contemporary issues, is essential to develop the skills needed to organize thoughts quickly and write effectively within the time constraints.

Staying current with global and national affairs is crucial for writing relevant and informed essays. It's prudent to prepare notes on evergreen topics like climate change, terrorism and women empowerment to provide a ready reservoir of content. Engaging in peer reviews and seeking feedback from mentors or coaching institutes can also be invaluable. Analysing the essays of previous toppers for their structure, content and presentation can offer insights and serve as benchmarks for your own writing.

On exam day, choose a topic you are well-versed in, allowing you to discuss it comprehensively and demonstrate a multifaceted understanding. Bharat advises, 'Before starting to write, build a framework on the rough sheets provided.' It sets the stage for a well-structured essay.

Begin with a compelling introduction that clearly states your thesis or main argument. You may start with a relevant quote, a startling fact, a question or a brief anecdote to capture the evaluator's attention. The body of the essay should be divided into paragraphs, each presenting a distinct point or argument supported by examples. Maintaining a logical flow with each paragraph seamlessly leading to the next is crucial. Subheadings can be used to break down complex arguments into manageable sections.

Conclude by summarizing the key points discussed and restating your thesis in a new light, emphasizing broader implications or future perspectives. The conclusion should leave a lasting impression, tying together the essay's main arguments coherently.

What sets a good essay apart from a mediocre one is the depth of content and quality of analysis. Presenting multiple perspectives on an issue demonstrates well-rounded understanding and critical thinking. Enhance your arguments with relevant examples, case studies, historical references or current events. Connecting these themes with areas of interest to the UPSC, such as governance, foreign policy, law, politics, economy and social equality, adds depth and relevance.

To show that your opinions are well-researched and grounded in facts, use data, statistics, quotes and reports from credible sources. Satyam, for instance, collected generic quotes on various issues like education, gender empowerment and climate change and used them appropriately in his essays.

Effective communication is another critical aspect. Write in clear, concise language, avoiding jargon and overly complex sentences. Maintain a consistent tone throughout the essay and avoid switching between formal and informal language. Write legibly and avoid excessive use of underlining or capital letters. Use bullet points sparingly and only when necessary.

Language Papers Need Attention, Too

The importance of language papers in the Mains often goes underestimated. English and one of the scheduled language papers are qualifying in nature, which leads many candidates to neglect their preparation, assuming they will easily pass. However, statistics reveal that around ten per cent of candidates fail to clear these language papers, rendering all their hard work for the Prelims and other Mains papers futile. Once you fail in these papers, none of your other papers are evaluated, causing the entire effort to go in vain.

Candidates, therefore, need to take these language papers seriously, especially if they have not studied the language after Class 10 or lack confidence in their proficiency. Among our seven heroes, Minnu opted for Malayalam as her second language. Recognizing her rusty language skills, she sought help from her mother and her friend Aishwarya, diligently practicing previous years' questions to regain fluency. Similarly, Waseem, who had studied Urdu only until Class 10, took lessons, particularly in grammar, from his sister Arzoo to brush up his skills.

Impressing the Interview Board

Clearing the Mains exam is a significant milestone, but the final formidable hurdle remains: the Personality Test, commonly known as the Interview. Lasting between twenty and thirty minutes and carrying 275 marks, the Interview plays a crucial role in determining your rank, service allocation and cadre in the IAS.

Unlike the Prelims and Mains, the Interview is not a test of knowledge but a comprehensive assessment of your personality. The Interview board evaluates qualities such as clear and critical thinking, analytical ability, logical exposition, balanced judgement, presence of mind, diplomatic skills, leadership, intellectual and moral integrity, confidence and overall suitability for a career in civil services.

You should be prepared to answer questions related to your interests, hobbies, education, work experience, optional subject and field of study. Additionally, questions about your state and the city you reside in are common. The board aims to gauge your personality's depth and breadth, ensuring you possess the traits necessary for a successful administrative career.

Several factors influencing the Interview are beyond your control, such as the timing of your interview, the composition of the panel, the chairman's mood and your position in the sequence of Interviews on that day. However, these variables are the same for all candidates, so it's best not to dwell on them. Instead, focus on aspects within your control and prepare diligently.

Let's briefly discuss how to prepare for this arduous challenge.

A Goldmine Named DAF

Candidates who cross the Prelims hurdle must submit a Detailed Application Form-1 (DAF-1). Those who clear the Mains and are called for the Interview must provide additional details in another form called DAF-2. These forms offer comprehensive information about a candidate to the Interview board, including educational background, place of residence, hobbies, work experience, areas of interest, achievements, service preferences, cadre choices and other personal particulars. The Interview board frequently frames its questions based on the information provided in the DAF-1 and DAF-2. Therefore, it is essential to fill out these forms honestly and with utmost care.

Once the Interview call is received, candidates should meticulously review their DAF and frame possible questions that could arise from the details mentioned. Thereafter, consider potential follow-up questions that may stem from your responses. Drafting well-thought-out responses to these questions is crucial. It is also important to have a plausible explanation ready regarding any gaps in education or employment history.

For instance, a candidate with a defence background should be prepared to discuss relevant topics such as necessary reforms in the defence sector, current issues and other pertinent information. Similarly, if a candidate lists cricket as a hobby, they should have a thorough understanding of the game's rules, recent performances of the Indian team, controversies related to the sport and the workings of the Board of Control for Cricket in India (BCCI).

Mastering Current Affairs

Staying abreast of current affairs is a vital component of preparing for the Interview. A comprehensive understanding of national and international events not only demonstrates your awareness but also showcases your ability to critically engage with contemporary issues. It also demonstrates your readiness for the multifaceted challenges of a career in civil services.

To stay updated, candidates should make it a habit to read daily newspapers and current affairs magazines. Complementing these readings with podcasts on current news analysis, watching debates and news on television channels will provide a well-rounded perspective. Beyond national and international issues, it is crucial to be well-versed on topics in news related to your home state, your optional subject and the subject of your graduation.

Developing informed opinions on various issues in advance, especially contentious ones, will be of immense help. Candidates should be able to forge linkages between a given topic and other related issues, a crucial skill to tackle cross-questioning during the Interview. For instance, if a news article discusses a report by the public accounts committee, the candidate should refresh the role and functions of the committee as covered in their textbooks. Such connections between current affairs and static knowledge enhance recall and comprehension during the interview.

Honing the Art of Communication

Effective communication skills are paramount during the Interview. While you don't need an extensive vocabulary or ornate language, articulating your thoughts with clarity and simplicity is essential. Your ability to convey ideas clearly can make a significant difference in how the interview board perceives your suitability for a career in civil services.

To enhance your communication skills, practice speaking clearly and confidently. Answer questions in a structured manner, ensuring your responses are coherent and logical.

Rehearsing answers to common and likely questions is important. Regularly practice in front of family members and friends to simulate the interview environment. Dress formally during these mock sessions to create a realistic interview scenario. Simulating the interview environment at home not only helps build confidence but also refines your delivery and identifies areas for improvement.

Certain questions are frequently asked during the interview, such as 'Tell me about yourself', 'Why do you want to join the civil services?', 'What are your strengths and weaknesses?', 'What's the meaning of your name?' and 'What are your achievements and failures?'. Preparing for these questions in advance ensures that you can respond thoughtfully and with composure.

It's also crucial to revisit your knowledge related to your optional subject, your graduation discipline and recent developments in these areas reported in the news. Many candidates share the questions they were asked by the interview board on various forums and study groups. Their PDF compilations are also available online, providing a sense of the types of inquiries you might face. Practice answering profile-specific questions from such current and past transcripts. Additionally, utilize questions posted online by coaching institutes for further practice.

The Vitality of the Mock Interviews

Just as test series are crucial for preparing for the Prelims and Mains, mock Interviews are essential for the Interview. They provide a realistic simulation of the actual Interview environment, allowing candidates to become comfortable with the setting. More importantly, mock Interviews offer invaluable feedback on performance, helping candidates improve their body language, communication skills and overall confidence.

Participating in too many mock Interviews can lead to diminishing returns. Therefore, it is advisable to attend three to four well-chosen mock Interviews at reputable coaching institutes. Reflect on the feedback provided and work diligently on areas needing improvement. Criticism should not be taken personally; instead, use it constructively to enhance your performance.

Satyam emphasized the importance of learning from others. He watched mock Interviews of previous years' candidates, who scored more than 200 marks. 'Don't get demotivated if you receive adverse feedback in a mock Interview,' he advised.

There are common mistakes that candidates often make during the Interview process, such as speaking too fast, displaying overconfidence or arrogance, giving vague or unsubstantiated answers, offering biased viewpoints, failing to maintain eye contact and lacking thorough knowledge of their DAF. Intense study and practice can help avoid these pitfalls.

Managing stress and staying calm is vital. Techniques such as deep-breathing exercises or meditation can help maintain a composed demeanour, enabling you to articulate your thoughts clearly and confidently. The day before the Interview, review your DAF one last time to ensure familiarity with every detail. Focus on relaxation the night before the Interview, as a good night's sleep is essential to ensure you are well-rested and alert.

Strategy for the Grand Finale

The day of the Interview demands meticulous preparation and composure. This is the moment where all your hard work culminates and your performance can determine your future. As the first impression matters a lot, dress formally and comfortably, ensuring your appearance is neat and tidy. Arrive at the venue well ahead of time to avoid any last-minute rush. Carry all necessary documents as specified in the call letter. While it's natural to feel nervous, strive to stay calm and composed.

The sequence in which you are interviewed is beyond your control and can have a bearing on your performance. For example, Minnu was the last to be interviewed before lunch during her first appearance and the chairman's remark about the approaching lunch time unsettled her. Conversely, Shruti was the first to be interviewed in the morning, leaving her little time to settle in, which affected her concentration. It's crucial to mentally prepare for such scenarios to ensure they don't disrupt your rhythm.

The actual Interview room setting can differ significantly from mock Interview rooms. UPSC rooms are smaller, with board members sitting closer to each other. Don't be taken aback by this difference.

When you enter the interview room, greet the panel politely and wait for an invitation to sit. Exhibit confidence, calmness, composure and a positive attitude. Your body language should convey confidence, attentiveness and respect. Maintain good posture, sit up straight and avoid excessive gesturing, although natural gestures are acceptable. Listen attentively to the panel's questions.

Address the Interview board respectfully and maintain a polite and courteous demeanour throughout. Maintain eye contact without staring, avoid fidgeting and manage any nervous habits. If you feel overwhelmed, take a deep breath. You need to sell yourself by proving that you are the best candidate for the job.

Unexpected questions can often trip candidates up. For instance, Minnu was asked, 'Tell us something about you that you haven't mentioned in your DAF?'

It's also wise to inform the board if any external noise is disturbing you or if you need them to speak louder. Waseem, for example, noticed heavy rain noise during his interview. He had the courage to inform the chairperson, which many candidates fail to do, leading to misunderstanding of questions and incorrect answers.

Remember, the Interview is a conversation, not a cross-examination. The board aims to understand you as a person and assess your suitability for a career in civil services. Be yourself, be honest and let your personality shine through. If you don't know the answer to a question, acknowledge your lack of knowledge politely and express a willingness to learn more about the topic. This honesty reflects character and is appreciated by the Interview board.

Epilogue

As you have seen through the life stories of the seven heroes in this book, the journey to becoming an IAS officer is indeed formidable. It demands a potent mix of intelligence, dedication and strategic planning, all sprinkled with a bit of luck. Cracking the UPSC's CSE is daunting, but with the right approach, unwavering dedication and a structured study plan, around 180 candidates achieve their dream of joining the IAS every year. Remarkably, some do it on their first attempt.

Do not be disheartened by the length of the journey or any perceived setbacks. These challenges are unearthing your potential, building resilience and instilling discipline. Believe in yourself, stay steadfast and embrace the understanding that there is no substitute for hard work. Remember, a journey of a thousand miles begins with a single step. Each day, as you adhere to your study plan and utilize your time efficiently, you inch closer to your goal. Every moment of struggle you overcome is transforming you into a future leader.

Drawing from my thirty years of experience serving the country as an IAS officer, I can emphatically say that the diversity, fulfilment, challenges and opportunity to serve people that IAS provides make the arduous trek to scale Mount UPSC really worthwhile. So, start your journey to ace the UPSC CSE exam today! This exam is not insurmountable; it is designed to be conquered by resilient aspirants like you.

Acknowledgements

At the outset, I would like to extend my deepest gratitude to Ms Nirmala Sitharaman, Union finance minister, for fostering a nurturing, motivating and stress-free environment and for providing unwavering support and encouragement.

I am immensely thankful to my mentor, an amazing person and a thorough professional, Dr T.V. Somanathan, Cabinet secretary, Government of India. His continuous encouragement and guidance have been invaluable, and this book could not have seen the light of day without his support.

I owe a debt of gratitude to the seven heroes of this book, who, with immense patience, spent hours with me, recounting their life journeys and sharing their strategies to scale Mount UPSC. Shruti Sharma, Waseem Ahmad Bhat, Anjali Sharma, Lavish Ordia, Bharat Singh, Satyam Gandhi and Minnu P.M., your stories are the heart of this work.

My heartfelt thanks go to all my dear friends who have been my pillars of strength through the highs and lows of writing this book. Your feedback and support have led to immense improvements, and I am deeply grateful for your staunch belief in me.

I am also immensely grateful to Manish Khurana, business and non-fiction editor at Penguin Random House India, for conceiving the idea of this book and for his constant guidance from inception to completion. His vision and insights have been crucial in shaping this book.

A special thanks to Dr Manoj Govil, Secretary Expenditure, and my colleagues in the department of expenditure, Sanjay Prasad, Parama Sen, Amit Negi, Manoj Sahay, Ashish Vachhani and Sanjay Aggarwal. Your support and camaraderie have been invaluable during this journey.

Lastly, I profoundly thank my wife Sunita, daughter Siya and son Karan, to whom this book is dedicated. They have borne with all the odd hours and efforts that went into this book without complaint and they have been my true pillars of strength. Your love and support have made this journey possible and I am forever grateful.

Appendix

Reading Material and Strategy of
Our Seven Heroes

Minnu P.M.			
Year of Selection in IAS	2021	Optional Subject	Geography
Key Strategy for Prelims	Proper planning, create and adhere to a timetable, consistent reading of newspapers and practicing previous years' questions and test series		
Key Strategy for Mains	Engage in extensive reading, participate in test series, practise daily answer-writing, solving previous years' questions and prioritize studying your optional subject		

Mains Paper-Wise Recommended Books/ Reading Material	
General Studies–I	**Indian Heritage and Culture:** Indian Art & Culture by Nitin Singhania **History:** – NCERT books (both old and new) from Class 6 to 12 – The Wonder That Was India by A.L. Basham – India's Struggle for Independence: 1857-1947 by Bipin Chandra – A Brief History of Modern India by Rajiv Ahir (Spectrum) – NCERT books **Geography:** NCERT books (both old and new) from Class 6 to 12; Geography of India by Majid Hussain; Oxford Atlas **Society:** NCERT books
General Studies–II	**Governance, Constitution, Polity:** NCERT books (new) from Class 6 to 12; Indian Polity by M. Laxmikanth **Social Justice:** Yojana and Kurukshetra magazines **International relations:** Newspaper and magazine articles

General Studies–III	**Economic Development:** NCERT books (new) from Class 6 to 12; Indian Economy: Key Concepts by Sankarganesh Karuppiah; Indian Economy by Ramesh Singh **Environment:** Coaching academy's book **Technology:** NCERT books, newspapers and current affairs magazines
	Disaster Management: Newspapers and magazines
General Studies-IV	A Practical Approach to Ethics Integrity and Aptitude by D.K. Balaji; Case Studies by IAS Score
Essay	Fundamentals of Essay and Answer Writing by Anudeep Durishetty
Optional Subject (Paper–1)	– Physical Geography by Savindra Singh – Human Geography by Majid Hussain – Class Notes by Nikhil from iLearnIAS – 500+ Questions by Himanshu Sharma – NCERT geography books (old & new) from Class 6 to 12

Optional Subject (Paper–2)	- India: A Comprehensive Geography by D.R. Khullar - Geography of India by Majid Hussain - Oxford World Atlas - Class Notes - 500+ Questions by Himanshu Sharma - NCERT books (old & new) from Class 6 to 12 - Magazines: Down to Earth, Tell Me Why, Yojana and Kurukshetra - Newspaper articles - YouTube channels (Topic-specific)
Key Strategy for Interview	Read transcripts of previous interviews, stay updated through newspaper reading, thoroughly understand your DAF, participate in select mock Interviews, engage in discussion groups and practice through one-on-one Interviews with friends and family members
Message to IAS Aspirants	More than memorizing facts, this exam tests your personality at every stage. Approach it with courage, a willingness to take risks and unwavering commitment. Stay true to yourself and strive to bring out your best self

Satyam Gandhi			
Year of Selection in IAS	**2021**	**Optional Subject**	**Political science and international relations**
Key Strategy for Prelims	Read NCERT and standard books, cover the syllabus thoroughly, ensure clarity on basic concepts, multiple revisions, focus on current affairs, practice mock tests and previous years' questions, improve analytical skills, manage time efficiently, be aware of negative marking and maintain good health		
Key Strategy for Mains	Engage in comprehensive note-making, regular answer-writing practice and systematic revision		
Mains Paper-Wise Recommended Books/ Reading Material			
General Studies–I	**Indian Heritage and Culture:** An Introduction to Indian Art Part-1&II (NCERT); coaching class notes **History:** A Brief History of Modern India by Rajiv Ahir (Spectrum); coaching class notes; Nitin Sangwan's notes on World History and Post-Independence History **Geography:** NCERT books; coaching class notes; selective reading of Certificate Physical and Human Geography by G.C. Leong **Society**: Coaching class notes		

General Studies–II	**Governance, Constitution, Polity:** Indian Polity by M. Laxmikanth; Vision IAS current affairs; newspapers; coaching class notes; NITI Aayog 3-year action agenda; NITI Aayog India @75 Action Plan **International Relations:** Monthly magazines and newspaper articles; coaching class notes
General Studies–III	**Economic Development:** Value Added Material of coaching academy; NITI Aayog 3-year action agenda; NITI Aayog India @75 Action Plan; current affairs magazines; coaching class notes **Technology:** Internet; magazines; coaching class notes
	Disaster Management: Value Added Material of coachng academy **Environment:** Coaching academy's book **Security:** Coaching class notes and Value Added Material of coaching academy; newspapers
General Studies–IV	Value Added Material of coaching academy; test series
Essay	Fundamentals of Essay and Answer Writing by Anudeep Durishetty; newspapers and current affairs magazines

Optional Subject (Paper–1)	– An Introduction to Political Theory by O.P. Gauba – A History of Political Thought: Plato to Marx by Mukherjee and Ramaswamy – Modern Indian Political Thought by Bidyut Chakrabarty – Foundation of Indian Political Thought by V.R. Mehta – Shubhra Ranjan's IAS crash course notes and model answers – Notes of Tushar Gupta – Indian Polity by M. Laxmikanth – Newspapers for value addition
Optional subject (Paper–2)	– Global Politics by Andrew Heywood and Ben Whitham – Shubhra Ranjan's notes and model answers – Globalisation of World Politics by Baylis, Smith and Owens
	– Tushar Gupta's notes – *Foreign Policy* magazine – *Indian Express* and *The Hindu* newspapers – Articles on Observer Research Foundation's (ORF) website – Coaching academy's material on PSIR – The Oxford Handbook of Indian Foreign Policy by Malone, Raja Mohan and Srinath Raghavan

Key Strategy for Interview	Ensure thorough preparation from the Detailed Application Form (DAF), review academic and optional subjects, participate in mock interviews and stay updated on current affairs
Message to IAS Aspirants	Before you begin, prepare a proper study plan and be honest with yourself about why you chose to take the exam. Study for ten to twelve hours daily and avoid distractions, including social media, relatives, friends and others

Bharat Singh			
Year of Selection in IAS	2021	Optional Subject	Political science and international relations
Key Strategy for Prelims	Focus on previous years' questions; attempt thirty to thirty-five mock tests; concentrate on five major subjects: political science, economics, history, geography and environment		
Key Strategy for Mains	Engage in answer-writing practice; update the static portion with current affairs; work on test series and previous years' questions; and focus on high-scoring papers such as the essay, GS-4 and your optional subject		

Mains Paper-Wise Recommended Books/ Reading Material	
General Studies–I	**Indian Heritage and Culture:** Indian Art and Culture by Nitin Singhania **History:** A Brief History of Modern India by Rajiv Ahir (Spectrum) **Geography:** NCERT (Class 11 and 12); Certificate Physical and Human Geography by G.C. Leong **Society:** Self-notes (updated with the current affairs)
General Studies–II	**Governance, Constitution, Polity:** Indian Polity by M. Laxmikanth; self-notes (updated with the current affairs) **International Relations:** Self-notes (updated with the current affairs) **Social Justice:** Self-notes (updated with the current affairs)
General Studies–III	**Economic Development:** Economy notes of coaching academy; Economic Survey; Union Budget (updated with the current affairs) **Environment:** Coaching academy's book (updated with current affairs)
	Technology: Self-notes **Security:** Coaching academy's notes (updated with the current affairs) **Disaster Management:** Self-notes

General Studies–IV	The Lexicon for Ethics, Integrity & Aptitude 2024 by Niraj Kumar, self-notes (updated with the current affairs); case studies, test series and previous years' questions
Essay	Anudeep Durishetty's Notes; self-notes (updated with the current affairs); test series and previous years' questions
Optional Subject	Shubhra Ranjan's class notes and supplementary reading materials; test series and previous years' questions; updating the static portion with the current affairs
Key Strategy for Interview	Focus on the DAF and current affairs, concentrate on optional and graduation subjects, be authentic and show your real personality and participate in three or four mock Interviews
Message to IAS Aspirants	It is one of the toughest exams in the country, demanding proper respect and focus from aspirants. Only wholehearted attempts lead to success.

Anjali Sharma			
Year of Selection in IAS	2023	Optional subject	Sociology
Key Strategy for Prelims	Previous years' questions, multiple revision from standard books, NCERT books		

Key Strategy for Mains	Previous years' questions; writing practice; compile data, facts and figures from value added materials and newspapers
Mains Paper-Wise Recommended Books/ Reading Material	
General Studies–I	Standard books for static portion, NCERT books, current affairs bulletins, previous years' questions, Value Added Materials of coaching academies
General Studies–II	Indian Polity by M. Laxmikanth, newspapers
General Studies–III	Newspapers, Economic Survey, Value Added Material on websites of coaching academies
General Studies–IV	Lexicon books for concept, Value Added Material
Essay	Newspapers, essay writing practice, Value Added Material
Optional subject	IGNOU material for basics; Essential Sociology by Nitin Sangwan, Seema and Shruti Jakhar; newspapers; previous years' questions
Key Strategy for Interview	Build self-confidence, thoroughly prepare every detail in your DAF, engage in mock Interviews and practice with peers
Message to IAS Aspirants	Patience and perseverance are key; having a Plan-B can also help in reducing stress

Waseem Ahmad Bhat			
Year of Selection in IAS	2023	**Optional subject**	**Anthropology**
Key Strategy for Prelims	Make diligent notes during coaching classes and supplement them later with information from standard books. Focus on mock tests, conduct multiple revisions and solve questions asked in Prelims at least in the last fifteen years		
Key Strategy for Mains	Study model answers from the past three years of coaching academies, stay updated with current affairs, practice writing as many previous years' questions may be repeated, self-evaluate and learn continuously, write test series and carefully consider feedback for improvement		
Mains Paper-Wise Recommended Books/ Reading Material			
General Studies–I	**Indian Heritage and Culture:** NCERT books; India's Struggle for Independence and India Since Independence by Bipin Chandra; coaching academy's model answers; self-notes		
	Geography: NCERT books; coaching academy's model answers for past 3 years; self-notes **Society:** Coaching academy's model answers for past three years; self-notes		

General Studies–II	**Governance, Constitution and Polity:** Coaching academy's model answers for past 3 years; self-notes **Social Justice:** Coaching academy's model answers for past three years; self-notes **International Relations:** Coaching academy's Mains 365 book; self-notes
General Studies–III	**Economic Development:** Coaching academy's model answers for past three years; self-notes **Environment:** Coaching academy's model answers for past three years; coaching academy's Mains 365 book; self-notes **Technology:** Coaching academy's Mains 365 book; self-notes **Security:** Coaching academy's model answers for past three years; coaching academy's Mains 365 book **Disaster Management:** Coaching academy's model answers for past three years; self-notes
General Studies–IV	Coaching academy's model answers for past three years; self-notes; short notes in tabular format containing quotes and examples
Essay	Non-fiction/fiction books, previous years' toppers' essays

Optional Subject	Anthropology by Ember and Ember Biological Anthropology by Susan C. Anton Physical Anthropology by P. Nath Books on Anthropology by Nadeem Hasnain If you have time, supplement your knowledge from books written by Jared Diamond, Chris Stringer, David Reich and others for biological anthropology; books by Napoleon Chagnon, Richard Lee, David Graeber and others for social anthropology; books by Yuval Noah Harari, Gaia Vince and others for general understanding; and books by Dr B.R. Ambedkar, M.N. Srinivas, Jean Dreze and others for Indian anthropology
Key Strategy for Interview	Thoroughly prepare from your DAF. Focus on understanding the context when reading current affairs. Utilize free time to read non-fiction. Enhance your personality through self-reflection, conducting SWOT analysis and discussing with friends. Watch online talks and debates by esteemed speakers. Attend mock Interviews but take reviews with caution
Message to IAS Aspirants	Confront your fears. Your success in this exam hinges on how you manage your fears and insecurities. Engage with your family and friends for support and don't hesitate to seek help when needed. Focus on understanding and internalizing what you study, rather than mere memorization. Stay proud of your efforts and maintain hope throughout your journey

Shruti Sharma			
Year of Selection in IAS	2022	**Optional Subject**	**History**
Key Strategy for Prelims	Manage current affairs without getting overwhelmed, solve previous years' questions thoroughly, analyse all four options for potential linked questions next year. Practice elimination techniques, create short or micro notes for effective revision, participate in mock tests, ensure adequate preparation for CSAT, stay calm and confident during exams and remain mindful of negative marking		
Key Strategy for Mains	Complete the syllabus well in advance of the Mains, compile a repository of data, quotes, graphs, diagrams, maps and key points for use in your answers. Create your own notes to aid retention and update them regularly. Prepare micro notes for quick revisions closer to the exams. Practice ample answer-writing and analyse your responses to pinpoint areas for improvement. Study past toppers' answer copies to glean insights for enhancing your own answers		

Mains Paper-Wise Recommended Books/ Reading Material	
General Studies–I	**Indian Heritage and Culture:** An Introduction to Indian Art Part-1&II (NCERT) **History:** A Brief History of Modern India by Rajiv Ahir (Spectrum); self-notes **Geography:** NCERT Class 11 and 12 books **Society:** Self-notes
General Studies–II	**Governance, Constitution and Polity:** Indian Polity by M. Laxmikanth; self-notes; coaching academy's Yellow Book; coaching academy's IAS PT & Mains 365; coaching academy's 'Most Probable Topics' for current affairs' selective reading of press releases by Press Information Bureau (PIB) and New India Samachar
General Studies–III	**Economic Development:** Current issues from newspapers and Zulfiqar's notes **Technology:** Ayaz Khan's notes, Mains 365 by Vision IAS, NCERT books of Class 9 and 10 for basic understanding, especially for non-science background aspirants **Disaster management:** Self-notes **Environment:** Coaching academy's book **Security:** Coaching academy's Yellow Book
General Studies–IV	Coachig academy's classroom notes; collection of numerous examples, quotes, case studies from newspapers which was used for essay paper as well

Optional Subject	Self-notes, combined package of maps and solved previous years' question papers from Self Study History; test series, newspapers for adding examples, arguments and perspectives beyond the basic books
Key Strategy for Interview	Read at least one newspaper daily post Mains exam. Listen to podcasts like 'Three Things' and 'Cut The Clutter'. Carefully analyse your DAF and formulate questions. Review model questions prepared by coaching academies related to your DAF. Record videos of yourself answering these questions and analyse them. Practice answering in front of a mirror
Message to IAS Aspirants	Limit your study sources and prioritize conceptual understanding.

Lavish Ordia			
Year of Selection in IAS	2020	Optional Subject	Mechanical Engineering
Key Strategy for Prelims	Utilize analysis of previous years' questions as a strategic tool to navigate through the extensive syllabus; conduct simulated practice tests under timed conditions, followed by meticulous analysis of weak areas and common mistakes; break down the syllabus into manageable targets and maintain a consistent study schedule		

Key Strategy for Mains	Focus on breadth rather than depth in your studies. No need for subject specialization; aim to have sufficient knowledge to write concise 200-word answers. Analyse previous years' questions to pinpoint crucial areas and allocate your efforts accordingly. Engage in rigorous answer-writing practice to ensure timely completion of exam papers. Simplify the examiner's task by emphasizing clear presentation and readability
Mains Paper-Wise Recommended Books/ Reading Material	
General Studies–I	**Indian Heritage and Culture:** Indian Art and Culture by Nitin Singhania **History:** Tamil Nadu Board's Class 11 textbook; A Brief History of Modern India by Rajiv Ahir (Spectrum)
	Geography: NCERT Class 11 and 12 books; Mrunal's Geography videos on YouTube
General Studies–II	**Governance, Constitution and Polity:** Indian Polity by M. Laxmikanth; Coaching academy's notes **Social Justice:** Coaching Institute's notes and Mains 365 book **International Relations:** Coaching academy's Mains 365 book

General Studies–III	**Economic Development**: Indian Economy by Sriram Srirangam and Mrunal's videos on YouTube **Environment:** A coaching academy's book on environment **Technology:** Coaching academy's notes and Mains 365 book
General Studies–IV	Decode Ethics by Mudit Jain & Amrita Jain
Essay	Studying other GS subjects and current affairs provide ample content to write essays, but it requires practice to integrate, structure and present everything in a comprehensive manner
Optional subject	Previous years' questions (solved) and test papers; coaching academy books; National Programme on Technology Enhanced Learning (NPTEL) lectures; and standard textbooks
Key Strategy for Interview	Analyse Interview transcripts of candidates from the past four or five years to identify questions related to your DAF. Continuously improve through daily mock Interviews with friends (four or five questions) and selective mock interviews at coaching academies
Message to IAS Aspirants	Give your best effort while preparing but avoid becoming obsessed with it

Scan QR code to access the
Penguin Random House India website